Explorin c Astrology

Exploring Professions *through* Vedic Astrology

Vol. 1

JATINDER PAL SINGH SANDHU

MOTILAL BANARSIDASS
PUBLISHING HOUSE • DELHI
Email: naraina@mlbd.in • Website: www.mlbd.in
@mlbdofficial

*First Edition : Delhi, **2023***

ISBN: 978-93-5676-020-2 (Hardcover)
ISBN: 978-93-5676-021-9 (Paperback)

Printed & Published by
Rajendra P Jain *for*
Motilal Banarsidass Publishing House
A-44, Naraina Industrial Area, Phase I,
New Delhi–110 028 (INDIA)
Email: naraina@mlbd.in Website: www.mlbd.in
Tel.: (+91-11)4751 1592

Showroom:
4637/20, F-2, Hari Sadan, First Floor, Ansari Road, Daryaganj
Delhi–110 002 (Opp. Fire Station) ***Tel.*** : (+91-11)4559 7999

Dedicated to lotus feet of Almighty God and astrology, from thy well I draw little at time and try to quench my thirst and then I share the rest with all interested.

Dedicated to all those who strive for genuine knowledge of the classics

Col. J.P.S. Sandhu and my parents

Contents

Introduction

Professions and evaluating the same through the horoscope has been a challenge area for the astrologers, there are not too many reference books around ,therefore the need was felt for a reliable source of interpretation and evaluation of professions and vocations through astrology.

This book of mine is an effort to simplify the process of evaluation based on certain specific combinations that repeat in pattern on a specific vocation group.

The combinations that I have devised are based on logic and knowledge based on classics, there is nothing out of context and out of the purview of Vedic astrology principles and fundamentals.

The purpose and objective of this book is simplifying the interpretation and evaluation of possibilities and probabilities as related to profession from the individual horoscope.

I have not used divisional charts as the way the charts are used by erstwhile astrologers is not as per the hints dropped in classics. Therefore the method of evaluation is based strictly on the natal chart assessment only.

1
Professions

Houses-Phal Deepika

लग्नं होरा कल्यदेहोदयाख्यं रूपं शिर्षं वर्तमानं च जन्म।
वित्तं विद्या स्वान्नपानाति भुक्तिं दक्षाक्ष्यास्यं पत्रिका वाक्कुटुम्बम्॥१०॥

[In a birth chart there are twelve houses. Each house has been given several names indicating the various subjects it deals with.] The names by which the first house or the Ascendant is known are Lagna,Hora, Kalya, Deha, Udaya, Rupa, Seersha, Vartmana (present) and Janma.

Significators – Karakas of Bhava As per Uttar kalamrita

The first Bhava (house) stands for (1) Body (2) Limbs (3) Happiness and misery (4) old age (5) knowledge (6) birth place (7) lame (8) dream (9) strength (10) dignity (11) politics (12) Longevity (13) tranquility (14) age (I5) hair (16) appearance (17) pride (18) livelihood (19) gambling for others (2) Stigma (21) honor (22) Skin (23) sleep (24) proficiency (25) Embezzlement (26) nature to insult others (27) freedom from sickness (28) detachment (29) nature (30) agency (31) perseverance in cattle breeding (32) loss of sense of decorum (33) blame from one's own Kin (34) Brain (35) Head.

The second house deals with Vitta (wealth), Vidya (learning). Swa, Annapana (riches, food and drinks), Bhukti (eating), the right eye, face (Asya), letter or document (Patrika), Speech (Vak) and Kutumba (family) and thus adopts these appellations.

Uttara Kalamrita—***The second Bhava*** (house) denotes: (1) speech (2) wealth (3) faith in sacred tradition (4) supporting others (5) nails (6) enjoyment (7) truth and false hood (8) tongue (9) eyes (10) clothes (11) diamond (12) copper (13) gems (14) pearl (15) determination (16) incense (17) family relationship (18) trade (19) softness of speech (20) liberality (21) effort to acquire Wealth (22) friendship (23) friend (24) splendor (25) miserliness in spending (26) pleasant oratorical ability (27) scholarship (28) gold (29) silver (30) com (31) modesty (32) selling Nose (33) firmness of mind (34) a close dependent (35) cycle of life and death (36) living power and (37) finance. (38) accumulated wealth (39) second marriage (40) observational power

दुश्चिक्योरो दक्षकर्णं च सेनां धैर्यं शौर्यं विक्रमं भ्रात्रं च
गेहं क्षेत्रं मातुल भागिनेयं बन्धुं मित्रं वाहनं मातरं च॥११॥

The names given (or the subjects allotted) to third house are Duschikya, Uras (breast), the right ear, army valour, prowess and brother.

Third Bhava (house) represents: (1) Courage (2) brothers (3) battle (4) ears (5) legs (6) roadside place (7) confusion of the mind (8) fitness (9) heaven or paradise (10) causing sorrow (11) dream (12) soldier (13) heroic valor (14) relatives (15) friend (16) wandering (11) throat (18) taking unspoiled or pure food (19) partition of property (20) ornaments (21) nobility (22) learning (23) pastime (24) physical strength (25) gain (26) Physical growth (27) noble descent (28) attendant (29) the part of the band between the forefinger and the thumb (sacred to the Manes) (30) maid servant (31) short journey by a good vehicle (32) a large undertaking (33) own religious duty.

राज्यं गोमहिषसुगन्धवस्त्रभूषाः पातालं हिबुकसुखाम्बुसेतुनद्यः।

The subjects or designations for the fourth house are kingdom, house, land, maternal uncle, a sister's son, a relation, a friend, conveyance, mother, kingdom, cow, buffalo, perfume, clothes, ornaments, the nadir, hibuka, sukha (happiness), water, bridge and river.

Uttara Kalamrit on 4th Bhava.

4th bhava (1) learning (2) kingdom (3) house (4) travel (5) vehicles like rickshaws and small boats (6) oil bath (7) mother (8) relatives (9) friend (to) caste (11) garment (12) well (13) water (14) milk (15) perfume (16) happy man (17) good name (18) lifesaving drug (19) trust (20) false allegation (21) tent (22) victory (23) tiresome work (24) land and agriculture (25) a garden (26) digging of a pond or well (27) wells for the public use (28) mother's side (29) sharp intellect (30) father (31) wife (32) accumulation of wealth (33) a palatial house (34) art (35) house opening (36) conclusions (37) disposition (38) damage to one's property (39) paternal property (40) celestial food (41) art of disclosing where a bouts of stolen property (42) an ant hill (43) f Vedic and Sacred "lore promotion (44) buffalos (45) cows (46) bones (47) elephants (48) surplus corn, wet lands are to be divined from the fourth house.

राजाङ्कं सचिवकरात्मधीभविष्यज्जानासून् सुतजटरश्रुतिस्मृतीश्च॥१२॥

The fifth house deals with (and has designations accordingly) the mark of the sovereign, taxes, soul, intelligence, knowledge of the future, life, progeny, belly, Vedic knowledge and other religious scriptures.

Fifth house: (1) progeny (2) fathers virtuous acts (3) a king (4) a minister (5) good conduct (6) mechanical art (7) mind (8) learning (9) pregnancy (10) discretion (11) umbrella (12) instructive Stories (13) auspicious letters (14) garments (15) a great desirable action (16) paternal property (17) foresightedness (18) fortune through wife's luck (19) liaisons with courtesans (20) Profundity (21) firmness (22) sacred (23) decorum (24) writing of news (25) well-being (26) friendship (27) long literary production (28) engaging oneself in any business (29) belly (30) invocation through mantras (31) Uncountable wealth (32) gift of cooked rice (33) discrimination between virtue and vice (34) chanting of Veda Mantras (35) Wisdom (36) ability for criticism (deep pondering) (31) ways of earning money (38) a festive occasion when drum or tabor is played (39) great contentment (40) profound learning (41) hereditary post of minister.

ऋणास्त्रचोरक्षतरोगशत्रून् ज्ञात्याजिदुष्कृत्याघभीत्यवज्ञाः।
जामित्रचित्तोत्थमदास्तकामान् द्यूनाध्वलोकान् पतिमार्गभार्याः॥१३॥

The sixth house deals with debts, arms, thieves, wounds, diseases, enemies, paternal relations, battle, wicked acts, sins, fear and humiliation.

6th Bhava (1) Disease (2) obstacle (3) fighting in combat (4) maternal uncle (5) phlegm (6) swelling in the body (7) cruel actions (8) insanity (9) a boil (10) enmity (11) miserliness (12) sickness (13) venereal wound (14) cooked rice (15) weariness (16) debt (11) reproach (18) enemy's satisfaction (19) consumption (20) heat (21) a wound (22) mental worry(23) intense anguish (24) enmity with many people (25) incessant eye trouble (26) receiving alms (21) untimely meals (28)a fall from a boat (29) trouble and fear from one's benefactors (30) Gain (31) exertion (32) poison (33) a severe colic or gout (34) fetters (35) guarding of one's own credit (36) urinary trouble (37) dysentery (38) the six flavors (39) severe reproach (40) Service (41) theft (42) calamity (43) prison house and (44) misunderstandings with brothers and the like are to be investigated from the 6th house.

The subjects dealt with by the seventh house are desire, passion, setting, sexual desire, a way, people, husband road and wife.

7th ***Bhava:*** (1) marriage (2) Unchastely (3) winning of a love (4) enmity with a debauched female (5) deviation from the right path (6) good perfume (7) music (8) flowers (9) savory food and drinks (10) chewing betel leaves with areca (11) break in a journey (12) curd (13) loss of memory (14) acquisition of garments (15) semen virility (16) faithfulness of the husband (17) a pair of wives (18) generative organs (19) urine (20) the anus (21) trade (22) sweet drink (23) tasting of nectar, soup, ghee, etc. (24) gifts (25) loss of power and status (26) victory over enemy (27) money kept in another place (28) controversy (29) sexual union (30) adopted son (31) relishing food prepared in ghee (32) foreign place (33) wife (34) all secret pleasures derived from sex (35) theft.

माङ्गल्यरन्ध्रमलिनाधिपराभवायुः
क्लेशापवादमरणाशुचिविघ्नदासान्।

For the eighth house subjects allotted are Mangalya (the living of the husband during the life time of the wife), Randhra, filthiness, mental pain, defeat or humiliation, longevity, sorrow, blame, death, impurity impediments and slavery.

8th bhava following should be ascertained (1) longevity (2) happiness (3) defeat (4) patrimony (5) an afflicted face (6) grief due to death of relatives (7) witch craft (8) quarrel over food (9) urinary disease (10) calamity (11) brother's enemy (12) wife's sickness (13) a tuft of braided hair (14) enemy's fortress (15) misery (16) idleness(17) punishment from the ruler (18) fear (19) loss of money (20) returning a debt (21) unintentional receipt of other's money(22) long standing property (23) meeting a wicked man (24) Vice (25) tilling of a living being (26) loss of limb (27) decapitation (28) formidable affliction (29) mental anxiety from story (30) chain of misfortune (31) overindulgence in doing cruel acts (32) battle and (33) great mental tension.

आचार्यदैवतपितॄन् शुभपूर्वभाग्यपूजातपःसुकृतपौत्रजपार्यवंशान्॥१४॥

The ninth house deals with preceptor (guru), deity (devta), father, auspiciousness, Poorv Bhagya (previous luck), worship, penance, virtuous act or virtue, grandson, and noble family. (Some of the learned in the North are of the view that all about father should be examined from the 10th house, because 10th is 7th to the 4th house dealing with the father. The view of Phal Deepika seems to be based on the logic that the 9th being 5th to 5th house (dealing with progeny) should be the most appropriate house to be connected with father).

Bhava 9—(1) giving alms (2) virtue and religion (3) pilgrimage (4) penance (5) reverence to elders (6) medicinal drugs (7) conduct (8) purity of mind (9) divine worship (10) hard work to acquire learning (11) splendor (12) conveyance (13) affluence (14) destiny (15) dignity (16) fable (17) travel (18) holy baths (19) nourishments' (20) good company (21) happiness (22) parental wealth (23) son (24) daughter (25) all sorts of wealth (26) horses (27) elephants (28) buffaloes (29)coronation ball (30) establishing the Brahminic faith (31) Vedic sacrifice (32) circulation of wealth are to be predicted from the 9th house.

व्यापारास्पदमानकर्मजयसत्कीर्तिं क्रतुं जीवनं
व्योमाचारगुणप्रवृत्तिगमनान्याज्ञां च मेषूरणम्।

The subjects (names) designated for the 10th house is business or trade, ranker position, honor, occupation, profession, sky or zenith, conduct, quality, inclination, gait, command and Meshurana (to give orders).

Bhava 10—(1) Trade (2) honor from the Sovereign (3) riding a horse (4) athletics (5) Government work (6) service (7) agriculture (8) doctor (9) fame (10) depositing of a treasure (11) sacrifice (12) pre-eminence (13) elders (14) talisman (15) incantations (16) mother (17) magnitude of moral merits (18) medicine (19) thigh (20) gods (21) accomplishment of a spell (22) prosperity (23) adopted son (24) a lord (25) road (26) honor (27) honorable living (28) a prince (29) fame (30) teaching (31) seal (32) supremacy (33) subjection and (34) the intension to command are to be determined from examination of 10th house.

लाभायागमनाप्तिसिद्धिविभवान् प्राप्तिं भवं श्लाध्यतां
ज्येष्ठभ्रातरमन्यकर्णसरसान् सन्तोषमाकर्णनूम् ॥१५॥

The matters to be considered from the eleventh house are gains, income, acquisition, receipt of wealth, accomplishment, splendor and prosperity, profits, veneration, elder brother or sister, left ear, anything juicy, delightful news.

Bhava 11—(1) Gain from all sources (2) wicked desires (3) all kinds or receipts (4) dependency (5) eldest brother sister (6) paternal uncle (7) worshipping deities (8) worshipping the good (9) learning (10) acquisition or gold and wealth (11) extremely clever (12) paternal property (13) the knee (14) a pre-eminent place (15) love or ornaments and pearls (16) master's wealth (17) loss or interest on capital (18) gold ornaments for one's lady love (19) wisdom (20) minister ship (21) brother-in-law (22) gain (23) dawn or fortune (24) wish fulfillment(25) easy gain (26) cooking (27) desire (28) mother (29) longevity (30) ear (31) the shank (32) beautiful paintings and (33) the skill in practical arts should be looked into from the 11th house.

दुःखांघ्रिवामनयनक्षयसूचकान्त्यदरिद्र्यपापशयनव्ययरिःफबन्धान्।
भावाह्व्या निगदिताः क्रमशोऽथ लीनस्थानं त्रिषड्व्ययपराभवराशिनाम्
॥१६॥

The significations used for the twelfth house are misery, leg, left eye, loss, spy, last rites, poverty, sins, bad expenditure and imprisonment or confinement.

Described above are the designations of the twelve houses or the subject matters to be examined from them. The 3rd, the 6th, the 8th and 12th are known as Leena Sthanas (hidden houses).

Bhava 12—(1) awakening from sleep (2) mental agony (3) the two feet (4) fear from enemy (5) imprisonment (6) liberation from pain (1) discharge of debts (8) elephants (9) horses (10) paternal wealth (11) enemy (12) entry into heaven (13) left eye (14) people's ellfllily (15) mutilation of a limb (16) Gallantry (17) loss through marriage (18) renouncing the Couch (19) termination of the appointment (20) the place of enemy's imprisonment in chains (21) mental agitation (22) wretchedness (23) harm (24) a blow to the idea of happiness of the parents and brothers (25) discussion or dispute (26) anger (27) physical injury (28) death (29) going to another place (30) expenditure through all sources (31) loss of wife are the issues to be deduced from the 12th house.

Described above are the designations of the twelve houses or the subject matters to be examined from them. The 3rd, the 6th, the 8th and 12th are known as Leen Sthaana (hidden houses).

Houses	Professions as per houses
1	Self-employment as it rules self.
2	Banking, investment, finance, teaching, writing and publishing. Securities, negotiable assets etc. Earning from speaking skills, food etc.
3	Mental inclinations in a way profession too, courage, short travels hands, ears, shoulders, neighbors, right ear, writing, sales professionals, means of communication, printing, editing etc., anything that involves the use of hands and shoulders. Psychology and psychiatrists, wrestlers, sports people etc.
4	lands, happiness, property, mind, chest, lungs, education, relatives, friendship. Places below the earth, agriculture, builders, sale purchase of vehicles, profession related to masses and mass communication etc.
5	Speculation, mantra chanting, teaching using and earning through skills and knowledge gained, learning, counseling, amusements, lottery etc.

Houses	Professions as per houses
6	Enemies, thieves, diseases, debts, cuts, wounds, uneasiness of mind, worries, legal court, servants, native 'sown work, labor, hygiene, sanitation, doctoring etc.
7	Trade, travel, death, marriage, litigation, recovery of lost property, vital powers, etc., success or failure in partnerships etc.
8	legacies, disgrace, degradation, murder, defeat, insult, sorrow and impediments, secret service, mining, insurance, research work, occult and astrology.
9	Religion, devotion, long journeys, travels, inventions, discoveries, publishing, Law etc.
10	Profession, occupations, rank, honor, government, position in life, success, respect, dignity, pilgrimage, reputation, authority, control, caste, customs, tradition, caste occupations, trade, wearing apparel, environmental Inheritance from father etc.
11	Gains from profession, income, 'elder brothers, friends, ornaments, profit from trade, Acquisition of money, social clubs etc.
12	Hospitals, institutions, jails, final resting places, professions that involve use of legs.

Apart from 10th house, the other houses that are capable of denoting profession are:

1. **2nd and 11th:** Both these houses rule earnings. 2nd house is the savings and 11th house is the source of money.
2. **6th house:** Although the 6th house is a dusthana, it is an important part of Artha trikon (2-6-10). In today's date and time, when loans and funding are important for bootstrapping a company, 6th house is an important asset. 6th house intimately rules healing and association with people and is important for services industry, e.g., the medical profession, hospitality sector, practice of law, etc.
3. **Lagna:** Lagna and lagna lord are the foundation of the chart. A strong lagna lord will imprint the profession as well.
4. **The 5th house -the 11th house,** as per Mantershwar (Phal Deepika) 5th house refers to Insignia of the State/Country/Government.

   राजाङ्कं सचिवकरात्मधीभविष्यज्जानासून्
   सुतजटरश्रुतिस्मृतीश्च ॥१२॥

   Here the word Rajaank (राजाङ्कं) refers to Government.
5. 11th house Signifies the High and important posting as per Kalidasa (Uttara Kalamrit) 10th

House signifies State or government. So, the 5th and 10th connection generally ends up in Government Service.

The high-level choices for a profession-based signification of the key planets are:

- **Sun:** Medicine, medical equipment, general administration, king's work, messenger, various services in government, dealing in gold, precious gems.
- **Moon:** Dealing with import/export, travel, professions related to water, ocean products, milk, liquids, artworks, especially made from earth, clothing & textile.
- **Mars:** Metals (except iron, which is governed by Saturn), providing security – police, military, etc., income tax, excise, liquids like petrol, petroleum products, chemicals, making money from any type of conflict, sports, etc.
- **Mercury:** Analysis, mathematics, astrology, teaching, literature, communication, marketing, priest, authorship, writing.
- **Jupiter:** Banking, advisors, consultants, teaching, finance, legal/judiciary, sales, astrology
- **Venus:** art, entertainment, selling precious and shiny items, dairy, restaurants, banking, vehicles, clothing & textile, etc.

- **Saturn:** General administration – dealing with large number of people, union, construction/ infrastructure area, iron ore, mining and cement industry, waste products, leather products, sale of grains

Sign based significations as related to professions

Aries—Vocations that require independence, daring and the pioneering spirit: entrepreneurs, pioneers in any field, idea people, those who initiate new projects, troubleshooters, directors, adventurers, executives. Vocations that involve fire, courage, metal, speed, energy, or daring: Firemen or fire fighters, forest rangers, engineers (metallurgical), members of the armed forces, firearms experts, police officers, machinists, mechanics, iron and steel workers, locksmiths, welders, athletics that involve speed and daring, race car drivers, contact sports, boxers, dancers, movement therapists, physical education instructors, surgeons.

Taurus—Vocations dealing with the earth and substance: farmers, ranchers, agriculture instructors, landscape architects, gardeners, rock collectors (semi-precious gems), builders, carpenters, building contractors, concrete pourers, chiropractors, massage therapists, computer programmers. Occupations involved with money and finance: bankers, bank tellers, stock brokers, financiers, money managers, investment advisors, securities analysts, treasurers, economists. Occupations involved with beauty, fashion, design or the voice: Artists, sculptors, jewelers, pottery makers, fashion designers, tailors, florists, musicians, singers, voice teachers, throat specialists.

Gemini—Vocations involved with communication or the media: authors, proofreaders, ad copywriters, screenplay writers, editors, reporters, teachers, lecturers, linguists, speech therapists, librarians, bookstore owners, publishers, magazine employees, radio operators or disc jockeys, television producers, telephone operators or repair persons, telemarketers, stationery store owners, journalists, salespeople, printers, book distributors, clerks, office workers, secretaries, typists, typesetters. Vocations involved with transportation: Messengers, mail carriers, taxi drivers, bus drivers, railway employees, plane pilots, accountants, jacks-of-all-trades. Can engage in two or more occupations at once.

Cancer—Vocations that nurture, physically or emotionally (especially through food): caterers, restaurant owners, chefs, cooks, bakers, waiters and waitresses, confectioners, dairy farmers, grocers, food distributors, nutritionists. Vocations involved with counseling, children or caretaking: Social workers, counselors, psychics, nurses, family therapists, preschool teachers, children's writers, caretakers. Water-related occupations: plumbers, swimmers, lifeguards, fishermen. All careers dealing with the home: realtors, landlords, hotel managers, innkeepers, homemakers, governesses, maids, laundry workers.

Leo—Performers/Entertainers of all types: actors and actresses, playwrights, entertainers, dancers, singers, musicians, movie stars, circus performers, jugglers, clowns, sports figures, teachers (good teachers are entertainers), amusement park owners, speculators, gamblers.

Leaders of all types: executives, managers, government officials, politicians, foremen, judges, athletes. Selling/Promoting: Salespeople, the profession of selling, promoters, diamond and precious metal brokers, gold workers, heart specialists. All vocations involving children.

Virgo—Vocations dealing with analysis, detail and technical expertise: statisticians, accountants, bookkeepers, computer programmers, teachers of technical subjects, stenographers, critics, inspectors of all types, draftsmen, graphic artists, technical illustrators, craftspeople, specialists, financial analysts. Health occupations and the social services: mental health workers, therapists, psychiatrists, psychoanalysts, social workers, employment counselors, nurses, doctors, massage therapists, respiratory technicians, dental hygienists, dentists, secretaries, office managers, food service workers, waiters and waitresses, dieticians, nutritionists, veterinarians, zoologists, sanitation workers, janitors, public health officials, house cleaners, butlers.

Libra—Vocations that pursue balance, harmony, and, justice: negotiators and counselors of all types, marriage counselors, wedding-related businesses, diplomats, labor arbitrators, judges, lawyers, managers, salespeople. Occupations dealing with beauty, art, creativity: artists, architects, painters, illustrators, photographers, fashion designers, fashion industry workers, milliners, color consultants, clothing store owners or salespeople, beauticians, hairdressers, cosmeticians, interior and exterior decorators, cosmetic manufacturers and dealers, jewelers, florists, candy makers.

Scorpio—Vocations that focus on uncovering hidden secrets: researchers, muckraking journalists, investigators, detectives, physicists, occultists, psychics, astrologers, numerologists. Those who work behind the scenes: espionage agents, vice squad workers. All matters dealing with death: funeral home directors, morticians, cemetery workers, insurance salespeople, soldiers, those working under the earth, undertakers. Those who work as healers: all medical practitioners, physicians, nurses, psychiatrists, psychologists, surgeons, pharmacists, pathologists, past-life investigators, hospice workers, chemists, music therapists, musicians.

Sagittarius—Vocations dealing with exploration, travel and adventure: explorers, astronomers, travel agents, airline employees, flight attendants, astronauts, import-export agents, foreign correspondents, language interpreters, traveling salespeople, promoters, customs officers, athletes of all types, archers, sporting goods manufacturers, horse trainers, breeders and jockeys. Occupations dealing with higher knowledge: philosophers, college professors, ministers, theologians, missionaries, preachers, orators, publishers, metaphysical writers, philanthropists, lawyers.

Capricorn—Vocations dealing with administering and organizing: administrators of all types, managers, business owners, executives, government officials, politicians, judges, manufacturers, coordinators, principals at schools, wardens, disciplinarians, buyers, consultants, vocational counselors. Occupations that work with form and structure: architects, contractors, builders, carpenters, civil and industrial engineers, economists, chiropractors, orthopedic specialists, osteopaths, miners, landowners, mountain climbers.

Aquarius—Vocations dealing with progress and invention: inventors, scientists, educators, researchers, astrologers, social workers, psychologists, futurists, humanitarians, social reformers, United Nations workers, employees of world relief organizations, future-oriented occupations, astronauts, airplane pilots, aviators, parachutists, hang glider pilots, solar energy researchers, physicists, radio and television technicians, electricians, electrical engineers.

Pisces—Vocations of a spiritual nature: religious workers, priests, monks, nuns, sisters of mercy, rabbis, clairvoyants, mediums, charity workers, prison workers. Vocations involved with healing: Physicians, faith healers, psychic healers, nurses, hospital workers, psychiatrists, psychologists, hypnotists, anesthesiologists, podiatrists. Vocations of an inspirational or artistic nature: Poets, musicians, writers (inspirational, fantasy, metaphysical, science fiction), actors, dancers, painters, artists, entertainers, comedians, singers, filmmakers. Water-related occupations: fishermen, sailors, sea captains, divers, swimmers, lifeguards, marine scientists, oceanographers, bartenders, oil industry workers.

Planet Significations as related to professions

Planet	Professions related to planets
Sun	Government service, chanting of hymns, gambling, wool, medicine, metalwork, gold, father, kings, fire arms, fire, poisons, and forests.
	The Sun denotes employment in the State Service, administration or management. It indicates people having much authority and power. The Sun indicates medicines and medical profession too. Mars/Ketu connected to sun /10th lord can be related to medicine. Jupiter influence likewise will cause chanting of mantras or priestly activities. Connected to 4th house it can be supplier of timbers or dealing in furniture. Satyacharya says in his work that the Sun rules over business in grass or straw, medical profession, embassy, trade in pearl and gold. If it is connected with Mars, or Ketu, the profession may be related to fire arms, electricity, radio etc.
Education stream	Political science, Medicine, Stats and Physics etc. Insurance or business actuary.

Planet	Professions related to planets
Moon	Being a feminine planet' It indicates earning through women also. This includes the cinema line where actors have to move with women. Connections with other female planets like Venus, combination with Mercury also has the same effect 'Cooks, nurse' Launderer are also ruled by the Moon'. Jataka Parijata says that one may be a musician playing on instruments, or one may be an agriculturist' One may be a cloth merchant, or he may be in the service of a queen'
	The Moon is a watery planet. It rues over all kinds of liquids, fresh water, milk and things produced from water'. Moon rules over agriculture, things produced in water, women, and interest on money. It signifies changes and travels also. Persons employed in shipping /fishing boats, trawlers etc.
Western Astrology	Nurses, midwives, dealers of liquids, public conveyance handler's, leaders, social reform personalities, sailors, fishermen, professions dependent on water element.

Planet	Professions related to planets
Education	Fine arts, music, Theater, Para medical, Chemistry etc.
Mars	Defense and police personnel, Brick kiln owners, It Signifies fires, firemen, warriors, military operations, blood, gold, copper, surgeons, gages, dentists, fire places, engineers, butchers, engines, iron and steel, chemists, dentists, druggists etc. People dealing in iron and steel or working in the kitchenware also ruled by Mars. Mars and Mercury can denote mechanical engineering; Mars and Sun can denote military hospitals. As per Satyacharya—buildings made of brick, masonry, oral discussions, argumentations, disputations, bold ventures; fire, administration of government, and murderous deeds are ruled by Mars'.
Education	Medicine/surgery, engineering, geology, mechanical engineering, logic, defense studies etc.
Mercury	Educated men, accountants, school teachers, secretaries, book-sellers, clerks, postmen, messengers, engineers, radio, wireless, telegraph, post, letters,

Planet	Professions related to planets
	typing, press, paper, cotton, representative, secretary, agent, clerk, astrologer, trade of foreign goods, import-export, thread, mercury, tin, accounts, auditing, able lawyer, expert, commissioners, ambassadors etc., are dl ruled by Mercury. Mercury represents Mathematics. It indicates lecturing too.
	Mercury represents learning, writing, arts, sculpture, medical profession, expertise, minister ship' message, wit, cleverness, duality, fame, astrology, wisdom, chanting Vedas, Priesthood, birds, fame, Literature, poetry, scriptures etc. Satyacharya says that Sculpture, astrology, recitation and composition of poetry, research work, dealing in cloths, and catching birds and animals are also ruled by Mercury.
Western astrology	Authors, accountants, educationists, communicators, publishers, book sellers,. postmen, businessmen, traders,
	technicians etc.
Education	Mathematics, accounts, journalism and astrology.

Planet	Professions related to planets
Jupiter	It rules over the power of reasoning, clear thinking, law and sciences. Western astrologers say that it rules over financial dealing, shipping business and foreign affairs.
	Jupiter indicates advocates, professors, priests, judges, ministers, administrators, divines, bankers, those working in revenue departments, palaces, law-courts, treasury, wealth, court, temples, religion, place of justice, treasures, banker, writers, mathematics, economics, religious lore, sastras, preaching, religious education, donation, physician, grammarian, turmeric, gold, valuable things etc. Jupiter is for knowledge. It denotes professors, philosophers' preceptors, gurus etc.
Education	Literature, philosophy, management, psychology.
Venus	Satyacharya says that Venus represents gold, precious stones, vehicles, women, cheating, curd, ghee, cow and perfumes. It rules over ornaments, adornments precious Stones, jaggery, young woman, music, cinema, cows.

Planet	Professions related to planets
	It can give employment connected with vehicles, transport, railway 'shipping etc. color, singers, cinema, drama, silk, perfumes, agriculture, silver, white things, diamond, diseases of women, assessment, careful judgment by weighing pros and cons, panchayat, jury, X-ray, glass, draughtsman, etc.
Western astrology	Fine arts, musicians, painters, singers, poets, actors, artists of all kinds, makers and dealers of fragrance or perfumes, flowers, ornaments, garments, fancy goods, luxuries, pastry cooks, sweet makers, confectioners, butlers, maid servants, sugarcane, sugar, diplomatic assignments, ministerial berth, power, politics etc.
Education	Fashion/jewelry designing, theater, music, painting, hotel management/ hospitality, computer graphics etc.
Saturn	Miners, merchants of coal and other commodities ruled by it, plumbers, watchmen, etc. Saturn indicates hard labour. Saturn denotes stone, mine ores, petrol, oil, coal, iron etc.

Planet	Professions related to planets
	Saturn represents leather and hides, agriculturists, farmers, miner, mason, sweeper, sexton, tanner, estate agent, dyer, plumber, cobbler, scavenger, potter, coal merchants, dealing in commodities ascribed to Saturn, jailers, watchmen, those who work at night, those who work underground etc.
	Saturn indicates service, positions of responsibility, and things within the earth, ores, oil, wells, coal, tin, lead, blue things, iron factory, poor homes, pension, bone, orthopedics, chronic ailments and hospitals for their treatment and so on.
Education	Labour laws, geology, engineering etc.
Rahu	It is considered to be strong in the tenth house, it is closely connected with inventions, politics, science, magic, and bad habits like drinking, gambling, treachery, poisonous drugs, sorcery, Witchcraft mountains, caves, buffaloes, jails, etc. computer hardware, cameras, communication, social media, it has connection with machinery photography printing etc.

Planet	Professions related to planets
Education	Research, pilot, space engineer, Air hostess, computer and photography hardware's
Ketu	occult sciences, philosophy, plotting, intriguing and quarrels It enhances the qualities of well-placed /exalted planet it is with and is called dwajh(flag)
Education	Linguistics, meteorologists etc.

2
Information and Characteristic Feature of Planets

The Sun is the singnificator of the person's collection of copper and gold, and of father, patience, valour, victory in war, one's soul (Atman), auspiciousness, happiness, prowess, power, light, any work relating to Lord Shiva, travels in forests and mountains, havans or yajnas, Inclinations for work, temple, acuteness, enthusiasm. Wise men should act according to these significations.

The Moon is the signiflcator of the welfare of the mother, tranquilityof the mind, bathing in the sea, white chamar, umbrella, good fan, fruits, flowers, tender objects, farming grains, fame, pearls, silver, bell metal, beauty. In other words, all about the above matters should be ascertained from the Moon.

All about one's strength (physical and mental), products produced from the earth, qualities of the brothers and sisters, cruelty, battle, courage, antagonism, the fire of the kitchen, gold, kinsmen, weapons, thieves, enemies, enthusiasm, sexual intercourse with another man's wife, falsehood, prowess, high thinking, sin, wounds, and acquisition of the position of a commander-in-chief should be ascertained from Mars. In other words, Mars is the significator of these matters.

From Mercury is to be ascertained all about learning, eloquence, proficiency in arts, praise by learned people, maternal uncle, dexterity in speech, aptness for acquiring knowledge, expertise in ways of worship, intelligence, religious acts relating to Lord Shiva, truthfulness, oyster, sports of recreation and enjoyment, skill in mechanical arts, kinsmen, heir apparent, friends, sister's sons and daughters etc.

Jupiter is concerned with matters relating to knowledge, noble qualities, sons (progeny), minister, good behavior, imparting knowledge or teaching, magnanimity, knowledge of shruties, shastras, smrities, progress in every direction, beatitude, devotion towards gods and Brahmins, sacrifice, penance, religious faith, treasury, mastering the senses, honour, kindness and happiness of the husband.

Note—In a female's horoscope Jupiter should be taken as the significator of the husband. In a male's horoscope Jupiter, among other matters, is the significator for progeny (San tan Karaka).

All about one's wealth, conveyances, clothes, ornaments, treasures (including hidden treasures), amalgam of song, dance and instrumental music, scents, flowers, co-habitation, bed, house, richness, fondness for poetry, Indulgence in all kinds of comforts and luxuries, minister ship, soft-spokenness, marriage and other holy deeds, celebrations, etc., should be ascertained through Venus.

Note—In a male's horoscope all about the happiness of wife and marital happiness should be considered through Venus. Venus is the significator for wife in such a chart.

Significator is of very great importance in assessing a birth chart. For example, on a particular case of Aquarius Ascendant, the native was of about 22 years with the Dasa of Venus in operation. Some astrologers predicted that the marriage of the native would take place in his 24th years after the commencement of the Dasa of the Sun lord of the 7th house. The marriage actually took place in the Dasa of Venus.

The significations of Saturn are longevity, death, fear, downfall, disgrace, sickness, unhappiness and misery, poverty, humiliation, sins, labour, filth, censure, misfortune, impurity of mind, observance of certain formalities after death in the family, stability, taking shelter from menials, buffalo, drowsiness, debts, articles of iron, service, slavery, confinement, getting arrested, agricultural implements etc.

The places governed by the Sun are a Shiva temple, open spaces, places where there is light, regions where there is no water and the Eastern quarter.

The Moon has jurisdiction over the temple of Goddess Durga, places inhabited by women, places where water, medicinal herbs, honey and wine are available and the North-Western quarter.

The places concerned with Mars are the battle field, those where there is fire, those inhabited by thieves and low people and the Southern quarter.

The governance of Mercury extends to places where there is a temple of Lord Vishnu, those frequented by men of learning, those of recreation, those where Mathematics is practiced and the Northern quarter.

Jupiter has jurisdiction over treasury, peepal trees, places, inhabited by gods and Brahmins, and the North-Eastern quarter.

The places coming under the administration of Venus are abodes of courtesans, the harem, bed rooms, dining halls, and the South-Eastern quarter.

Saturn rules over places inhabited by low class people, temple of Shasta (a deity), those which are full of filth and the Western quarter.

The places belonging to Rahu and Ketu are the ant-hills, the dark holes of serpents and the South-Western quarter.

Sun—A worshipper of Lord Shiva, a physician (Vaidya), a king, one who performs yajna, a minister, tiger, deer and chakor (the ruddy goose) are the significations of the Sun.

The Moon rules over worship of Shasta (a deity) females, a washerman, a cultivator, an animal living in water, a hare, an antelope crane, birds known as Bagula(crane) and Chakor.

Mars—has jurisdiction over a cook (in the kitchen), an armed person, a goldsmith, a ram, a cock, a jackal, a monkey, a vulture and a thief.

Mercury—is concerned with a milkman, a person of learning, an artisan, an expert accountant, a devotee of Lord Vishnu, Garuda, a Chataka , a parrot and a cat.

Jupiter—An astrologer, a minister, a Brahmin, a preceptor, a sanyasi, and important personage, a pigeon, a horse and swan belong to Jupiter.

Venus—A wealthy man, a songster, a Vaishya (businessman), a sensualist, a dancer, a weaver, a prostitute, a peacock, a cow, a buffalo and a parrot are represented by Venus.

Saturn has influence over a seller or buyer of oil. servant, a mean person, a hunter, a blacksmith, an elephant, a crow and a cuckoo.

Rahu—A Buddhist, a snake catcher, a donkey, a wolf, a camel, a serpent or snake, mosquitoes, a bug, insects, an owl and a place of darkness are signified by Rahu and Ketu.

Planet Significations as per Uttara Kalamrit

Sun- Significations

1) The soul (2) power (3) intense severity (4) fortress (5) Good strength (6) heat (7) splendor (8) fire (9) worship of Shiva (10) courage (11) thorny trees (12) being in royal favor (13) bitterness (14) old age (15) cattle (16) wickedness (17) land (18) father (19) taste (20) self-realization (21) skyward look (22) one born of a timid woman (23) world of mortals (24) square (25) bone (26) valor (27) grass (28) the belly (29) strenuous effort (30) forest (31) half a year (32) eye (33) wandering over the mountain's (34) quadruped (35) king (36) travelling (37) dealing (38) bite (39) scorch (40) circular shape (41) eye disease (42) body (43) timber (44) mental purity (45) lordship of the whole country (46) freedom from disease (47) Lord of Saurashtra state (48) ornament (49) disease in the bead (50) pearls (51) Lord of sky (52) short like a dwarf (53) Lord of the East (54) copper (55) blood (56) kingdom (57) a red cloth (58) a stone (59) public life (60) river bank (61) coral (62) strong at mid-day (63) east (64) mouth (65) long standing anger (66) capture of the enemy (67) sattvic (pure) (69) red chandan (sandal) or saffron (69) hostility and (70) thick cord.

Moon Significations

(1) Intelligence (2) flower (3) good perfume (4) going to a fortress (5) disease (6) Brahmin (7) idleness (8) Phlegmatic humor (9) epilepsy (10) enlargement of the spleen (11) mental disposition (12) heart (13) woman (14) virtue or vice (15) sourness (16) sleep (17) happiness (18) anything like water (19) silver (20) thick sugarcane (21) typhoid (22) travel (23) well (24) tank (25) mother (26) impartiality (27) mid-day (28) pearls (29) consumption (30) whiteness (31) waistband (32) bell-metal (33) salt (34) short stature (35) mind (36) ability (37) pond (38) diamond (39) winter season (40) break of 48 minutes Muhurta (41) facial luster (42) white color (43) belly (44) worshipping Goddess Gauri (45) honey (46) joking (47) nourishment (48) wheat (49) pleasure (50) splendor (51) face (52) sharp in thought (53) love of curd (54) mendicant (55) fame (56) beauty (57) strength at night (58) facing westward (59) learned (6) saline (61) getting a job (62) love for west (63) the middle World (64) nine gems (65) middle age (66) life (67) eating (68) going too far of countries (69) ailment of the shoulders (70) umbrella or any other royal insignia (71) good fruits (72) blood purity and vitality (73) fish and other water creatures (74) serpent (75) silk garments (76) good budding (77) brilliant things (78) clean crystal and (79) soft and velvety.

Mars Significations

1) Prowess (2) land (3) strength (4) carrying arms for the battle (5) Kingship (6) loss of virility (7) thief (8) battle (9) hostility (10) enemy (11) generosity (12) love for deep red color things (13) owning a garden (14) sound of a trumpet (15) affection (16) quadruped (17) king (18) fool (19) anger (20) going to a foreign country (21) firmness (22) supporter (23) fire (24) controversy (25) bile (26) heal (27) wound (28) service under a ruler (29) day (30) sky (31) seeing (32) shortness (33) disease (34) fame (35) tin (36) sword (37) lance or spear (38) minister (39) fracture of a limb (40) jewel (41) praying to God Subrahmanyam (42) youth (43) pungent (44) Dumar Hall (45) earthen pots (46) obstacles (47) flesh eater (48) calumniating others (49) victory over enemy (50) bitter (1) strong at the end of the night (52) gold (53) summer season (54) valor (55) enemy's strength (56) profundity of character (57) strength (58) man (59) tendency (60) God Brahma (61) axe (62) forester (63) Village headman (64) state inspection (65) pain while passing urine (66) square (67) goldsmith (68) rogue (69) burnt place (70) good dinner (71) leanness (72) deft in archery (73) blood (74) copper (75) a beautiful cloth (76) facing South (77) inclining towards South (78) desire (79) anger (80) scandal (81) house (82) army commander (83) Cannon and weapons (84) a tree

(85) Sama Veda (86) brother (87) spade or hatchet (88) looking after the wild animals (89) independence (90) persistency (91) land (92) judge (93) serpent (94) world (95) speech (96) fickle mindedness (97) mounting a vehicle (98) sight of blood (99) coagulation of blood.

Mercury Significations

(1) education (2) horses (3) treasury (4) mathematics (5) wisdom (6) speech (7) Brahmin (8) infantry (9) writing (10) new garment (11) palatial building (12) green color (13) sculpture (14) astrology (15) pilgrimage to holy places (16) wise lectures (17) temple (18) trading (19) best ornaments (20) courteous speech (21) Vedanta philosophy (22) maternal-grand-father (23) bad dreams (24) eunuch (25) facing North (26) skin (27) we (28) bell metal (29) renunciation (30) Ritu (season) (31) beautiful house (32) Doctor (33) neck (34) influencing through recitation of mantras (33) child (36) crooked look (37) heave (38) Modesty (39) paternal relation (40) rear (41) dancing (42) devotion (43) humorous temperament (44) powerful in the morning (45) Hemant Ritu (46) stone to sharpen knives (47) tranquility (48) navel (49) family prosperity (SO) mixed items (51) proficiency in language (52) worship of lord Vishnu (53) Sudra (54) bird (55) after-born (56) depth of language (57) The Directions (58) Atharav Veda (59) religious action (60) tower (61) dust (62) garden (63) pudendum virile (64)

even (65) benefic (66) moving in villages (67) impartial nature (68) fond or Northwest quarter (69) well versed in the legends or the past (70) specialist in grammar (71) expert in testing or the precious stones (72) a scholar (73) maternal uncle (74) sacred prayer (75) an amulet and (76) spells or a high order.

Jupiter Significations

(1) Brahmin (2) Guru (3) one's duty (4) Chariot (5) cow (6) infantry (7) savings (8) Meemamsa (9) treasure (10) horse (11) curd, etc. (12) large body (13) Valor (14) reputation (15) logic (16) astrology (17) son (18) grandson (19) dropsy (20) wealth of elephants (21) philosophy (22) great grandfathers (23) palatial house (24) gems (25) eldest brother (26) grandfather (27) Lord loon (28) cold season (29) wrath (30) jewel (31) merchant (32) physical health (33) beautiful mansion (34) royal honor (35) thigh (36) Gods (37) penance(38) Charity (39) religious duty (40) helping others (41) impartiality (42) facing North (43) circular (44) yellow color (45) moving in villages (46) North (47) close friend (48) swinging (49) Orator (50) rat (51) old garment (52) new house (53) happiness (54) old (55) Mantras (56) twice born (57) holy water (58) Knee (58) movement in heaven (60) I house granting all comforts (61) intellect (62) proficiency in learning (63) literature (64) tower (65) charming an audience (66) throne (67)

installation of God Brahma (68) strong at all times (69) month (70) Vessels (71) Lapis Lazuli (72) fruits of Agnisthoma rite (73) sweet juice (74) being Good (75) happiness (76) misery (77) length (78) gentleness (79) reading other's mind (80) gold (81) ornamentation (82) device (83) wind (84) phlegm (85) topaz (86) Vedic text (87) brilliancy (88) softness (89) Stone (90) (91) performing one's religious duties and (92) travelling in a well-decorated carriage (93) Memory

Venus Significations

(1) while umbrella (2) good cowrie (3) garment (4) marriage (5) income (6) a biped (man) (7) woman (8) Brahmin (9) Sabha (10) Wily (11) wife (12) sexual happiness (13) short (14) sour (15) flower (16) command (17) fame (18) Youthful vigor (19) Vehicle' (20) silver (21) Southeast quarter (22) Salty (23) ogling (24) quarter (25) scratching (25) half a month (27) the quality of passion (28) strong (29) pearl (30) Yajur Veda (31) Vaisya (32) beauty (33) buying and selling (34) love-making (35) watery resort (36) elephant (37) horse (38) variegated color (39) poetry (41) dancing (42) middle age (43) singing (44) enjoyment (45) happiness from the wife (44) gems (45) fond of humor (46) swimmer (47) servant (48) luck (49) variegated color (50) handsome Youth (51) Kingdom (52) scents (53) garland (54) Veena (55) flute (56) amusement

(57) lovely gait (58) eight kinds of wealth (all sorts of pleasures) (59) well-formed limbs (60) sparing in meals (61) spring season (62) ornaments (63) inclined towards maintaining several women (64) eye (65) truth speaking (66) proficiency in art (67) semen (68) water sports (69) profundity of character(70) Pre-eminence (71) sharp-witted (72) musical instrument (73) decoration for the stage (74) fond of amorous sports (75) broken health (76) love, as chief business (77) greatly respected and highly esteemed (78) fondness for white garments (79) Bharat Natyama (a form of dance) (80) Government seal (81) a lord (82) worshipping Goddess Parvati and Lakshmi (83) sexual pleasures (84) gentleness (85) much emaciated (86) day silting mothers (87) literary composition, deft at writing Poetry (88) black hair (89) auspicious (90) mysterious or genital organs (91) urine (92) moving in the region of good serpents (93) afternoon (94) knowledge of the generative organs and the secret connected with it.

Saturn Significations

(1) Laziness (2) obstruction (3) horse (4) elephant (5) skill (6) gain (7) proof or witness (8) distress (9) sickness (10) misunderstanding (11) misery (12) death (13) happiness through a woman (14) maid servant (15) asses and mules (16) outcaste (17) one with disfigured limbs (18) haunting woods (19) handsome look (20) gift

(21) a lord (22) a portion of life (23) eunuch (24) one born of the lowest caste (25) birds (26) the three sacred fires (27) a servile duty (28) unrighteous conduct (29) one without manliness (30) telling lies (31) long lasting (32) wind (33) old age (34) tendons and muscles (35) strong at the end of the day (36) Shishir Ritu or winter (37) great-anger (38) exertion (39) born of a very low mother (40) bastard (41) Golaka (42) dirty clothes and house (42) wicked mind (44) friendship with the wicked (45) black color (46) evil (47) cruelty (48) ashes (49) black grain (50) gems (51) iron (52) nobility (53)a year (54) Shudra (55) Vaisya (56) one representing the father (57) learning the trade of another class (58) crippled (59) sharp (60) a blanket (61) facing West (62) lifesaving drugs (63) downward look (64) living by agriculture (65) arsenal (66) student belonging to another caste (67) external position (68) fondness for the North-Eastern quarter (69) serpent world (70) downfall (71) lost battle (72) wandering (73) a spear (74) lead (75) misdirected strength (76) a Turk (77) worn out (78) oil(79) wood (80) Brahmin (81) the Tamas (82) travelling through forests and over mountains (83) hard-heartedness (84) fear (85) long standing distress (86) hunter (87) ugly hair (88) entire sovereignty (89) 81ann (90) goats and the like (91) buffalos and the like (92) indulging in sex pleasure (93) dressing oneself for amorous appeals (94)

worshipping God Yama (95) dog(96) theft (97) cruel-hearted.

Rahu significations

(1) Umbrella (2) Cowrie (3) kingdom (4) gathering (5) fellacious argument (6) hurling by speech (7) outcast (8) wicked woman (9) decorated vehicle (10) an irreligious man (11) gambling (12) strong at twilight (13) intriguing with a wicked woman (14) going abroad (15) impurity (16) bone (17) enlargement of spleen (18) falsehood (19) downward look (20) perplexity (21) emerald (22) facing the Southern quarter (23) shelter of outcast or low people (24) painful swelling (25) a big forest (26) wandering in rugged places (27) mountain (28) pain (29) staying outside (30) tending towards south-west (31) wind (32) phlegm (33) sorrow (34) serpent (35) night breeze (36) sharp (37) long (38) reptile (39) reading of dreams (40) travel (41) a Muhurta (42) old age (43) a vehicle (44) world of serpents (45) other (46) Grandfather or maternal grand-father (47) air (48) an acute or sharp pain (49) catarrh (50) breathing (51) great prowess (52) forest (53) Worshipper of Goddess Durga (54) wickedness (55) cohabitation with quadruped's (56) Urdu script (58) harsh words (59) Argument.

Ketu significations

(1) Worship of God Ganesh, and many other gods (2) doctor (3) dog (4) a cock (5) vulture (6) salvation (7) all kinds of wealth (8) consumption (9) pain (10) fever (11) bathing in the Holy Ganges (12) great penance (13) wind (14) a Hunter (15) friendship (16) conferring of prosperity (17) stone (18) wound (19) witchcraft (20) inconstancy (21) knowledge of Brahma (22) belly (23) eye-sore (24) stupidity (25) thorn (26) deer (27) knowledge (28) observing silence as a fast (29) philosophy (30) all sorts of luxuries (31) luck (32) trouble from enemies (33) loss of appetite (34) indifference to the world (35) paternal grandfather (36) hunger (37) severe inconstancy (37) severe stomachache (38) boils and the like skin troubles (39) revoking the orders of arrest and (42) the association of Shudra.

Source of livelihood Based on Navamsa Position of 10th Lord.

If Sun is the Navamsa lord of the 10th.

The sources of livelihood of the native will be through fruit bearing trees, by the recitation of mantras, by fraud and cunningness, by gambling, by speaking lies, through wool, medicines and the like, by working on metals or through service under a king or respectable person, if the lord of the 10th house be placed in the Navamsa of the Sun.

Moon

The sources of income or livelihood will be through trade in water- products (pearls, corals etc.), agriculture and cattle breeding, pilgrimage to holy places, service under a woman and trade in drapery. If the Navamsa occupied by the lord of the 10th house is that of the Moon.

Mars

The sources of income or livelihood will be through metals, serving for fighting battles, cooking, lands, gold, causing troubles to others, weapons, adventure, association with wicked men, spying or through theft if the lord of the 10th house occupies the Navamsa of Mars.

Mars

In a nativity where the lord of the 10th house is posited in the Navamsa owned by Mercury, the earning will be through composition of poem, study of sacred scripture, by being a writer, or through clerical work or through tricks, through the knowledge of astrology, through the study of Vedas, by recitation of Mantras, through priesthood or by some pretext.

Jupiter

If the Navamsa be that of Jupiter, the sources of livelihood or earning will be through dependence on Brahmins, or through dependence on temples (serving as priests etc.) or religious Ashramas, through the beneficience of the king (Government), through study of Puranas, Shastras, or Vedas, through practicing of righteous paths and actions, or by religious instruction.

Venus

If the Navamsa be that of Venus, the sources of earning will be through dependence, serving a woman (she may be wife, prostitute, queen, a film actress or any other woman), through cows, buffaloes, elephants, horses, etc., through teaching music or through musical performances, by singing or dancing, through silver (sale and purchase), scents, milk, curd etc., ornaments, through silken and other expensive dress materials, by being a companion or aides of a lady of high standing, or by his poetic talents.

Saturn

If the Navamsa be that of Saturn, the sources of income or livelihood, will be through dealing in roots and fruits, by hard physical labour, through servants or menials, rogues and through the earnings of men of low morality, through grains of bad quality, by carrying loads, by following low kind of professions, through sculpture, wooden materials, and by serving under a butcher.

Will the lively hood be in the Native Place or Some where else?

If the lord of Navamsa be strong, there will be accrual of wealth without any obstacle or exertion.

If it be weak, very little earning may be expected. The country from which the accrual of wealth will be Indicated by the sign representing the 10th house or the Navamsa occupied by the lord of the 10th house. If the sign be occupied or aspected by its lord, the source of income will be found in his own country. The same will happen when the Navamsa occupied by the lord of the 10th house by a fixed sign. If the sign of the 10th house be occupied or aspected by planet other than its lord, the person concerned will earn in the place other than his native land.

GOVERNMENT SERVICE

राजाङ्कं सचिवकरात्मधीभविष्यज्जानासून्
सुतजटरश्रुतिस्मृतीश्च ॥१२॥

The fifth house deals with (and has designations accordingly) the mark of the sovereign.

10th house deals with the state, 11th house an important high-ranking post (Uttara Kalamrit).

Example 1

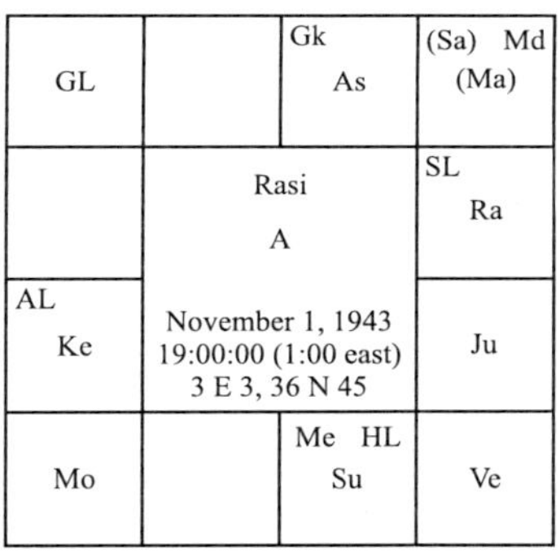

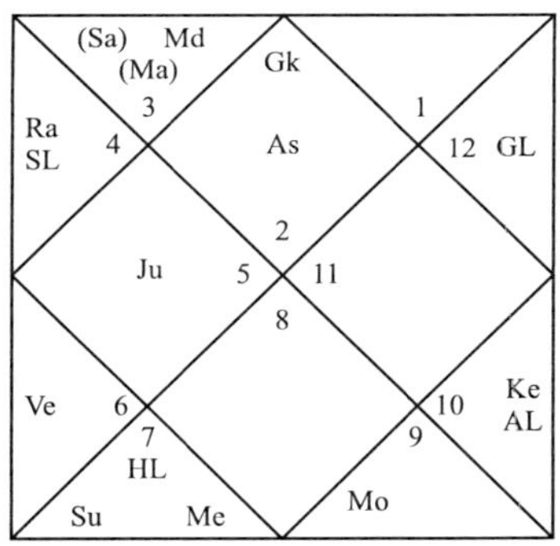

As:	9 Ta 31	Su:	16 Li 29-AK	Mo:	2 Sg 29-PiK	Ma (R):	0 Ge 06-DK
Me:	10 Li 59-AmK	Ju:	2 Le 22-PK	Ve:	0 Vi 43-GK	Sa (R):	4 Ge 11-MK
Ra:	19 Cn 28-BK	Ke:	19 Cp 28	HL:	8 Li 30	GL:	27 Pi 16

French Government official. Exchange of Sun and Venus, relates Sun, Mercury, Jupiter and Venus. Saturn the 9th,10th lord is in the sign of mercury links with 5th and 2nd lord Mercury, Mercury is also linked with Jupiter the lord 11th. So, there is a link of 5th, 10th and 11th.

Example 2: Former IAS

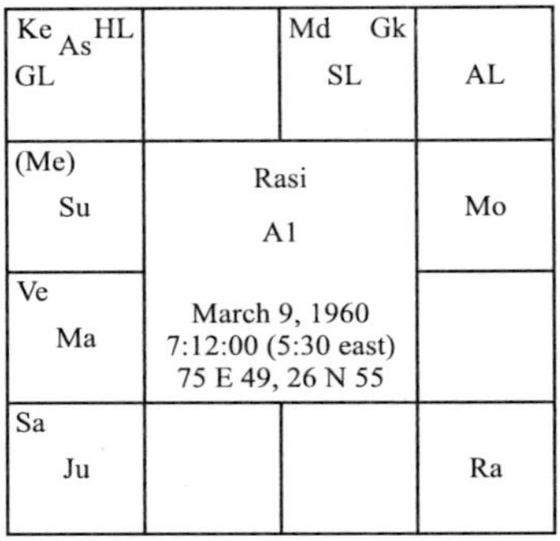

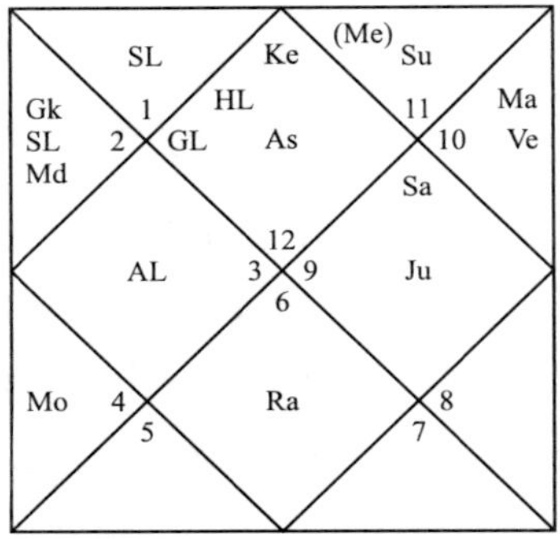

As: 5 Pi 06	Su: 26 Aq 18-MK	Mo: 5 Cn 54-DK	Ma: 19 Cp 11-PK
Me: 29 Aq 50-AK	Ju: 8 Sg 46-GK	Ve: 29 Cp 11-AmK	Sa: 24 Sg 18-PiK
Ra: 2 Vi 28-BK	Ke: 2 Pi 28	HL: 8 Pi 55	GL: 27 Pi 51

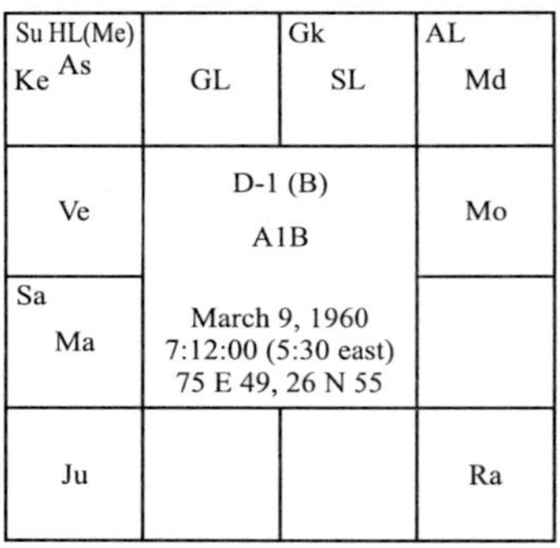

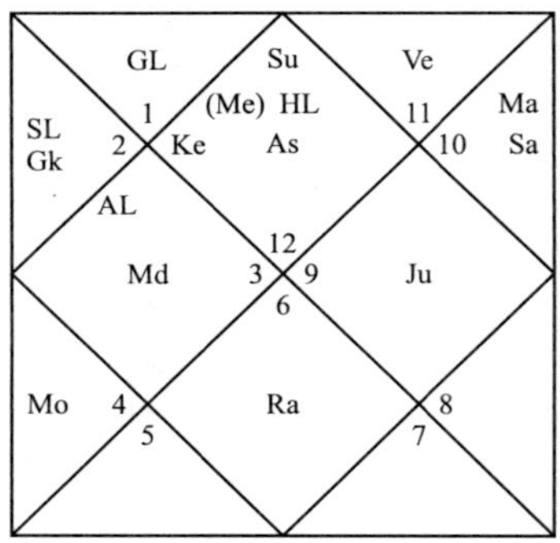

As: 15 Pi 53	Su: 26 Pi 44-MK	Mo: 23 Cn 06-DK	Ma: 22 Cp 41-PK
Me(R): 28 Pi 26-AK	Ju: 18 Sg 54-GK	Ve: 22 Aq 35-AmK	Sa: 8 Cp 40-PiK
Ra: 22 Vi 16-BK	Ke: 22 Pi 16	HL: 20 Pi `13	GL: 10 Ar 41

Moon the 5th lord in 5th related to Mars 2nd ,9th and Venus the 8th and 3rd, Mars is in the sign of Saturn which is related to 10th lord Jupiter, here the 5th ,10th and 11th are related through dispositor's.

Example 3: IAS Lady, Government Service

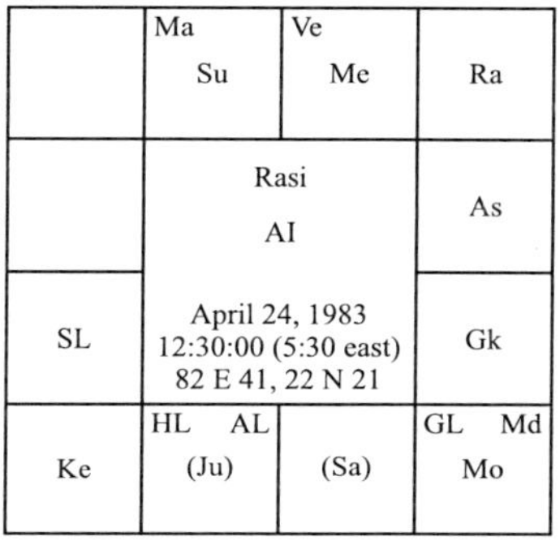

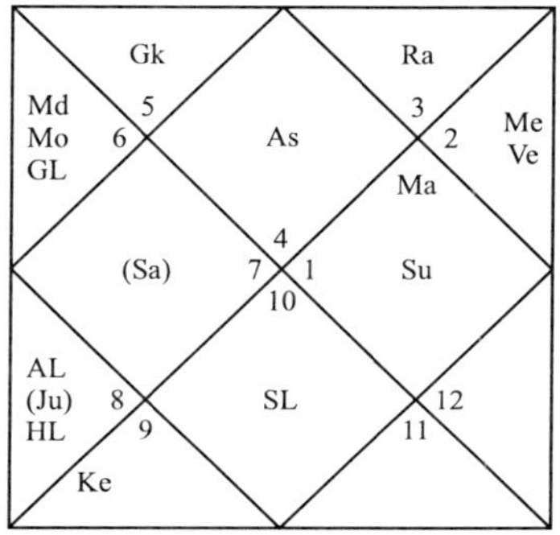

As: 21 Cn 29	Su: 11 Ar 01-PiK	Mo: 2 Vi 45-GK	Ma: 21 Ar 15-AmK
Me: 0 Ta 29-DK	Ju (R): 17 Sc 16-MK	Ve: 20 Ta 08-BK	Sa (R): 8 Li 24-PK
Ra: 3 Ge 58-AK	Ke: 3 Sg 58	HL: 7 Sc 29	GL: 17 Vi 36

Lord of 5th and 10th Mars in 10th Related to Sun the 2nd, Mercury 3rd and 12th, Saturn the 7th and 8th, Jupiter the 6th and 9th, the 11th ,4th lord Venus is related to Jupiter and through Jupiter to Mars, so the lords of 5th ,10th and 11th requirement is fulfilled for the high-ranking government service.

Example 4: Government Employee

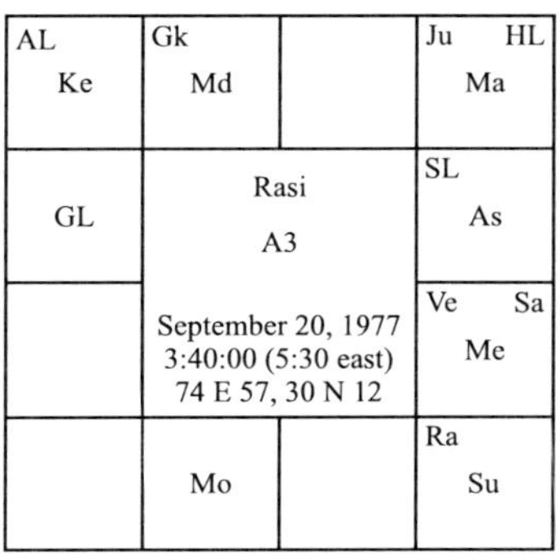

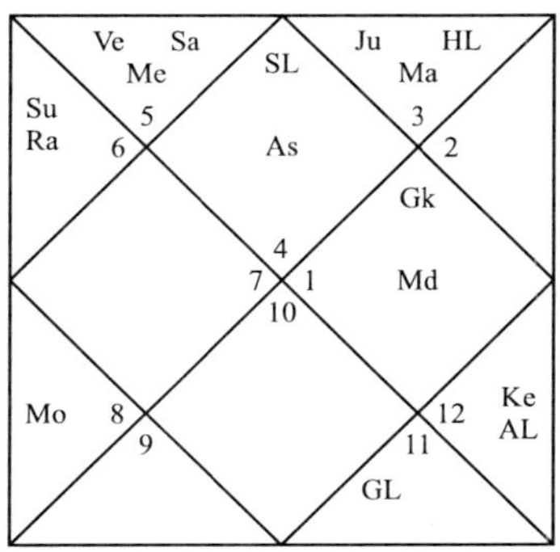

As: 29 Cn 45	Su: 4 Vi 24-PK	Mo: 29 Sc 55-AK	Ma: 18 Ge 50-AmK
Me: 16 Le 40-BK	Ju: 11 Ge 48-MK	Ve: 4 Le 16-GK	Sa: 21 Le 37-DK
Ra: 22 Vi 55-PiK	Ke: 22 Pi 55	HL: 13 Ge 17	GL: 12 Aq 56

The 5th ,10th lord Venus is in 10th and is under aspect from the 11th and 4th lord Mars, So the condition requirement of the lords of the 5th ,10th and 11th is there as lords as mentioned are connected.

Note – Another noteworthy condition is that 5th, 10th lord and bhava be of strength.

Example 5: Doctor employed in Government hospital

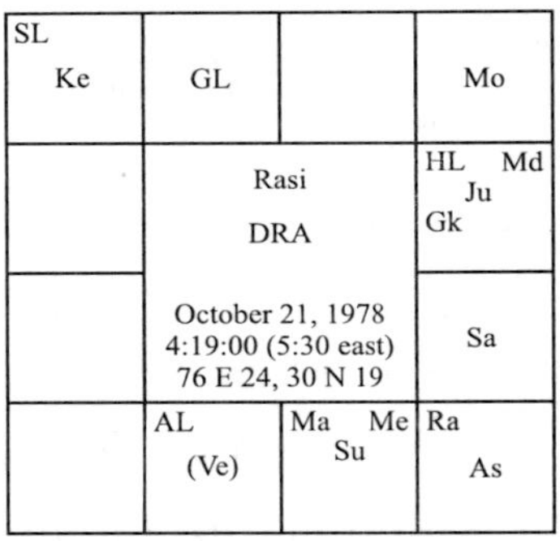

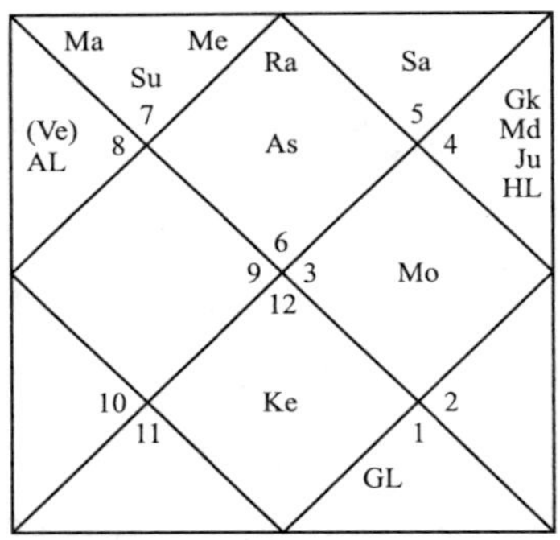

As: 5 Vi 31	Su: 4 Li 44-PK	Mo: 0 Ge 53-GK	Ma: 28 Li 56-AK
Me: 18 Li 03-BK	Ju: 14 Cn 35-PiK	Ve (R): 0 Sc 11-DK	Sa: 17 Le 55-MK
Ra: 3 Vi 52-AmK	Ke: 3 Pi 52	HL: 26 Cn 37	GL: 15 Ar 49

5th, 6th lord Saturn aspects the 10th lord by 3rd aspect, further its placed in the sign of Sun the 12th lord, this Sun is related to the 10th, Ascendant lord Mercury, Saturn also aspects the 11th lord Moon through the 10th aspect, the condition of 5th, 10th and 11th connection is fulfilled here, therefore the government service.

Example 6: Government Service.

JAG is army, currently a Major.

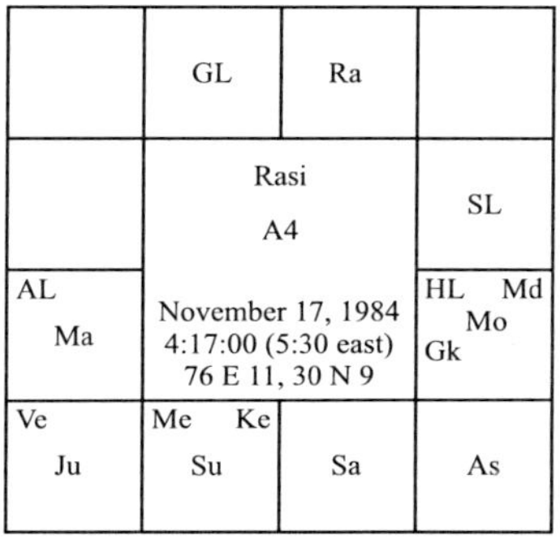

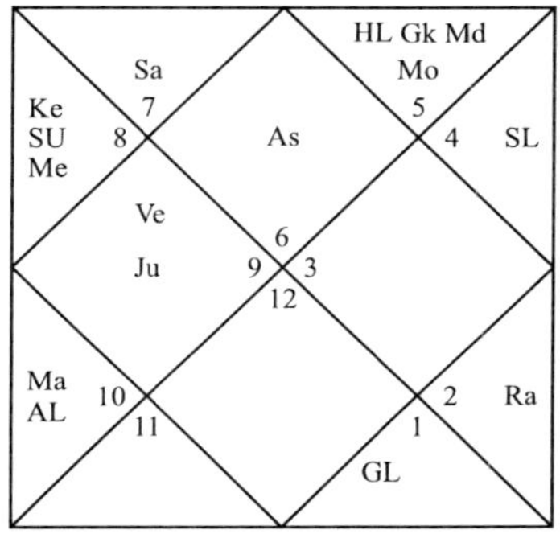

As:	28 Vi 23	Su:	2 Sc 14-DK	Mo:	10 Le 46-PK	Ma:	8 Cp 21-GK
Me:	22 Sc 12-BK	Ju:	19 Sg 10-MK	Ve:	11 Sg 01-PiK	Sa:	27 Li 13-AK
Ra:	4 Ta 54-AmK	Ke:	4 Sc 54	HL:	12 Le 04	GL:	13 Ar 12

5th lord Saturn in sign of Venus, while 10th lord Mercury is in the sign of Mars, which is placed in Saturn's sign, Saturn the 5th lord connects to 10th lord Mercury through Mars, as the 10th lord is in sign of mars, 11th lord Moon also connects through the aspect of mars to moon. The connection of 5th, 10th and 11th is also established in this case.

Example 7: Ex-accountant General

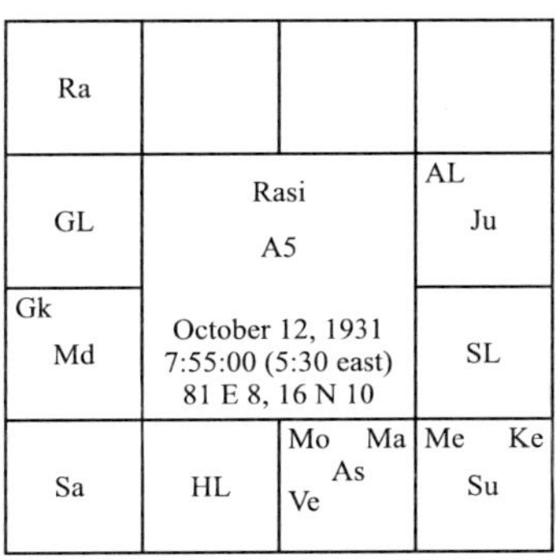

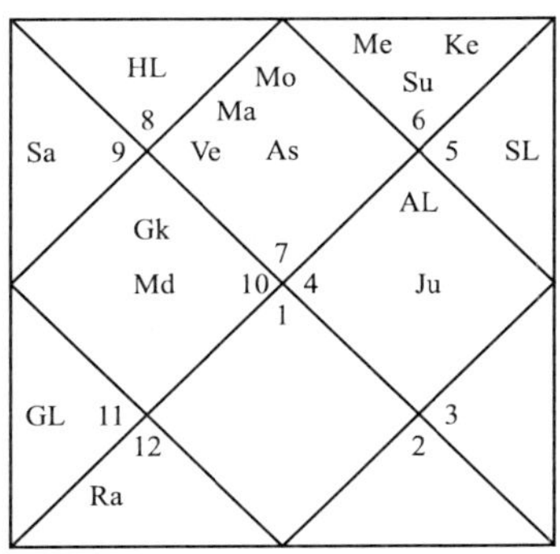

As:	22 Li 54	Su:	25 Vi 60-AK	Mo:	3 Li 52-DK	Ma:	25 Li 08-MK
Me:	21 Vi 11-PiK	Ju:	25 Cn 49-AmK	Ve:	5 Li 01-GK	Sa:	25 Sg 11-BK
Ra:	13 Pi 36-PK	Ke:	13 Vi 36	HL:	23 Sc 11	GL:	19 Aq 06

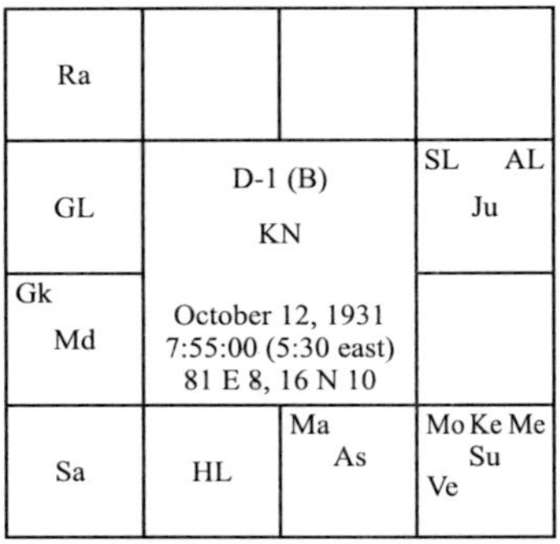

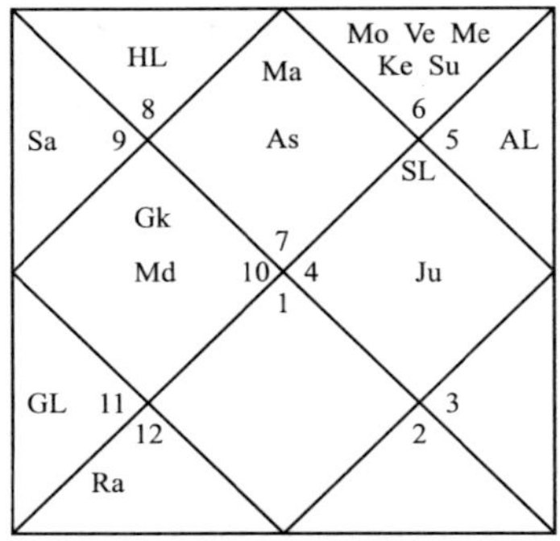

As:	26 Li 04	Su:	23 Vi 59-AK	Mo:	4 Li 47-DK	Ma:	16 Li 14-MK
Me:	10 Vi 43-PiK	Ju:	22 Cn 19-AmK	Ve:	15 Vi 08-GK	Sa:	16 Sg 36-BK
Ra:	2 Pi 22-PK	Ke:	2 Vi 22	HL:	28 Sc 42	GL:	21 Aq 50

The 5th lord Saturn establishes a clearer connection through the Bhava Chalit chart as, the connection with 10th and 11th is established there. In natal chart the connection is established through Jupiter which is in Kendra relationship within 10th lord and it owns the placement sign of Saturn, while Saturn aspects the 11th lord & own bhava the 5th.

Example 8: Government Administrative Service

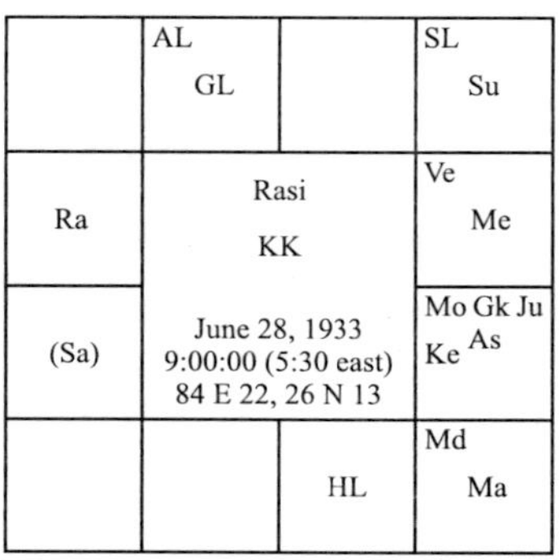

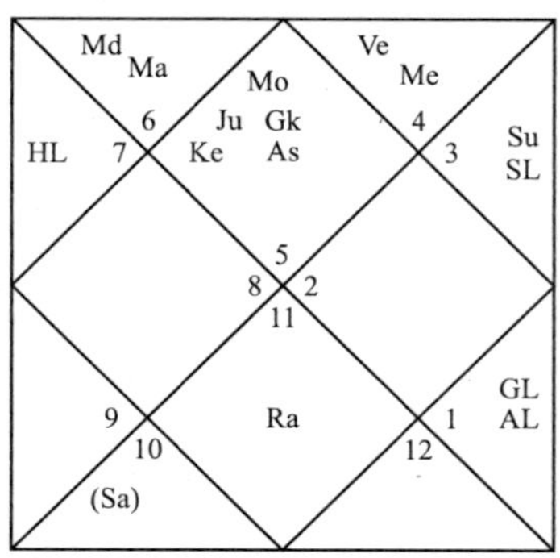

As:	4 Le 55	Su:	14 Ge 09-MK	Mo:	11 Le 01-PiK	Ma:	3 Vi 33-GK
Me:	9 Cn 30-PK	Ju:	24 Le 47-AK	Ve:	2 Cn 10-DK	Sa (R):	23 Cp 44-AmK
Ra:	7 Aq 59-BK	Ke:	7 Le 59	HL:	10 Li 47	GL:	5 Ar 58

5th lord in the ascendant it, aspects the 5th house, the bhava that is under aspect by the lord owning it prospers, Jupiter is related to moon the Sign placement lord of 10th lord Venus and 11th lord mercury, The Moon here, therefore the link of 5th, 10th and 11th as required is fulfilled here.

Example 9: Government Service, An ex-Judge at district courts.

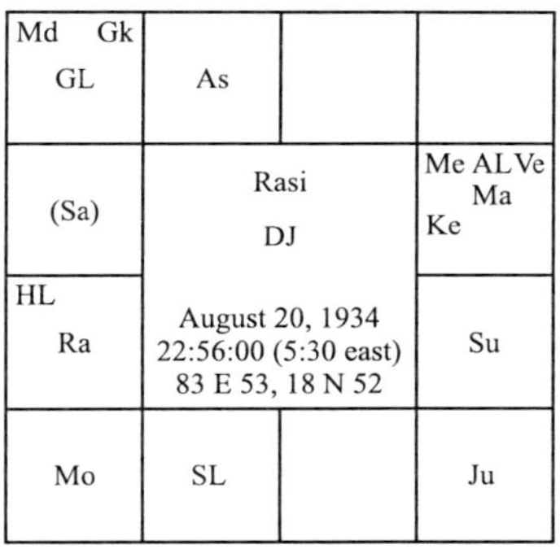

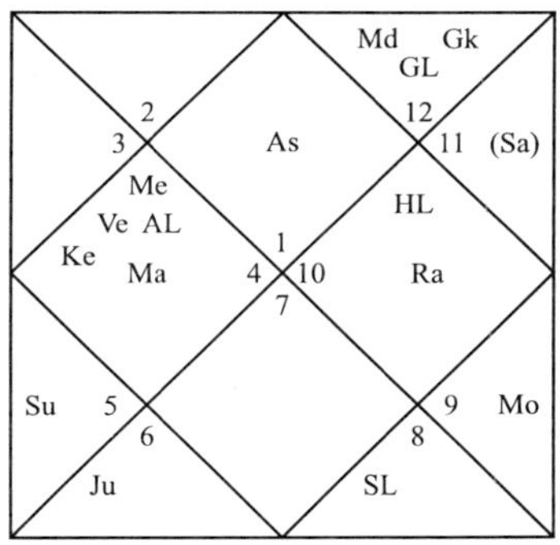

As: 29 Ar 45	Su: 4 Le 03-PK	Mo: 7 Sg 03-PiK	Ma: 0 Cn 44-DK
Me: 28 Cn 19-AK	Ju: 26 Vi 58-AmK	Ve: 10 Cn 48-MK	Sa (R): 1 Aq 42-GK
Ra: 17 Cp 15-BK	Ke: 17 Cn 15	HL: 11 CP 12	GL: 7 Pi 59

5th lord is in 5th in relation with the 10th and 11th lord Saturn due to the mutual aspect. The native was a government appointed judge at district courts. Notice the presence of Jupiter in 6th or influencing the 6th leads to the profession aligned to law.

Example 10: A BAMS employed in Government medical services.

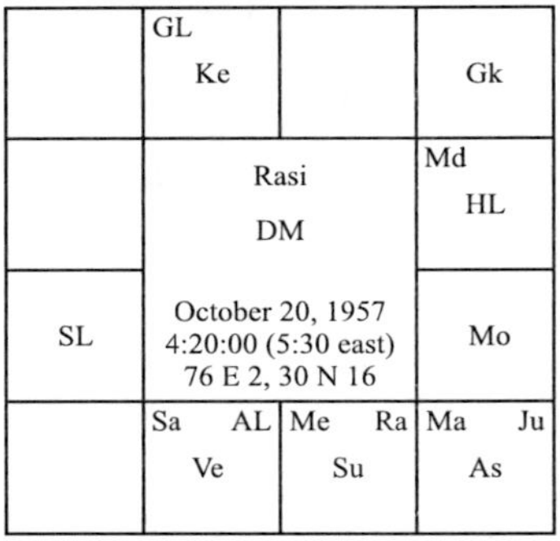

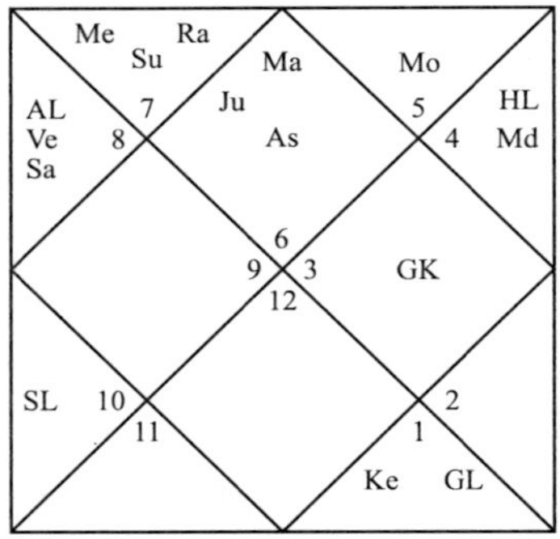

As: 3 Vi 50	Su: 3 Li 01-GK	Mo: 18 Le 01-BK	Ma: 23 Vi 32-AK
Me: 0 Li 09-DK	Ju: 21 Vi 58-AmK	Ve: 17 Sc 58-MK	Sa: 17 Sc 58-PiK
Ra: 17 Li 19-PK	Ke: 17 Ar 19	HL: 25 Cn 01	GL: 14 Ar 22

5th lord aspects the own house the 5th and is related to Venus, the sign placement lord of 10th and 11th lords the Mercury and the moon. So the conditional requirement of 5th, 10th and 11th connection is met.

Example 11: Government service, Engineer in irrigation department.

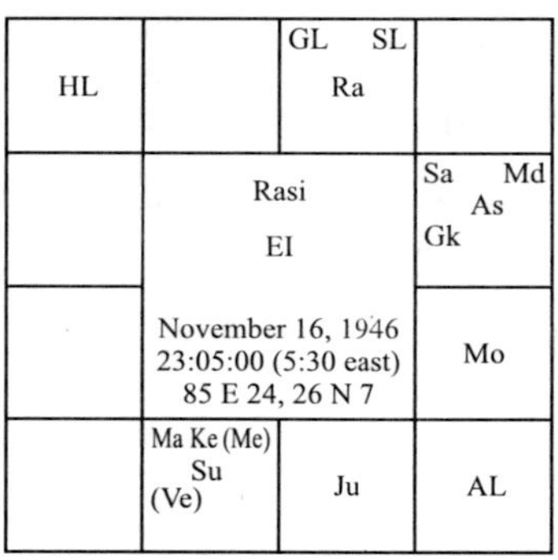

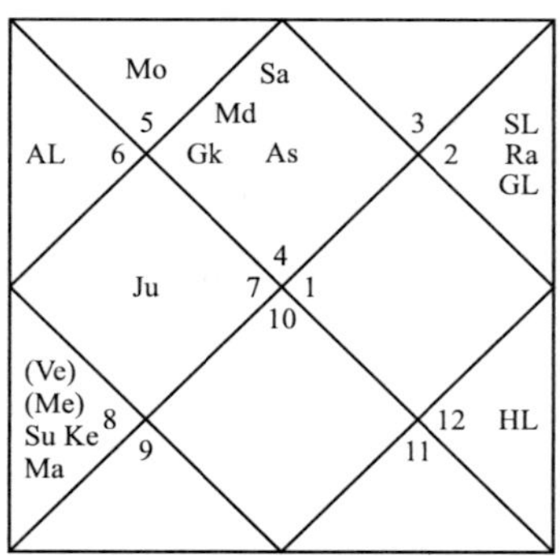

As: 26 Cn 21	Su: 0 Sc 40-DK	Mo: 10 Le 31-PK	Ma: 14 Sc 06-BK
Me (R): 11 Sc 43-MK	Ju: 18 Li 09-AK	Ve (R): 2 Sc 22-GK	Sa: 15 Cn 46-AmK
Ra: 18 Ta 47-Pik	Ke: 18 Sc 47	HL: 26 Pi 58	GL: 7 Ta 29

The 5th, 10th lord Mars is related to 4th, 11th lord Venus as they are all in 5th along with Sun the second lord, Mercury the 3rd, 12 lord. The requirement of the government job is fulfilled here as 5th, 10th and 11th lord connect to create the yoga for being employed by the state.

Example 12: Government Service (Retired Col)., Army medical corps.

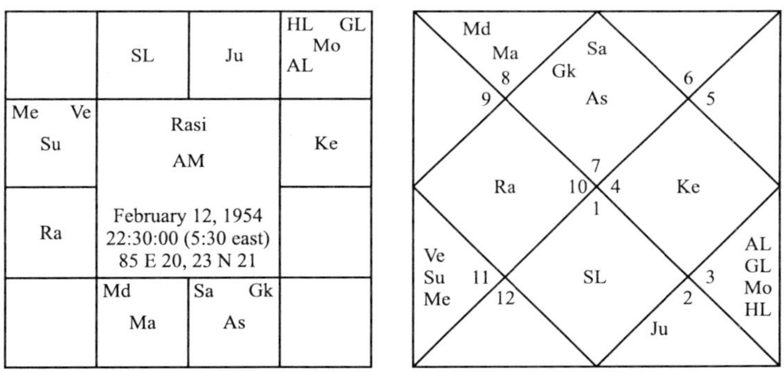

As: 6 Li 26	Su: 0 Aq 15-GK	Mo: 0 Ge 02-DK	Ma: 8 Sc 24-PiK
Me: 18 Aq 19-BK	Ju: 23 Ta 12-AmK	Ve: 3 Aq 33-PK	Sa: 16 Li 07-MK
Ra: 0 Cp 32-AK	Ke: 0 Cn 32	HL: 0 Ge 46	GL: 2 Ge 33

Exchange between the 5th, 6th lord Saturn and the ascendant lord is there, so Saturn, Venus and 9th, 12th lord Mercury are related, while the 11th lord Sun is related to Saturn, the 10th lord Moon falls in the Sign of the mercury a planet related to the Saturn the 5th, 6th lord.

Example 13: Indian Revenue Service–(High ranking officers)

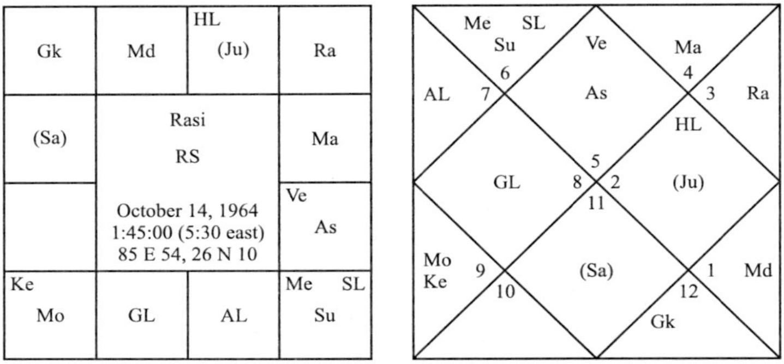

As: 2 Le 51	Su: 27 Vi 10-BK	Mo: 28 SG 40-AK	Ma: 23 Cn 46-PiK
Me: 25 Vi 47-MK	Ju (R): 1 Ta 23-DK	Ve: 15 Le 57-PK	Sa (R): 5 Aq 17-GK
Ra: 1 Ge 57-AmK	Ke: 1 Sg 57	HL: 24 Ta 49	GL: 22 Sc 33

The 10th lord is in Kendra position to 5th lord, 10th lord Venus and 11th Mercury are linked due to the Sun, sun is related to mercury and dispositor of 10th lord Venus. Jupiter the 5th, 8th aspects the Sun and mercury combination in 2nd, Saturn is related to the 10th, Mars aspects the Saturn a planet related to 10th lord Venus.

Govt hi ranking job Combination-5th Jupiter is linked to Venus the 10th, mercury the 11th and Sun the ascendant.

Example 14: IRS a former tax commissioner

5th, 12th lord Venus and 8th, 9th lord Saturn are in exchange, the planets in 5th and 8th become related planets due to this exchange.

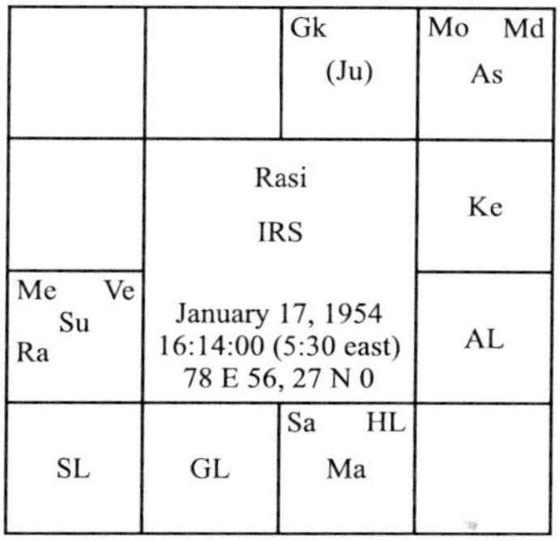

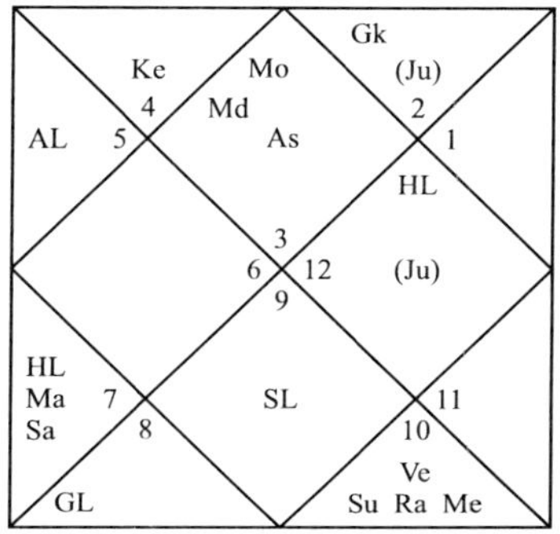

As:	14 Ge 56	Su:	3 Cp 35-GK	Mo:	13 Ge 21-PiK	Ma:	23 Li 26-BK
Me:	5 Cp 19-PK	Ju (R):	24 Ta 09-AmK	Ve:	0 Cp 35-DK	Sa:	15 Li 19-MK
Ra:	0 Cp 48-AK	Ke:	0 Cn 48	HL:	5 Li 40	GL:	24 Sc 23

5th Lord Venus is linked to 11th through an exchange with Saturn, 10th lord Jupiter is in the sign owned by Venus the 5th, 12th lord Venus and it also aspects the 5th lord, Jupiter's link with Mars and Saturn is through common dispositor Venus.

Govt job- The link of 5th, 10th and 11th house lords is present in the horoscope.

JOURNALISTS

Mars is pen and mercury is the ink, third house represents authorship and writing ,4th the masses, the 10th sign is represented by mercury from ascendant from moon the 10th sign is Venus, from Sun the 10th is again Venus. Mercury is exalted and in own sign forming Bhadra Panchmahapursh Yoga but is hemmed in malefic, Venus the 10th from both Sun and moon is the lord of 6th Servitude and 11th income and gains in 9th with lord of 9th Sun and Mars Lord of 5th and 12th Mars aspects 3rd and 4th houses, while Sun and Venus Aspect 3rd on their own and the 4th through Mars. The influence of the mars on 3rd house 4th house through aspect and on 6th /11th lord Venus through relationship is there, Mars also has a relationship with the 9th lord as well, Mercury is exalted and in 10th therefore being strong it will represent profession of the nature of sign Virgo and planet Mercury. The native is a journalist.

Note– Mars influence on 3rd, 5th, 6th, 8th, 10th and 12th is vital constituent here.

Note– One of the 5th house signification is writing the news.

Example 1

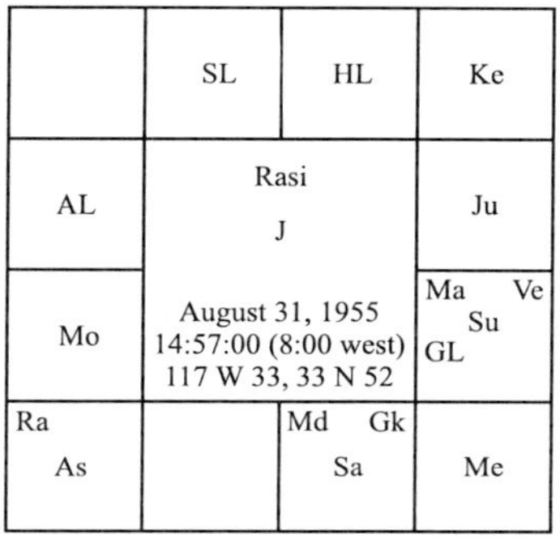

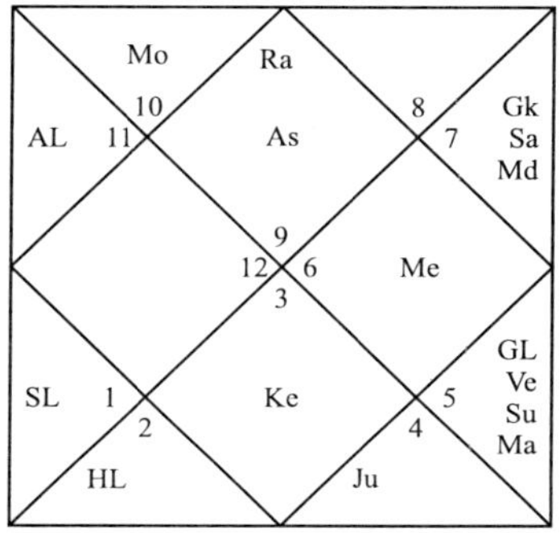

As:	15 Sg 20	Su:	14 Le 31-PiK	Mo:	27 Cp 55-AmK	Ma:	9 Le 39-GK
Me:	5 Vi 58-DK	Ju:	23 Cn 53-BK	Ve:	14 Le 25-PK	Sa:	22 Li 46-MK
Ra:	0 Sg 19-AK	Ke:	0 Ge 19	HL:	29 Ta 11	GL:	6 Le 46

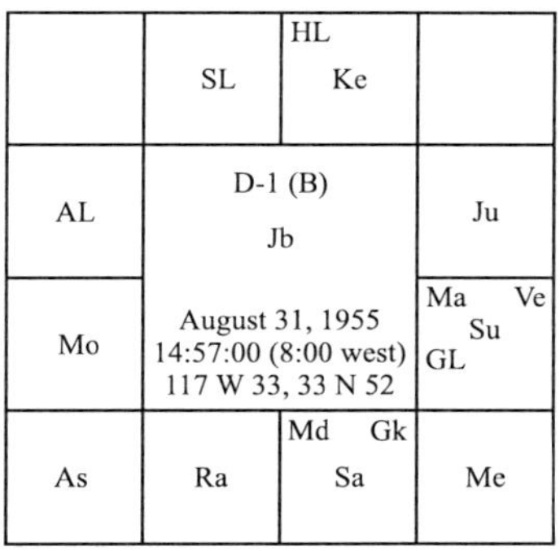

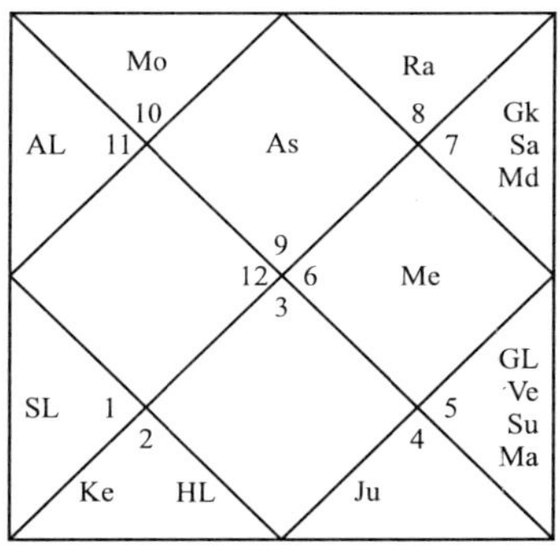

As:	18 Sg 00	Su:	10 Le 37-PiK	Mo:	11 Cp 12-AmK	Ma:	26 Le 51-GK
Me:	23 Vi 38-DK	Ju:	4 Cn 56-BK	Ve:	9 Le 45-PK	Sa:	24 Li 52-MK
Ra:	2 Sc 52-AK	Ke:	2 Ta 52	HL:	22 Ta 41	GL:	0 Le 58

Mars is pen and mercury is the ink, third house represents authorship and writing, 4th the masses, the 10th sign is represented by mercury from ascendant from moon the 10th sign is Venus, from Sun the 10th is again Venus. Mercury is exalted and in own sign forming Bhadra, Panch Mahapursh.

Yoga, but is hemmed in malefic, Venus the 10th from both Sun and moon is the lord of 6th Servitude and 11th income and gains in 9th with lord of 9th Sun and Mars Lord of 5th and 12th Mars aspects 3rd and 4th houses ,while Sun and Venus Aspect 3rd on their own and the 4th through Mars .The influence of the mars on 3rd house 4th house through aspect and on 6th/11th lord Venus through relationship is there ,Mars also has a relationship with the 9t lord as well, Mercury is exalted and in 10th therefore being strong it will represent profession of the nature of sign Virgo and planet Mercury. The native is a journalist.

Note–Mars influence on 3rd, 5th 6th 8th, 10th and 12th is vital constituent here.

Note–One of the 5th house significations is writing the news.

Example 2

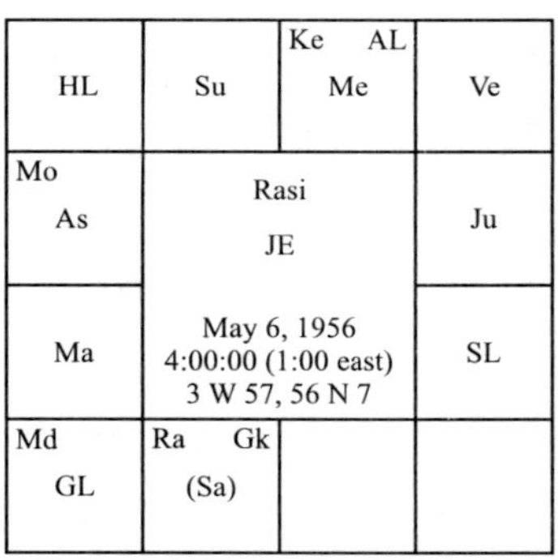

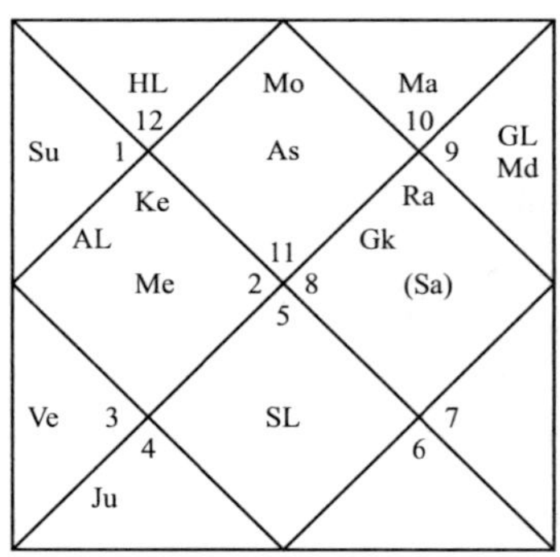

As: 21 Aq 35	Su: 22 Ar 19-BK	Mo: 26 Aq 27-AmK	Ma: 20 Cp 04-MK
Me: 12 Ta 41-PiK	Ju: 28 Cn 46-AK	Ve: 5 Ge 23-DK	Sa (R): 7 Sc 20-GK
Ra: 15 Sc 06-PiK	Ke: 15 Ta 06	HL: 7 Pi 28	GL: 29 Sg 18

Mars is the lord of 3rd and 10 in relation with Sun the 7th lord, Mars is also related to Jupiter the 2nd and

11th lord. Mars is sign exchange with ascendant and 12th lord Saturn, there is another exchange of 4th and 5th lords who are also the lords of 8th and 9th. Both from ascendant and moon the Scorpio sign and the lord Mars figures as the profession providing planet, the mars is exalted and quite strong, as a 3rd and 10th lord its aspects 3rd, 6th and 7th house, from sun the 10th sign is Capricorn with exalted mars housed in it and that too involved in exchange with the sign lord of Capricorn Saturn. the Native is a journalist. The 8th and 10th lords also connect through Saturn.

Example 3

Note–Mars influence on 3rd, 5th, 6th, 8th, 10th and 12th is vital constituent here.

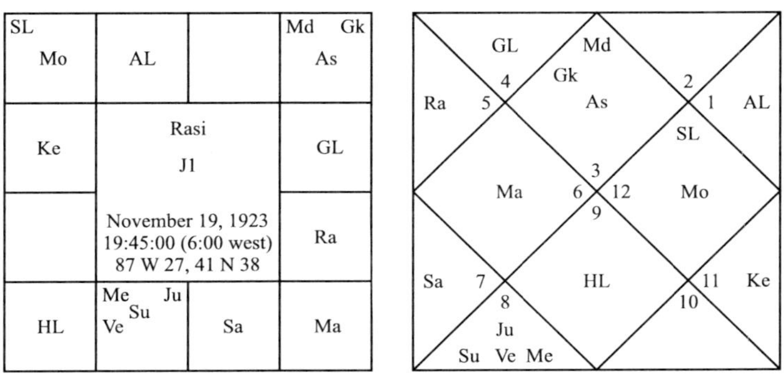

As: 24 Ge 06	Su: 3 Sc 56-DK	Mo: 26 Pi 16-AmK	Ma: 28 Vi 14-AK
Me: 6 Sc 16-PiK	Ju: 6 Sc 11-PK	Ve: 22 Sc 01-BK	Sa: 4 Li 15-GK
Ra: 15 Le 31-MK	Ke: 15 Aq 31	HL: 2 Sg 01	GL: 14 Cn 59

10th lord Jupiter is related to mercury and Mars, through an exchange between Mars and Mercury, Mars is lord of 11th and 6th, it is also the depositor of 12th and

5th lord Venus and 3rd lord Sun, Mars also aspects the 10th house. From ascendant the 10lord is Jupiter, from moon and sun, Mercury, Mars incidentally influences both Mercury and Jupiter as both of them are in its sign Scorpio, further there is an exchange relationship between Mars and Mercury.

Example 4

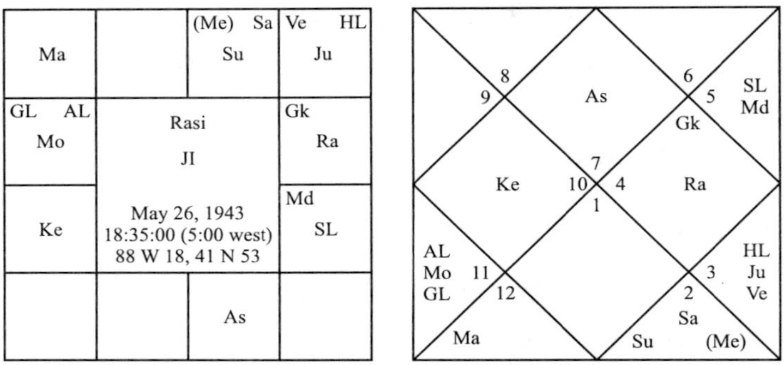

As:	22 Li 58	Su:	11 Ta 46-PiK	Mo:	17 Aq 10-MK	Ma:	6 Pi 38-GK
Me (R):	6 Ta 38-GK	Ju:	29 Ge 59-AK	Ve:	24 Ge 24-AmK	Sa:	21 Ta 26-BK
Ra:	26 Cn 00-DK	Ke:	26 Cp 00	HL:	14 Ge 01	GL:	3 Aq 10

Mars is in 6th, aspects 12th house, it also aspects the Jupiter (6th and 3rd lord) along with Venus the ascendant lord placed in 9th, there is an exchange relationship between Venus and Mercury as well, Saturn is related to the 10th lord from ascendant and it also aspects 10th house. From Moon the 10th lord is Mars, from Sun, Saturn.

The 8th and 10th lord connect through the dispositor of 10th Saturn.

Note– Mars influence on 3rd, 5th, 6th, 8th, 10th and 12th is vital constituent here.

Example 5

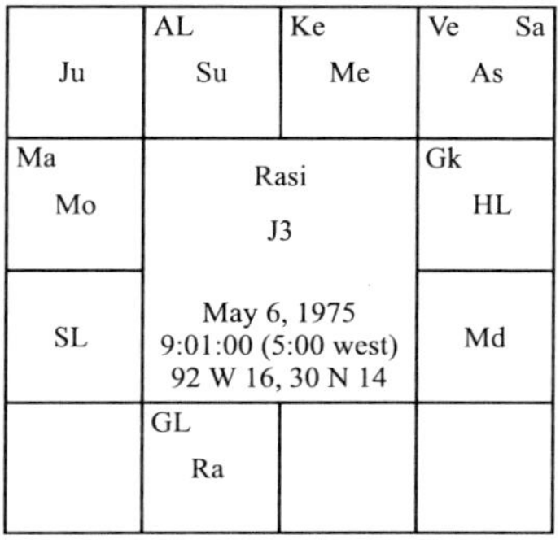

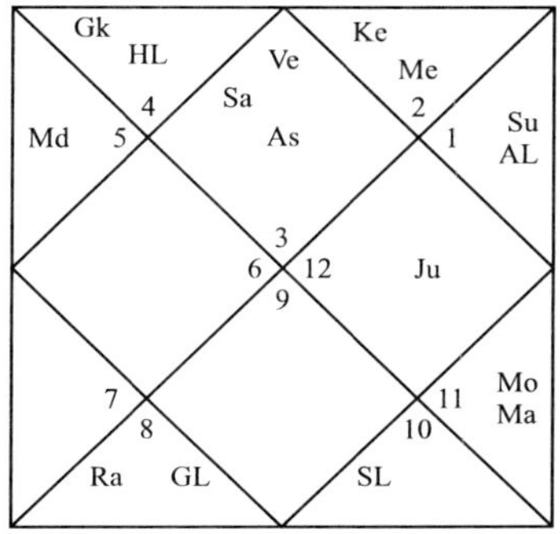

As: 3 Ge 11 Su: 21 Ar 55-MK Mo: 28 Aq 30-AK Ma: 25 Aq 21-AmK
Me: 10 Ta 04-GK Ju: 17 Pi 60-PK Ve: 2 Ge 48-DK Sa: 20 Ge 54-PiK
Ra: 7 Sc 30-BK Ke: 7 Ta 30 HL: 9 Cn 15 GL: 5 Sc 24

Mars is the lord of 6th, aspects 3rd and 12th. Mars also aspects mercury in the 12th, 3rd lord Sun is in the sign of mars. 8th lord Saturn aspects the 10th lord and house, Mars is in sign of Saturn. 10th from moon is the sign of Mars, 10th from Sun the sign of Saturn, here all the constituent 10th houses are connected through aspect or depositor relationship. Mars and mercury relation are there.

Example 6

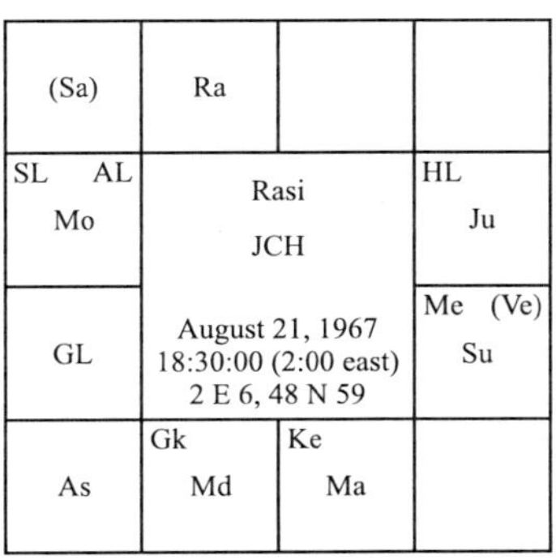

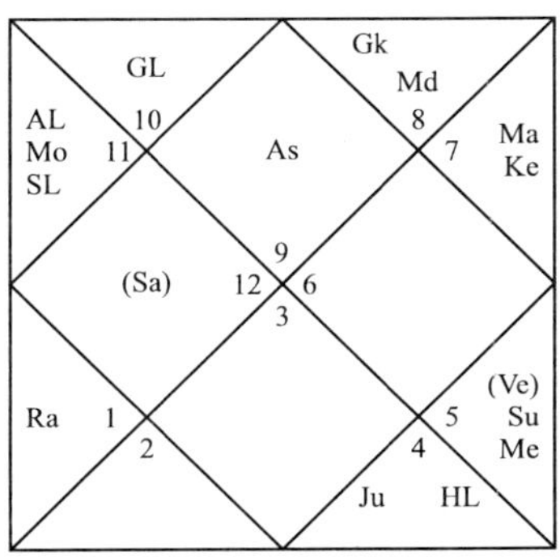

As: 15 Sg 16 Su: 4 Le 32-GK Mo: 22 Aq 46-MK Ma: 24 Li 24-AmK
Me: 1 Le 28-DK Ju: 24 Cn 58-AK Ve (R): 17 Le 10-PK Sa (R): 18 Pi 26-PiK
Ra: 6 Ar 17-BK Ke: 6 Li 17 HL: 20 Cn 46 GL: 0 Cp 49

8th lord Moon connected to 10th lord Mercury, Mars Aspects The 6th is lord of the 12th and its dispositor Venus is with lord of 10th and 9th. Mars and mercury link are established. Saturn is dispositor of 8th and related to ascendant and 4th lord.

10th from moon's sign lord is Mars, 10th from Sun Venus, 10th from ascendant is Mercury, Venus and mercury are related, while Venus is dispositor of Mars.

Example 7

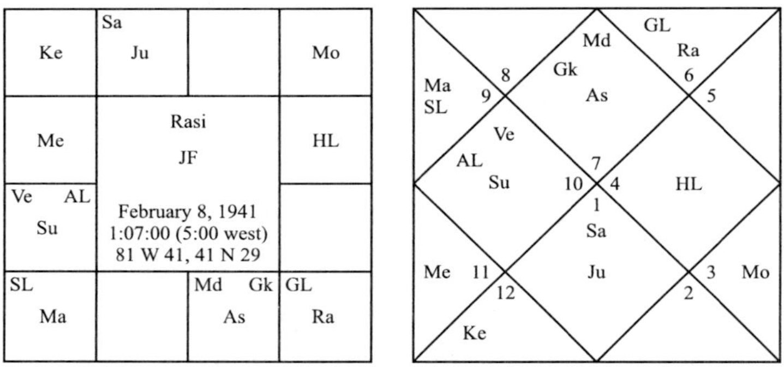

As: 22 Li 19	Su: 26 Cp 05-AK	Mo: 8 Ge 40-PK	Ma: 0 Sg 19-DK
Me: 13 Aq 51-PiK	Ju: 15 Ar 10-MK	Ve: 8 Cp 39-GK	Sa: 15 Ar 40-BK
Ra: 9 Vi 43-AmK	Ke: 9 Pi 43	HL: 10 Cn 14	GL: 17 Vi 36

Saturn connects with both the 5th and 10th lord, Mars is in 3rd aspects 6th, 9th and 10th. Jupiter and Saturn are related, while Mars is in exchange with Jupiter, 12th lord mercury is in the sign of Saturn, mars connects because it is in relation to Saturn, so Mars is in 3rd, aspects 6th and has an indirect relationship with mercury through Saturn as Saturn is the dispositor of Mercury. 10th from Moon is Jupiter, 10th from Sun, Venus, 10th from Ascendant Moon. Venus and Jupiter in Kendra to each other and

Moon is under aspect by Saturn a planet related to Jupiter, so all the 10th house constituents again connect.

Example 8

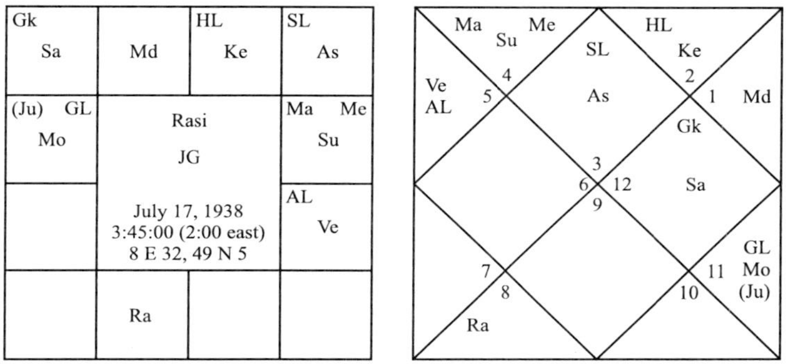

As: 6 Ge 07	Su: 0 Cn 50-DK	Mo: 20 Aq 12-MK	Ma: 3 Cn 13-GK
Me: 23 Cn 43-BK	Ju (R): 8 Aq 14-PK	Ve: 10 Le 17-PiK	Sa: 24 Pi 53-AmK
Ra: 1 Sc 54-AK	Ke: 1 Ta 54	HL: 0 Ta 38	GL: 1 Aq 39

Mars is the 6th lord with 3rd lord and dispositor of 12th lord. Exchange between 10th and 8th lord Saturn. 10th from moon is the Mars, 10th from Sun is the Mars, 10th from Ascendant is Jupiter and it is related to Moon the dispositor of the Mars, so again the constituent of 10th from ascendant, the moon and Sun are connected.

Example 9

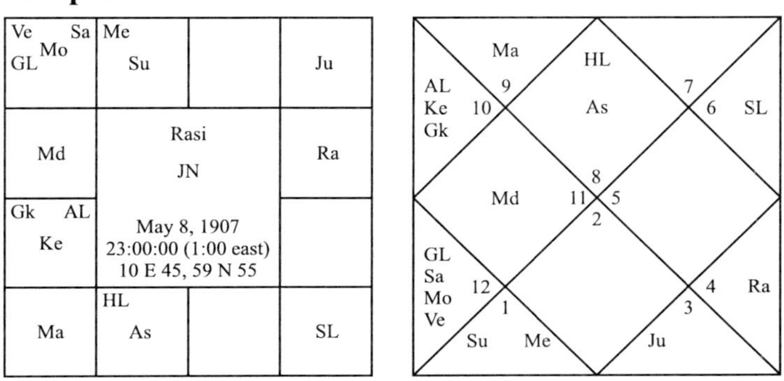

As: 20 Sc 05	Su: 24 Ar 35-AmK	Mo: 14 Pi 18-PK	Ma: 22 Sg 10-BK
Me: 7 Ar 57-GK	Ju: 15 Ge 44-PiK	Ve: 21 Pi 02-MK	Sa: 1 Pi 54-DK
Ra: 3 Cn 36-AK	Ke: 3 Cp 36	HL: 19 Sc 40	GL: 28 Pi 25

Mars is the 6th lord and aspects 3rd lord Saturn and 12th lord Venus.10th lord Sun is in the sign of mars. 8th and 10th lord is together in 6th. Saturn aspects the Dispositor of 8th and 10th Mars, so it also completes the requirement. Mars and Jupiter are related and 12th lord Venus, 3rd, 4th lord Saturn and 9th lord Moon all are in Sign of Jupiter, so they have an indirect relationship with Mars also.

Example 10

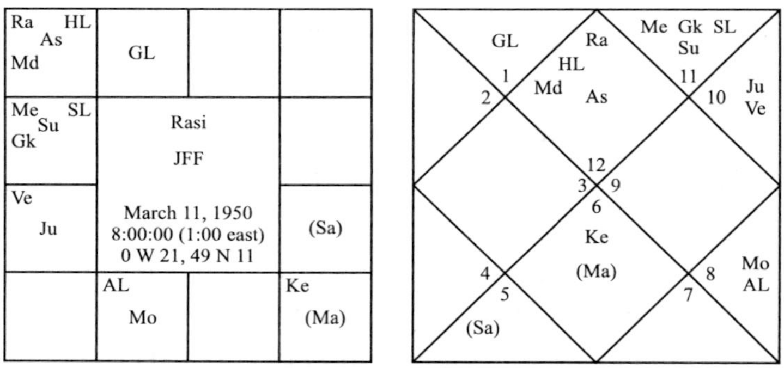

As: 13 Pi 27	Su: 26 Aq 59-BK	Mo: 29 Sc 19-AmK	Ma (R): 13 Vi 15-GK
Me: 12 Aq 27-DK	Ju: 29 Cp 35-AK	Ve: 15 Cp 53-PiK	Sa (R): 22 Le 34-MK
Ra: 14 Pi 25-PK	Ke: 14 Vi 25	HL: 12 Pi 01	GL: 4 Ar 36

The dispositor of Mars, Saturn is related to 9th lord Sun and the lord of 11th and 12th Saturn, the depositor of 3rd is Saturn so mars establish a link with 12th, 3rd and 6th the 8th and 10th lords are conjunct in 11th in the sign owned by Saturn here also the link of Saturn with 8th and 12th is established. The mars and mercury link are also present in the chart.

LEGAL PROFESSION
(Judges/Jurists/Attorneys/Lawyers)

The 6th house is an important factor in evaluating the legal profession, Influence of Jupiter, mars and Saturn on 6th is the key here, 6th house signifies litigations, Jupiter is considered to be the planet signifying Judges, jurists and legal profession, Saturn is the Significator of karma and also the significator of 6th, 8th and 12th houses, therefore Saturn owns both the houses of Litigation and the legal punishments through the 6/12th axis. Jupiter Mercury connection is predominant. Jupiter connection with 10th is also a factor quite common and predominant. Saturn, Mars and Jupiter's influence on 6th and 10th is observable Connection of 2nd lord/house with Mercury is also common observable factor arguments and debate is a significant factor in legal profession. 2-6-9-3 link as Per Col gaur From Astrology of Professions.

Example 1

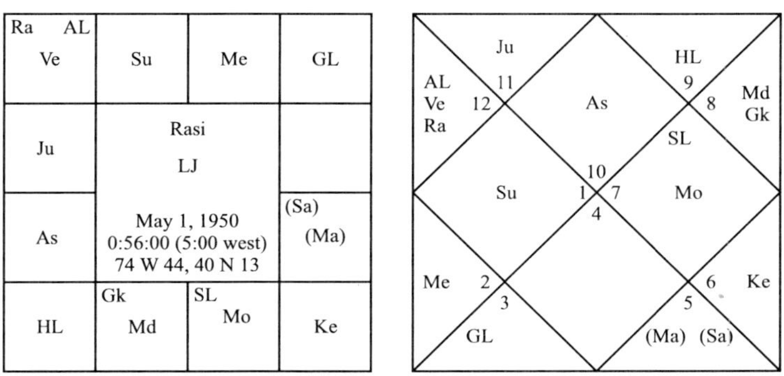

As: 10 Cp 01	Su: 17 Ar 08-BK	Mo: 3 Li 14-GK	Ma (R): 28 Le 53-AK
Me: 4 Ta 06-PK	Ju: 9 Aq 33-PiK	Ve: 1 Pi 55-DK	Sa (R): 19 Le 35-AmK
Ra: 13 Pi 59-MK	Ke: 13 Vi 59	HL: 11 Sg 46	GL: 4 Ge 55

Jupiter aspects 6th house and is related to Mars and Saturn. Mars aspects the 11th, 3rd and 2nd house and 10th house through the related planet Saturn, 10th lord Venus is in sign of Jupiter, Saturn aspects the 6th lord Mercury, Jupiter also aspects the 10th. 2nd Lord Saturn Connects to mercury through an aspect.

Since it is Government position, the 5th and 10th lord will have a link, here the 5th and 10th lord is Venus, further Exalted Sun aspects the 10th.

Example 2

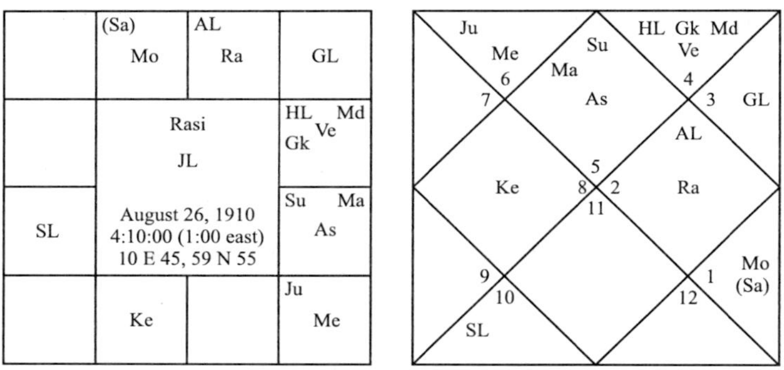

As:	1 Le 22	Su:	9 Le 24-GK	Mo:	19 Ar 57-MK	Ma:	20 Le 09-BK
Me:	6 Vi 07-DK	Ju:	21 Vi 08-AmK	Ve:	15 Cn 47-PiK	Sa (R):	13 Ar 56-PK
Ra:	0 Ta 11-AK	Ke:	0 Sc 11	HL:	13 Cn 24	GL:	5 Ge 48

Jupiter aspects the 6th, 8th and 10th house, Saturn aspects the 11th, 3rd and 6th house, dispositor lord of 10th lord Venus, the moon is related to Saturn. The 6th, 12th house axis lords are together and the lord of 10th is in 12th, Jupiter and exalted mercury represent a glib speaker.

2nd lord mercury exalted in 2nd house.

Example 3

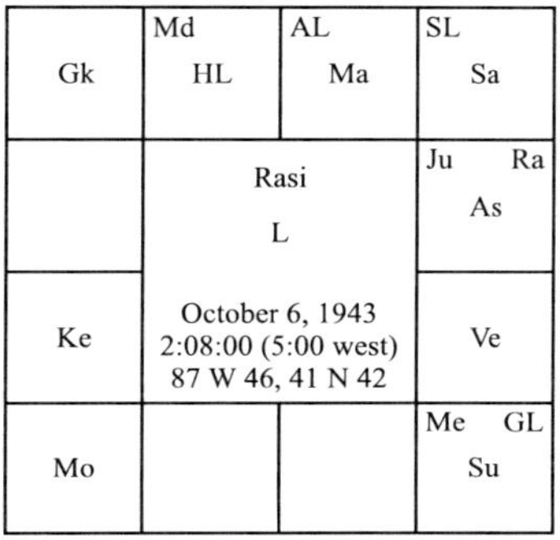

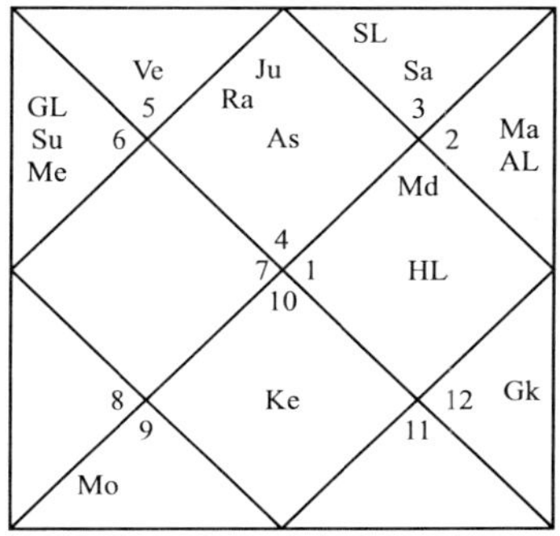

As: 22 Cn 41	Su: 19 Vi 06-BK	Mo: 12 Sg 05-PiK	Ma: 25 Ta 59-AmK
Me: 2 Vi 10-DK	Ju: 27 Cn 21-AK	Ve: 12 Le 46-MK	Sa: 3 Ge 33-GK
Ra: 21 Cn 02-PK	Ke: 21 Cp 02	HL: 24 Ar 21	GL: 18 Vi 25

Jupiter is the lord of 6th in exchange with ascendant lord, Saturn is also related to the moon in the 6th on account of mutual aspect relationship, Mars the 10th and 5th lord also aspects the 6th. Jupiter is in Kendra to tenth house. Mercury is with 2nd lord Sun, thus Mercury again connects with the 2nd lord.

Example 4

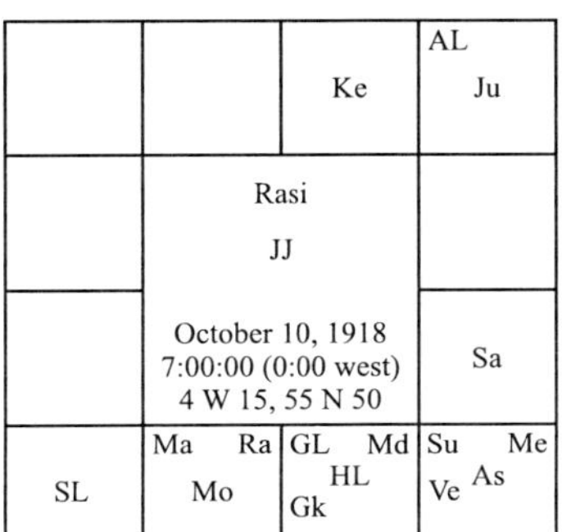

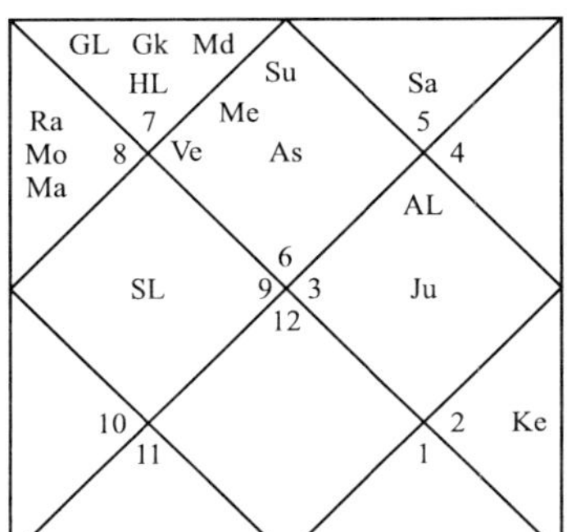

As: 26 Vi 24	Su: 23 Vi 27-AK	Mo: 19 Sc 47-BK	Ma: 13 Sc 38-PiK
Me: 19 Vi 36-MK	Ju: 22 Ge 09-AmK	Ve: 12 Vi 07-PK	Sa: 2 Le 22-DK
Ra: 21 Sc 52-GK	Ke: 21 Ta 52	HL: 2 Li 22	GL: 15 Li 47

Jupiter aspects the 6th, Saturn is the 5th and 6th lord in 12th, Mars aspects the 6th and 10th as a 3rd and 8th lord. The sign of the Saturn is Sun in conduction relationship with 10th and ascendant lord and 9th and 2nd lord Venus, Since Judge as vocation is Government service, the 5th lord Saturn is in the Sign of Sun, who is in relationship with 10th lord mercury, therefore the condition of Government service is fulfilled (5th and 10th lord linked and with some relation with Sun).

Mercury Connects to second lord Venus through being in same sign.

Example 5

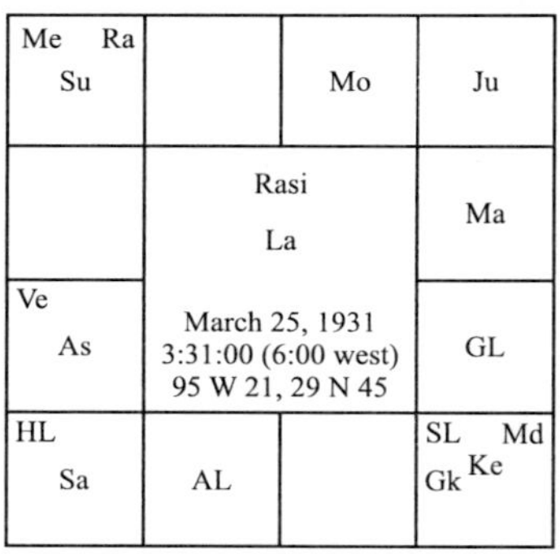

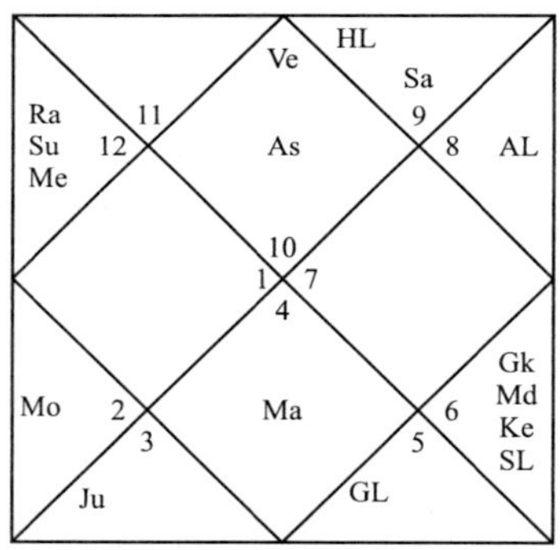

As: 12 Cp 44	Su: 10 Pi 53-PK	Mo: 18 Ta 51-MK	Ma:6 Cn 08-DK
Me: 20 Pi 20-BK	Ju: 18 Ge 05-PiK	Ve: 29 Cp 37-AK	Sa: 29 Sg 10-AmK
Ra: 21 Pi 31-GK	Ke: 21 Vi 31	HL: 12 Sg 48	GL:1 Le 58

Jupiter in 6th in exchange with 6th lord mercury. Saturn aspects Jupiter and the 6th house, Mars is under aspect from Rahu and mercury the 6th lord through Rahu (it's also in trine to Mercury And related as per Phaldeepika). So, all three Jupiter, Mars and Saturn have an influence or receive influence from the 6th house or lord. Mars is also in relation with the 10th lord venus,10th lord Venus is in the Sign of Saturn therefore Saturn is the dispositor, while Saturn is related to Jupiter, so all three Saturn, Jupiter and Mars also establish link with 10th Lord. 2nd Lord Mercury and Mercury both connect through common depositor Jupiter.

Example 6: A typical but difficult chart.

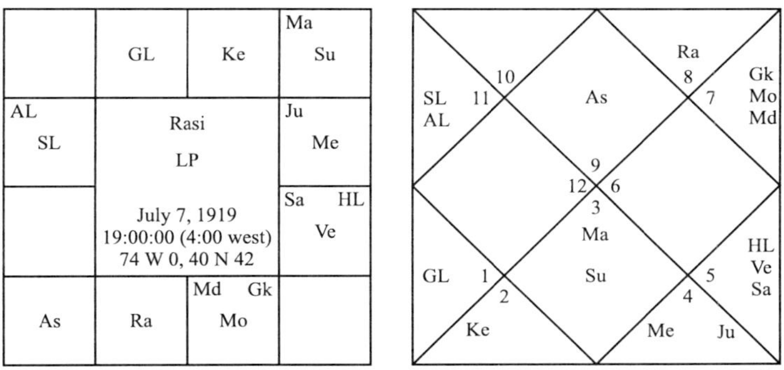

As: 1 Sg 49	Su: 22 Ge 01-AmK	Mo: 22 Li 52-AK	Ma: 6 Ge 46-PK
Me: 16 Cn 13-MK	Ju: 1 Cn 37-DK	Ve: 7 Le 27-PiK	Sa: 3 Le 05-GK
Ra: 10 Sc 29-BK	Ke: 10 Ta 29	HL: 3 Le 22	GL: 6 Ar 11

Mars is in relationship with depositor of 6th lord, Saturn aspects the 6th house and is in relationship with 6th lord as well, the depositor of Jupiter and the 10th lord Mercury the moon is in Kendra to them therefore related according to Phal Deepika, 6th lord Venus is the Sign lord owner of the Moon, the moon is the Sign owner of Jupiter and 10th lord Mercury. Saturn and Venus are related and Venus exerts Influence on The Moon through Saturn. Incidentally mars also aspects the 10th house, Jupiter is with 10th, Saturn aspects the depositor of 10th lord the moon. Here mercury aspects 2nd house along with exalted Jupiter.

Example 7

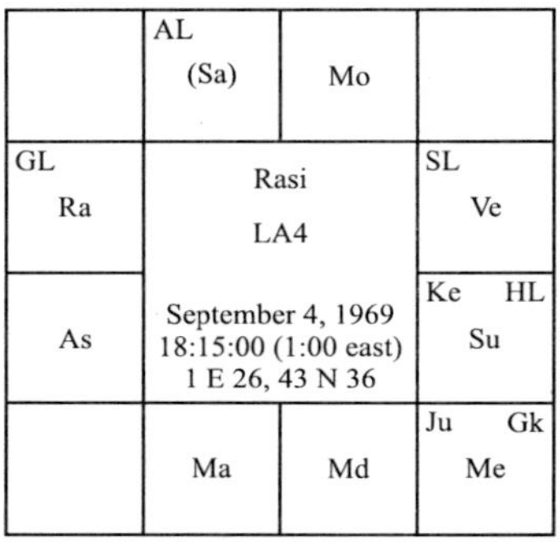

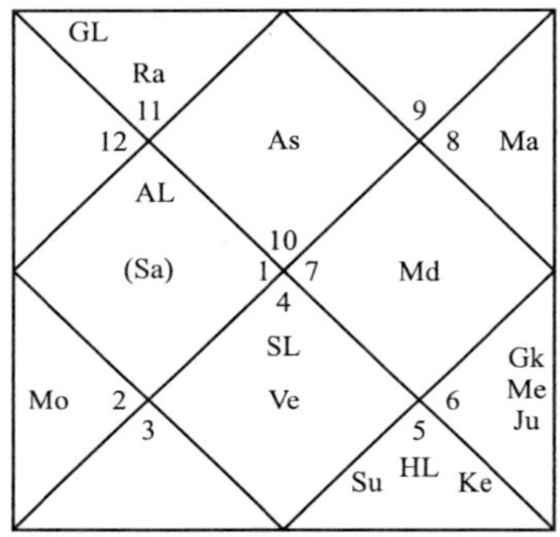

As: 21 Cp 47	Su: 18 Le 33-BK	Mo: 29 Ta 45-AK	Ma: 26 Sc 57-AmK
Me: 15 Vi 32-MK	Ju: 15 Vi 31-PiK	Ve: 14 Cn 24-GK	Sa (R): 15 Ar 20-PK
Ra: 27 Aq 44-DK	Ke: 27 Le 44	HL: 12 Le 47	GL: 4 Aq 51

Jupiter is with 6th lord, mars aspects the 6th house, Saturn also aspects the 6th, 10th and the ascendant, there is an exchange of 7th lord the moon and 10th/5th lord Venus, the 7th lord is also in relation with Mars, so mars has connection with 10th lord as well, Venus the 10th lord is also in Kendra from Saturn. Venus is the lord of 10 from ascendant and Sun.

For independent profession like Attorney or Lawyer– The rule is that if you have more planets between 7th and ascendant then the work you will do will be self-oriented.

Example 8

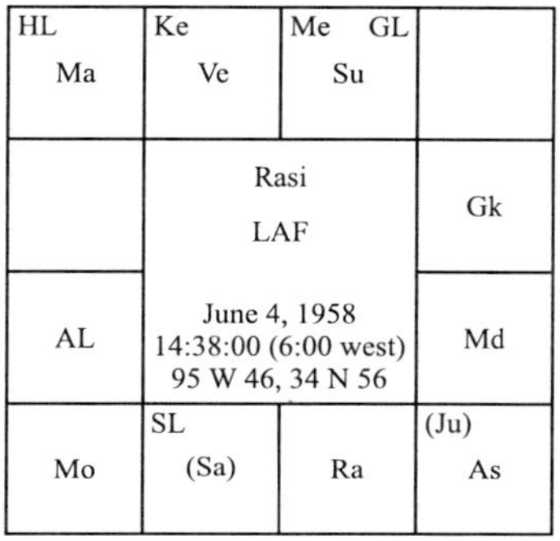

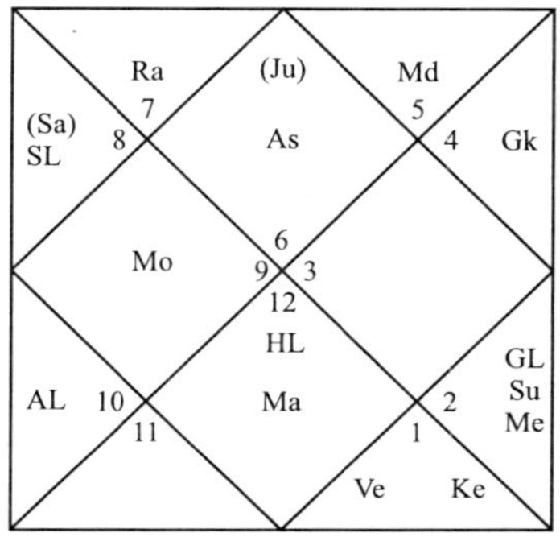

As: 20 Vi 31 Su: 20 Ta 26-PiK Mo: 29 Sg 03-AmK Ma: 5 Pi 00-GK
Me: 4 Ta 49-DK Ju (R): 28 Vi 47-PiK Ve: 10 Ar 58-PK Sa (R): 29 Sc 48-AK
Ra: 7 Li 09-MK Ke: 7 Ar 09 HL: 1 Pi 54 GL: 4 Ta 41

6th lord Saturn is in the sign of Mars and it is related to the 10th lord Mercury, Jupiter aspects its dispositor Mercury and 12th lord Sun, therefore Jupiter also has a connection with 10th, Mars aspects the 10th house, Jupiter and Mars are related on account of the mutual aspect, while Saturn the 6th lord is in the sign of the Mars therefore connects through related planet Mars. Mercury in the sign of 2nd and 9th lord, so connected to 2nd.

Example 9

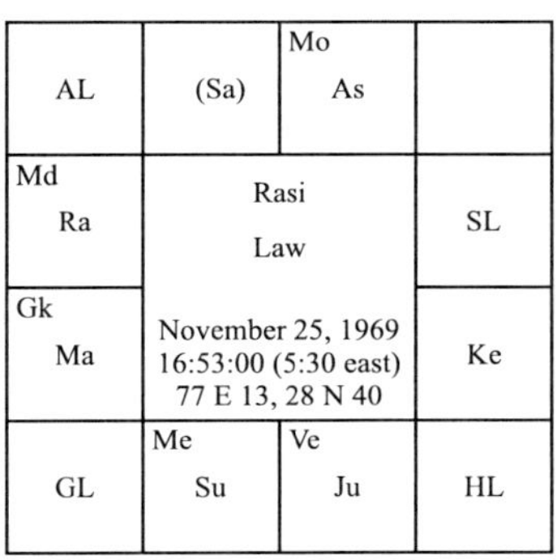

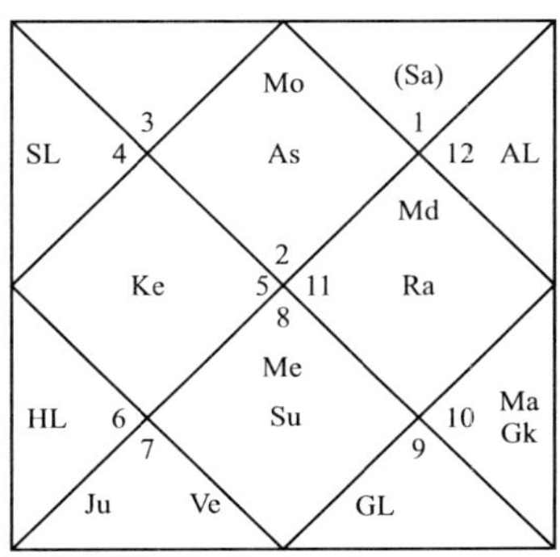

As: 2 Ta 02 Su: 9 Sc 36-PK Mo: 26 Ta 29-AK Ma: 21 Cp 38-BK
Me: 14 Sc 46-MK Ju: 2 Li 45-DK Ve: 25 Li 06-AmK Sa (R): 9 Ar 58-PiK
Ra: 24 Aq 27-GK Ke: 24 Le 27 HL: 7 Vi 49 GL: 5 Sg 47

Jupiter in 6th with 6th lord, Saturn in relationship with lord of 6th and Jupiter, Mars is in exchange relationship with Saturn so it is also connected to the 6th, Mercury itself is 2nd lord in sign of Mars, therefore connected to Jupiter through mars, 10th lord Saturn is connected to both Mars and Jupiter.

Example 10

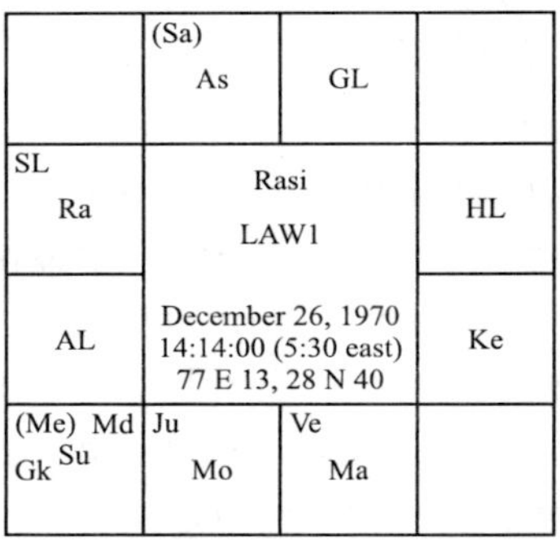

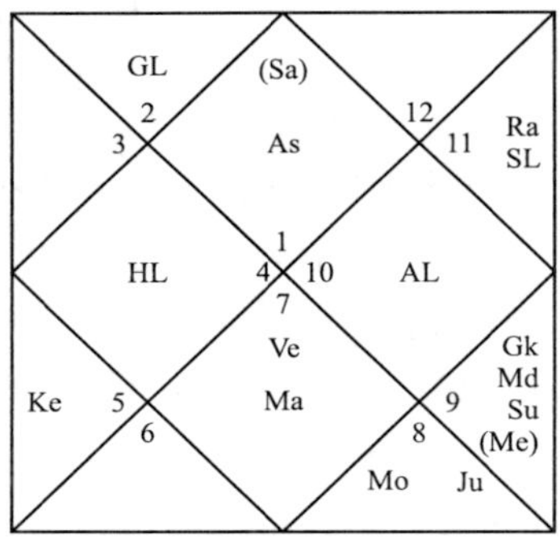

As:	20 Ar 45	Su:	10 Sg 43-K	Mo:	13 Sc 58-PK	Ma:	19 Li 02-MK
Me (R):	15 Sg 55-PiK	Ju:	3 Sc 03-DK	Ve:	26 Li 57-AmK	Sa (R):	22 Ar 42-BK
Ra:	1 Aq 25-AK	Ke:	1 Le 25	HL:	9 Cn 21	GL:	22 Ta 44

10th lord Saturn is related to Mars and Venus and Jupiter is in sign owned by Mars. The 6th lord Mercury is in 9th in a Sign owned by Jupiter, while the Sign owner of Jupiter placement Mars and Saturn are related, so they connect with 6th lord Mercury through Jupiter the sign owner of mercury's placement. Jupiter the dispositor of mercury, Jupiter also establishes connection to 2nd house through an aspect.

Example 11: Jawahar Lal Nehru

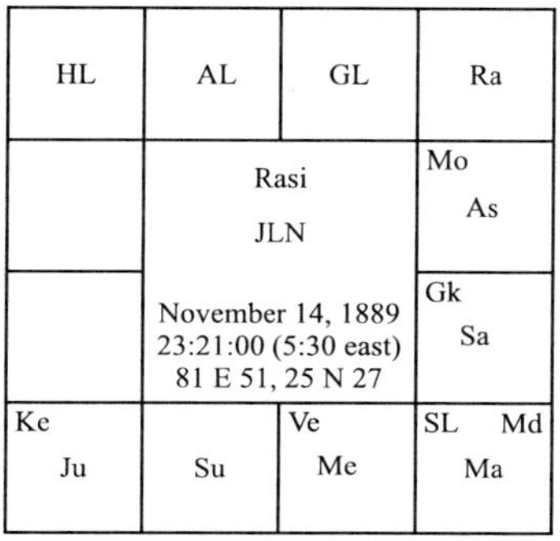

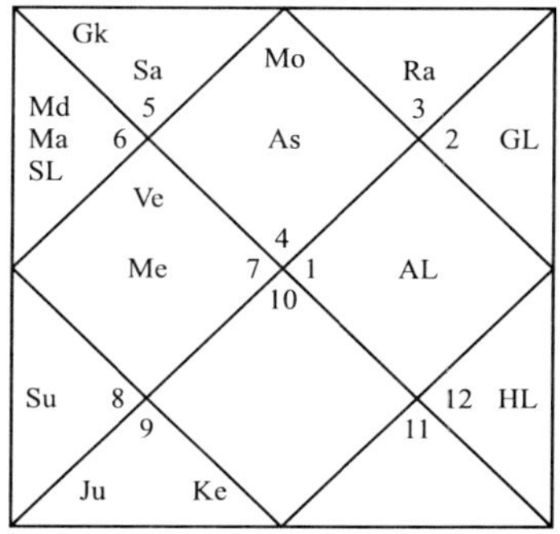

As: 26 Cn 19	Su: 0 Sc 17-DK	Mo: 18 Cn 00-AmK	Ma: 9 Vi 00-PK
Me: 17 Li 10-BK	Ju: 15 Sg 11-MK	Ve: 7 Li 23-GK	Sa: 10 Le 48-PiK
Ra: 11 Ge 27-AK	Ke: 11 Sg 27	HL: 28 Pi 26	GL: 11 Ta 43

The first prime minister of India was also a barrister of law.

Jupiter is the 6th lord in 6th its also the lord of 9th, Saturn is under aspect from the Jupiter, so Saturn has a 6th lord influence, Mars aspects the 6th, Mars is also the lord of 10th, Jupiter aspects the 10th house as well, Mercury has an aspect from planet in 2nd the Saturn, Mercury owns the Sign placement of Mars and aspects the 10th house as well.

MEDICAL PROFESSION
(Doctors, Surgeons, Psychiatrics, psychologists, dentists, technicians -Doctors and Surgeons)

Sun represents the Herbs & medicine, 5th and 11th houses represent the healing houses, 6th is diseases and 12th the hospitals, 8th represents critical diseases.

So, planet suns connection with 5th, 11 is a strong constituent for being a doctor.

Connection of 6th, 8th and 12th lords is also a common observable factor. 6th is diseases, 12th hospital and 8th stands for critical diseases& research.

Suns connection to 5th and Mars connection to 6th and 10th, Jupiter connects to 5th house or lord and 10th house or the lord.

Jupiter in 11th, 6th, 5th or 12th or influencing these.

Jupiter's influence on 5th and 11th

The 5th and 10th lord connection is a common factor. if sun completes the same there is possibility of career in medicine.

Example 1: Doctor Teacher Anatomy

Planet sun with 5th lord ,10th lord Mars related to 6th lord and aspects the 5th, while being placed in 11th, the 5th house 11th house axis is healers/doctor's axis. Saturn aspects the 5th and 10th and is the lord of 12th and ascendant, Jupiter is in sign exchange with 10th lord and is related to the 6th, 8th, 10th and 3rd lords, while Saturn the 12th lord is in 8th in the Sign of planet related to Jupiter the Mercury.

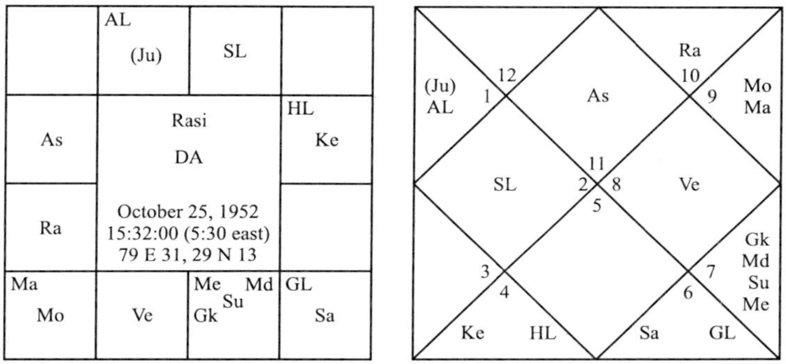

As: 27 Aq 50	Su: 8 Li 45-GK	Mo: 28 Sg 59-AK	Ma: 16 Sg 21-PiK
Me: 27 Li 31-AmK	Ju (R): 24 Ar 34-MK	Ve: 10 Sc 44-PK	Sa: 26 Vi 29-BK
Ra: 25 Cp 13-DK	Ke: 25 Cn 13	HL: 12 Cn 37	GL: 4 Vi 00

The native is a teacher of Anatomy

Example 2: Anesthesia specialist

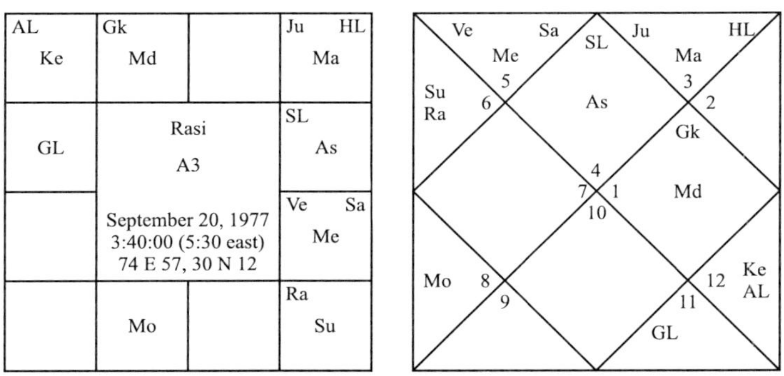

As: 29 Cn 45	Su: 4 Vi 24-PK	Mo: 29 Sc 55-AK	Ma: 18 Ge 50-AmK
Me: 16 Le 40-BK	Ju: 11 Ge 48-MK	Ve: 4 Le 16-GK	Sa: 2 Le 37-DK
Ra: 22 Vi 55-PiK	Ke: 22 Pi 55	HL: 13 Ge 17	GL: 12 Aq 56

Mars is the 5th and 10th lord and it, aspects the Sun, so Sun connects with 5th and 10th lord. Jupiter is the 6th and 9th lord in relationship with Mars and they jointly aspect the 6th while being placed in 12th in the sign of mercury the 12th and 3rd lord, another relation that the Sun enjoys with 5th, 10th lord Mars and 6th, 9th lord Jupiter is that they all have a common dispositor Mercury. 7th, 8th lord Saturn is with 11th lord Venus and Mercury Dispositor of Mars, Sun and Jupiter. So, the lords of 6th, 8th and 12th are also connected, through placement and sign lords.

Example 3: Doctor of Forensic science

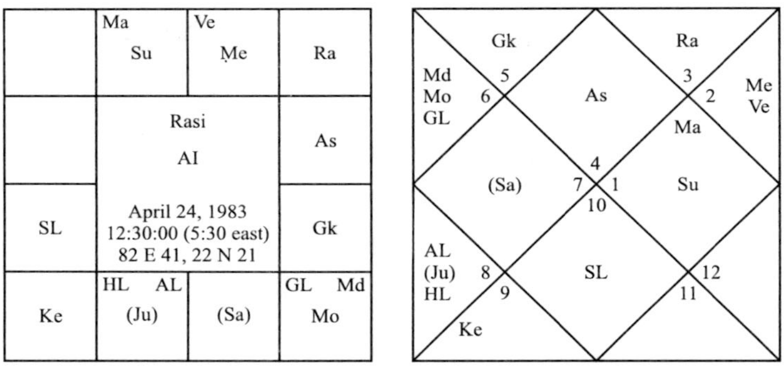

As: 21 Cn 29	Su: 11 Ar 01-PiK	Mo: 2 Vi 45-GK	Ma: 21 Ar 15-AmK
Me: 0 Ta 29-DK	Ju (R): 17 Sc 16-MK	Ve: 20 Ta 08-BK	Sa (R): 8 Li 24-PK
Ra: 3 Ge 58-AK	Ke: 3 Sg 58	HL: 7 Sc 29	GL: 17 Vi 36

5th lord Saturn Aspects Sun the 12th lord, the 10th lord mercury and 8th lord Mars, Saturn is the lord of 5th, 6th, so there is connection between 6th, 8th, 12th. Jupiter aspects the 5th while in 11th, 5th lord in sign of Sun and connects with Sun, mercury and Mars, Malefic influence on 5th is through Rahu. The 5th and 10th lord connect that indicates a Government service, particularly when 5 planets are there in 1st to 6th (Indicates Service rather than independent practice). 10th lord mercury is with

Mars, Sun and under aspect from Saturn, While Jupiter is in Kendra to it. The 6th 12th Link is evident here.

Example 4: Physician in Army

5th lord moon in relation to 6th lord Sun and 4th ,7th lord Mercury, Jupiter is in 5th and related to 5th as it, aspects moon the 5th lord placed in its sign Pisces. Mars aspects the 6th and 10th house, Saturn aspects 10th house,6th and 5th lord. Here again the 6th lord Sun ,8th lord Venus and 12th lord Saturn connect through aspect or dispositors. The 5th and 10th lord connect so the doctor is in Government Service and in Army as Physician.

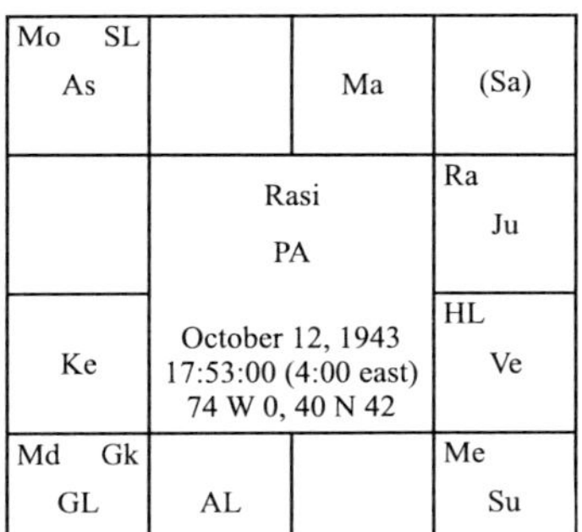

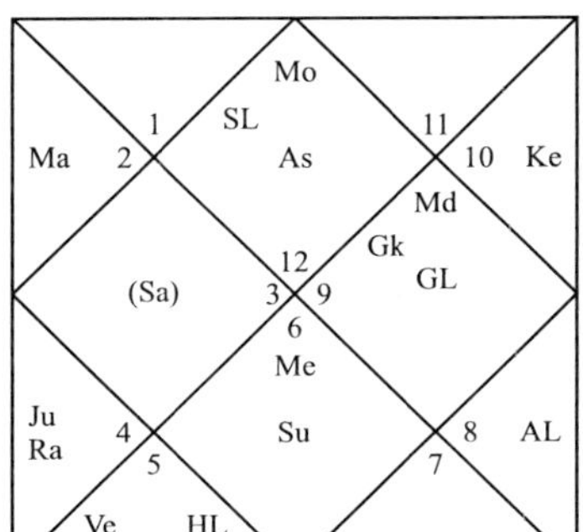

As: 15 Pi 19	Su: 25 Vi 38-BK	Mo: 16 Pi 60-MK	Ma: 27 Ta 34-AmK
Me: 8 Vi 05-GK	Ju: 28 Cn 27-AK	Ve: 15 Le 32-PiK	Sa (R): 3 Ge 33-DK
Ra: 20 Cn 46-PK	Ke: 20 Cp 46	HL: 17 Le 53	GL: 21 Sg 56

Example 5: Cardiologist

Sun with 5th lord and in mutual aspect relationship with Saturn, Jupiter and Mars are in 5th, Mars and Saturn establish a connection with 10th lord Saturn through the 5th aspect of Jupiter to 9th and 10th lord Saturn. Mars is the 12th lord with 8th lord Jupiter and is related to 3rd

lord Moon as well, The dispositor of 6th lord is related to Mars and Jupiter.

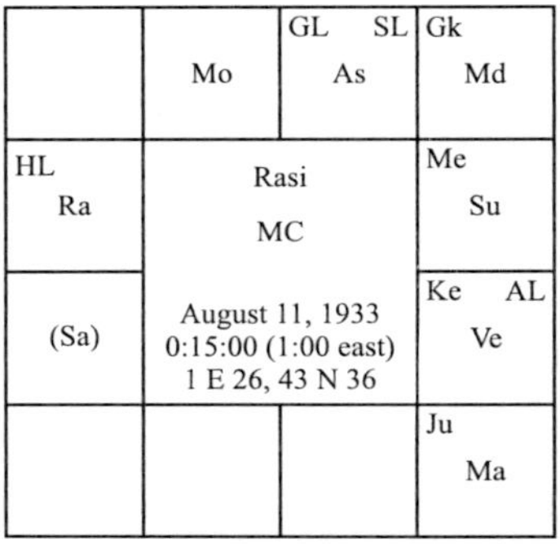

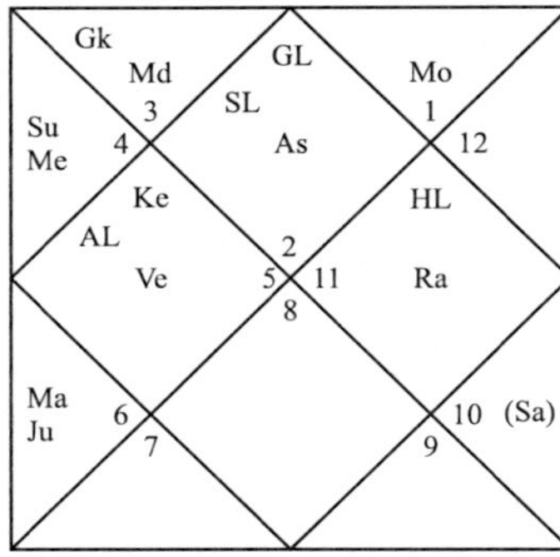

As: 9 Ta 19	Su: 24 Cn 54-AmK	Mo: 0 Ar 01-DK	Ma: 27 Vi 25-AK
Me: 9 Cn 13-PK	Ju: 0 Vi 53-GK	Ve: 24 Le 22-BK	Sa (R): 9 Cp 43-PiK
Ra: 5 Aq 42-MK	Ke: 5 Le 42	HL: 2 Aq 57	GL: 16 Ta 08

Example 6: Surgeon

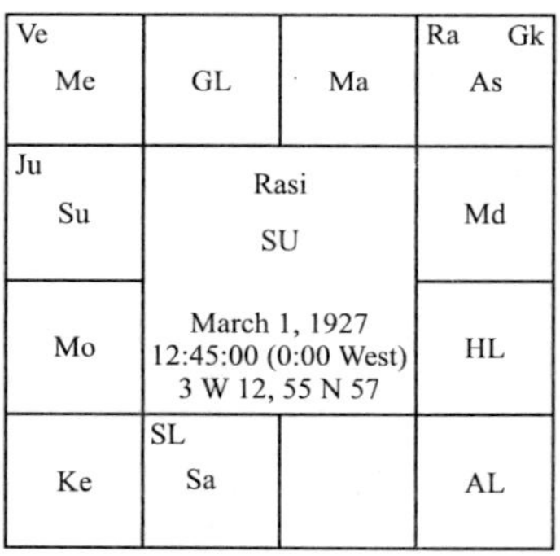

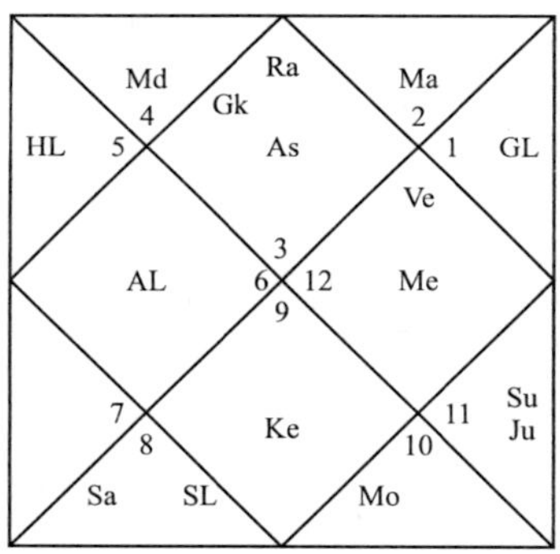

As: 28 Ge 09	Su: 17 Aq 07-AmK	Mo: 15 Cp 18-MK	Ma: 11 Ta 05-PK
Me: 4 Pi 04-DK	Ju: 17 Aq 03-BK	Ve: 10 Pi 52-GK	Sa: 14 Sc 36-PiK
Ra: 12 Ge 12-AK	Ke: 12 Sg 12	HL: 2 Le 50	GL: 11 Ar 47

For Surgeon Mars link to 6th is important.

The dispositor of 5th lord Venus is with Sun, Jupiter is related to the Sun and aspects the 5th house. Mars aspects the 6th, Mars Aspects the Saturn and they become related because Mars is the dispositor of Saturn and that the aspect is mutual, Mars is in the sign of 5th lord Venus. In the Horoscope. Saturn is in Kendra to 10th lord while the 10th lord Jupiter is in the sign of Saturn. Mars is also in Kendra relationship to the 10th lord as well. The 6th lord Mars, the 12th lord Venus and 8th lord Saturn have a connection.

Example 7: Surgeon

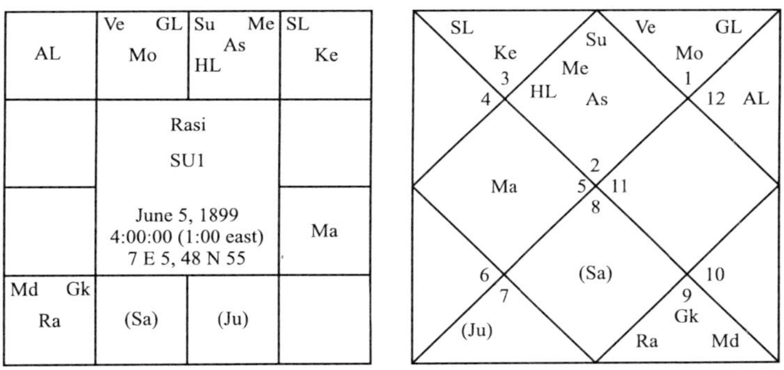

As:	10 Ta 52	Su:	21 Ta 45-Mk	Mo:	14 Ar 36-PiK	Ma:	1 Le 31-DK
Me:	10 Ta 18-PK	Ju (R):	8 Li 36-Gk	Ve:	24 Ar 21-GK	Sa (R):	28 Sc 25-AK
Ra:	7 Sg 03-BK	Ke:	7 Ge 03	HL:	2 Ta 25	GL:	4 Ar 48

Sun is with 6th lord, 6th lord Venus in sign of Mars, Saturn is the lord of 10th related to mars, Jupiter is in 6th related to lord of 6th Venus, Jupiter also aspects the 10th, just like mars, the sign lord of the mar's placement is Sun and its related to 5th and 2nd lord Mercury so Mars has a connection through Sun with 5th lord. Jupiter is 8th lord related to 6th lord, while 6th lord Venus is in the sign of 12th lord Mars, being placed in 12th, So the 6th ,8th and 12th connect, while Jupiter is also the lord of 11th a healing house.

Example 8: Surgeon

Sun is related to 5th lord Saturn, 10th lord Moon in relation with 6th lord Jupiter, Mars the 2nd, 7th lord, 8th lord jointly they aspect 5th and aspect 6th through Mars, the sign lord of 8th lord placement is Moon its with 6th lord Jupiter, the 8th lord Venus is the sign placement lord of the 12th, so the link between 6th ,8th and 12th is there as well.

Influence of Saturn, Jupiter, Mars on 5th and 10th is there.

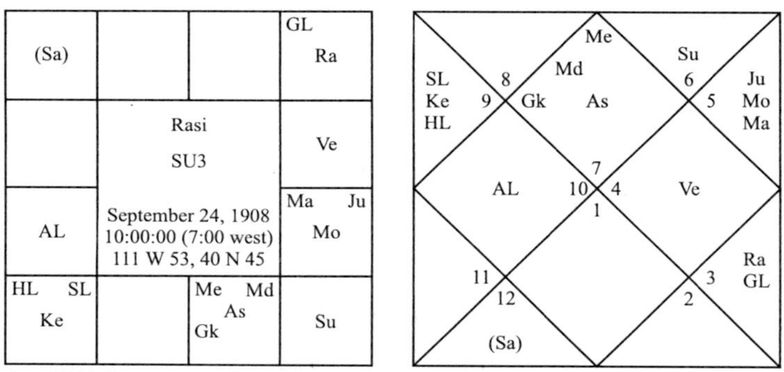

As: 21 Li 41	Su: 8 Vi 39-GK	Mo: 28 Le 30-AK	Ma: 27 Le 28-AmK
Me: 2 Li 18-DK	Ju: 9 Le 59-PK	Ve: 22 Cn 56-GK	Sa (R): 14 Pi 36-PiK
Ra: 7 Ge 60-MK	Ke: 7 Sg 60	HL: 27 Sg 56	GL: 2 Ge 04

Example 9: Surgeon

The sun and fifth lord Jupiter share a common sign lord Mars ,so they connect through it .Mars is related to Lord of 10th Venus and lord of 12th and aspects 5th and 6th house. Jupiter the 5th, 8th lord is also related to 12th lord moon and 10th lord Venus, Saturn and sun aspect the 10th house, while their placement sign lord Mars aspects the 10th lord, 2nd and 11th lord mercury is also related to Jupiter, here the lords of 6th Venus, 8th Jupiter and 12th also connect.

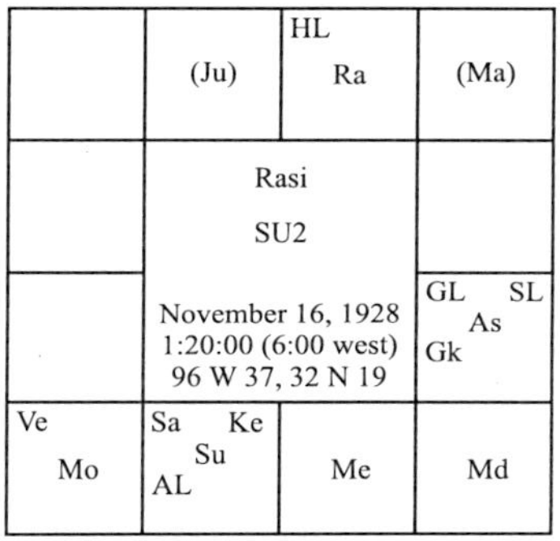

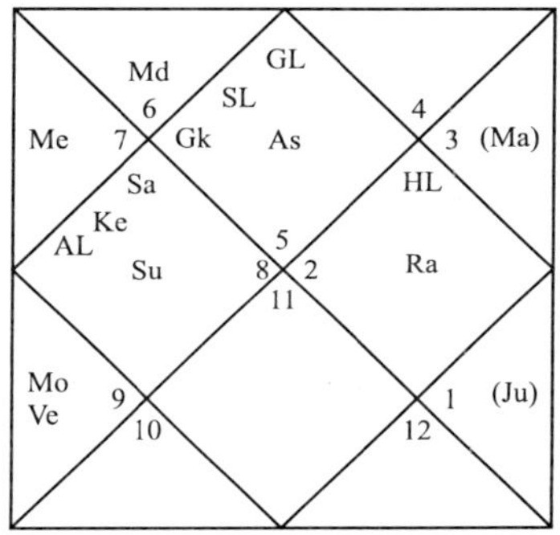

As: 18 Le 47 Su: 0 Sc 51-DK
Me: 13 Li 38-MK Ju (R): 10 Ar 07-PK
Ra: 7 Ta 36-AmK Ke: 7 Sc 36

Mo: 13 Sg 01-PiK Ma (R): 16 Ge 19-BK
Ve: 5 Sg 60-GK Sa: 25 Sc 32-AK
HL: 10 Ta 00 GL: 24 Le 53

Example 10: Surgeon

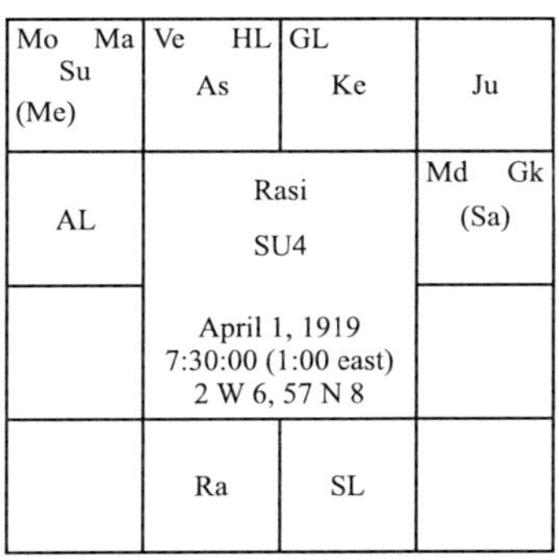

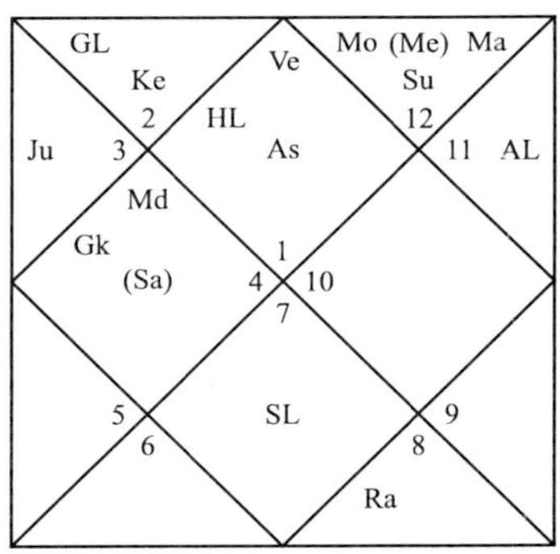

As: 18 Ar 37 Su: 17 Pi 45-PK
Me (R): 28 Pi 57-AmK Ju: 14 Ge 25-DK
Ra: 12 Sc 29-GK Ke: 12 Ta 29

Mo: 23 Pi 18-MK Ma: 26 Pi 48-BK
Ve: 17 Ar 59-PiK Sa (R): 29 Cn 04-AK
HL: 9 Ar 15 GL: 11 Ta 32

Sun is the 5th lord in 12th with Sign lord of 10th the Moon, Mars and mercury are also there Mercury the 3rd. 6th lord is in exchange with 9th and 12th lord Jupiter, There is a connection of 6th, 8th and 12th, Mars is with

5th lord and aspects 6th house, it also has a relation with the 6th lord, Saturn also aspects the 6th.

Example 11: Doctor of Homeopathy

Sun aspects the 5th house and has relationship with 1st, 6th Venus and 8th,11th Jupiter. Mars aspects 5th and is in sign of 5th and 2nd lord Mercury, 5th lord Mercury is related to 10th lord Saturn, 6th lord Venus, 8th lord Jupiter are related and 12th lord Mars is in Kendra to 6th and 8th lords so 6th, 8th and 12th are linked.

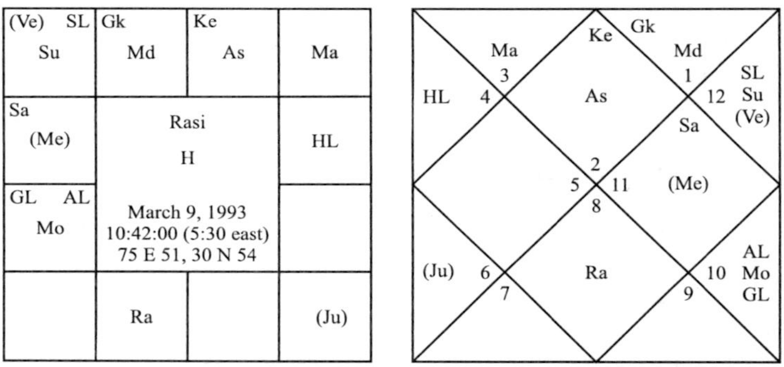

As:	22 Ta 33	Su:	4 Pi 51-GK	Mo:	20 Cp 23-AmK	Ma:	20 Ge 16-BK
Me (R):	17 Aq 05-PiK	Ju (R):	17 Vi 28-MK	Ve (R):	24 Pi 60-AK	Sa:	1 Aq 32-dK
Ra:	22 Sc 05-PK	Ke:	22 Ta 05	HL:	7 Cn 41	GL:	12 Cp 10

Example 12: Doctor of Ayurveda

Sun aspects the 5th as a 10th lord placed in 11th, Mars is in 10th as an ascendant lord, 6th lord, Venus is also there as 12th and 7th, mercury as 8th and 11th, Saturn aspects the 6th and is in the sign of Venus placed in 10th, Jupiter is the 5th lord related to Mars.

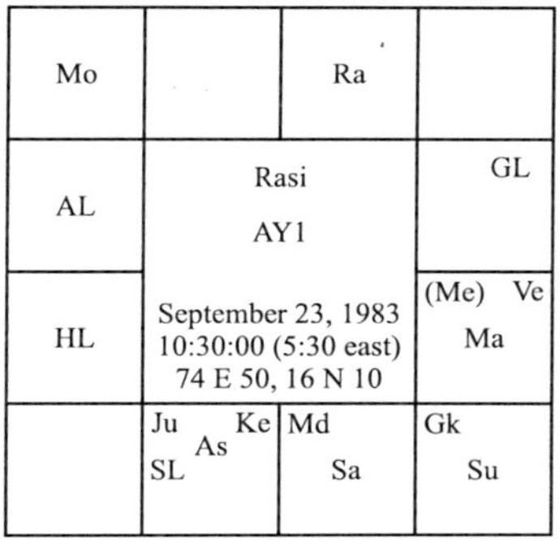

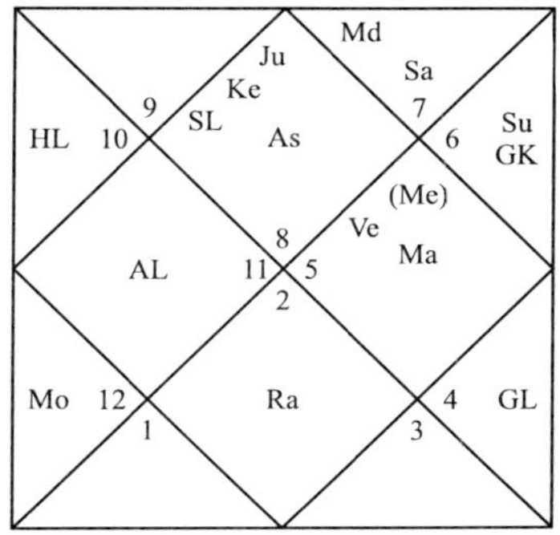

As: 4 Sa 01	Su: 5 Vi 59-PiK	Mo: 16 Pi 32-AmK	Ma: 2 Le 09-GK
Me: 22 Le 59-AK	Ju: 11 Sc 51-BK	Ve: 0 Li 37-DK	Sa: 9 Li 12-MK
Ra: 25 Ta 44-PK	Ke: 25 Sc 44	HL: 9 Cp 15	GL: 14 Cn 25

Example 13: Doctor of Ayurveda

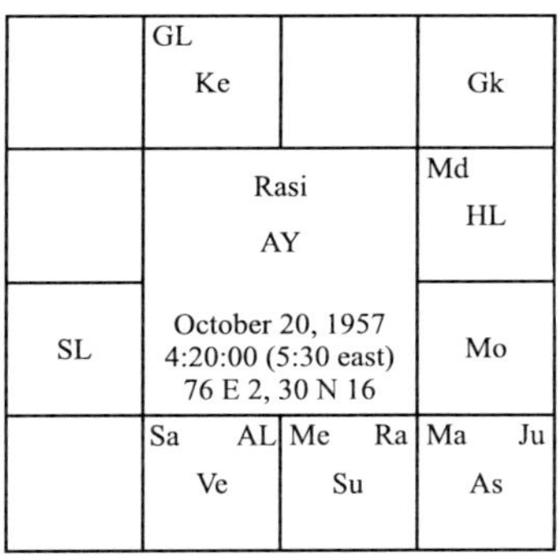

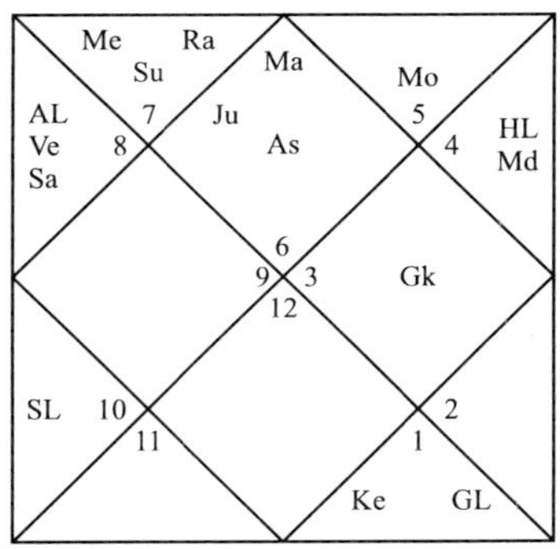

As: 3 Vi 50	Su: 3 Li 01-GK	Mo: 18 Le 01-BK	Ma: 23 Vi 32-AK
Me: 0 Li 09-DK	Ju: 21 Vi 58-AmK	Ve: 17 Sc 58-MK	Sa: 17 Sc 58-PiK
Ra: 17 Li 19-PK	Ke: 17 Ar 19	HL: 25 Cn 01	GL: 14 Ar 22

Sun is with 10th lord Mercury, while the sign lord of Sun and mercury placement Venus is with Saturn the 5th and 6th lord. Jupiter and Mars are related and influence the 5th house through an aspect from Jupiter. The sign lord of 5th lords Placement is Mars, so Mars and Jupiter also have an influence on the lord of 5th and 6th, 6th lord Saturn and 8th lord Mars have a link, because mars owns the sign of 6th lord placement ,similarly 12th lord Sun is in the sign of Venus which is related to Saturn so the link is established of 6th, 8th and 12th.

Example 14: Doctor of Ayurveda

Jupiter the 5th lord aspects the Sun, Sun is in the Sign owned by mercury which shifts impact in Bhav chalit to third house to be with Venus the 10th lord, Jupiter owns the 5th house and aspects the 10th, while in 6th it also owns the 8th and aspects the 12th lord, while being placed in the sign of 6th lord Saturn. So, the link of 6th ,8th and 12th is again established. Saturn aspects the 5th and the 5th lord is in the sign of Saturn, Jupiter also aspects the 10th, Mars is the only planet related or influencing the 10th lord Venus.

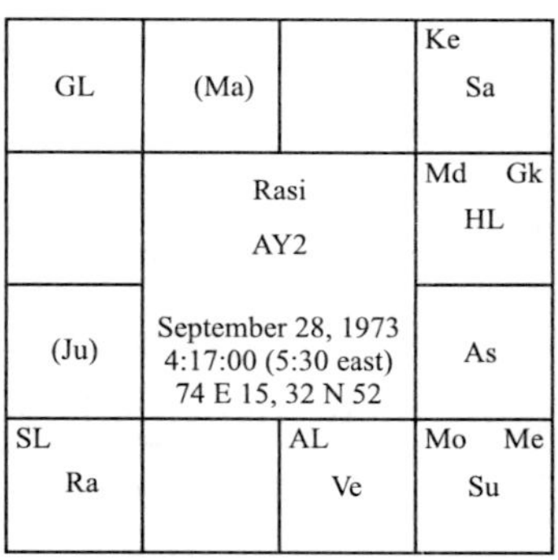

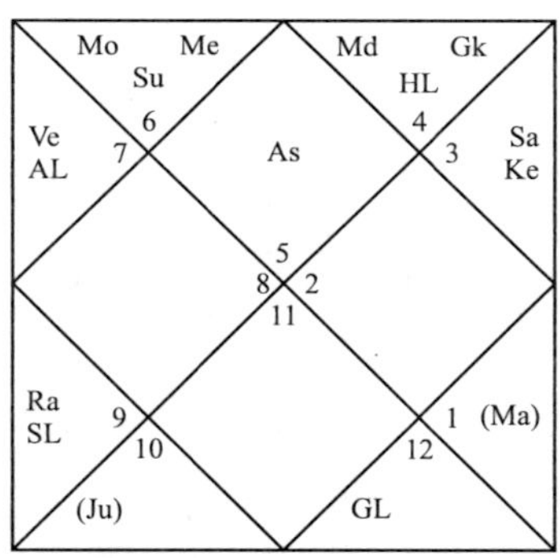

As: 13 Le 15	Su: 11 Vi 11-PK	Mo: 28 Vi 06-AmK	Ma (R): 15 Ar 18-PiK
Me: 29 Vi 25-AK	Ju (R): 8 Cp 48-DK	Ve: 23 Li 28-BK	Sa: 10 Ge 55-GK
Ra: 9 Sg 21-MK	Ke: 9 Ge 21	HL: 4 Cn 45	GL: 26 Pi 26

The following chart is Bhav cjhalit Chart of the above, it gives clearer impetus of the derivation then the Rashi chart.

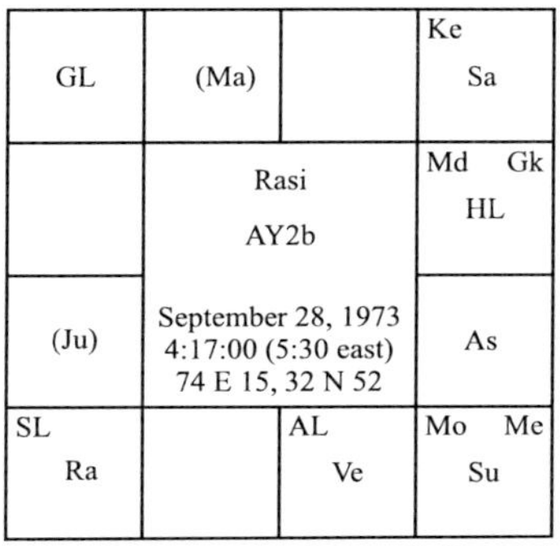

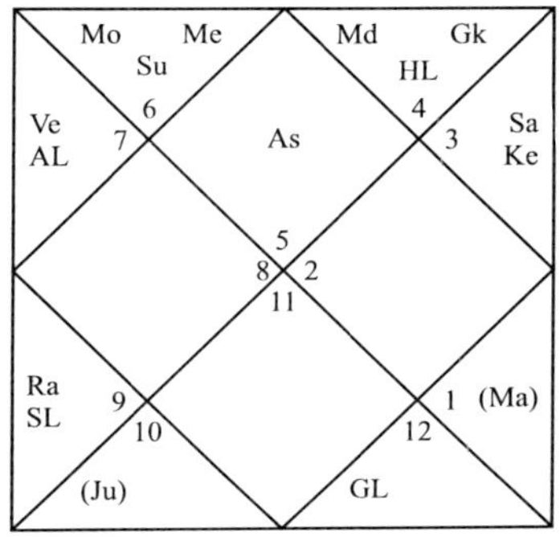

As: 13 Le 15 Su: 11 Vi 11-PK Mo: 28 Vi 06-AmK Ma (R): 15 Ar 18-PiK
Me: 29 Vi 25-AK Ju (R): 8 Cp 48-DK Ve: 23 Li 28-BK Sa: 10 Ge 55-GK
Ra: 9 Sg 21-MK Ke: 9 Ge 21 HL: 4 Cn 45 GL: 26 Pi 26

In the above Bhav chalit chart Mercury shifts signs to be with Venus the 10th lord and creating a link between Sun and 10th lord through Mercury the Sign owner of the Sun placement.

Example 15: Ayurveda doctor

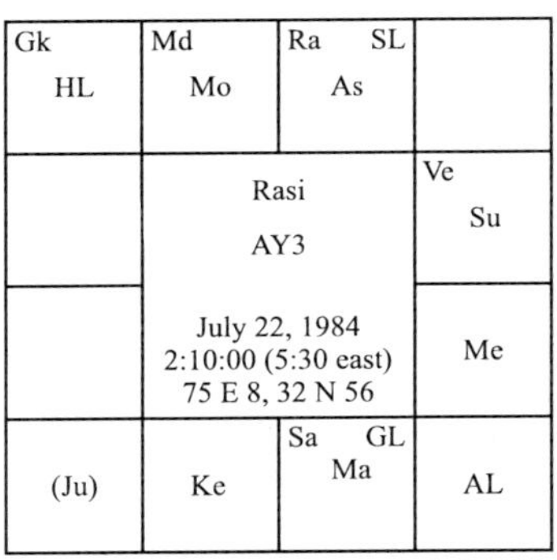

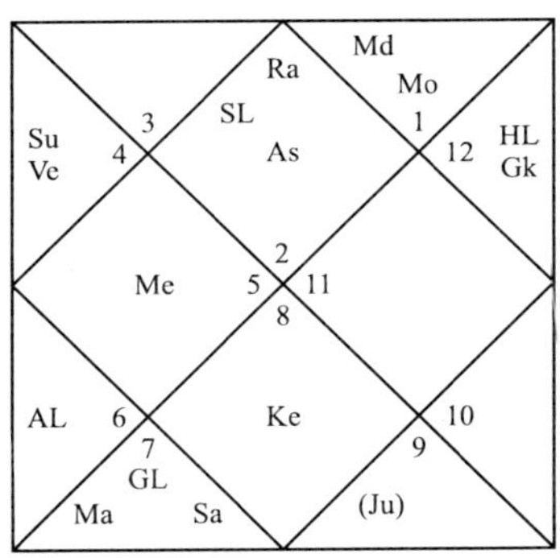

As: 18 Ta 08 Su: 5 Cn 36-GK Mo: 13 Ar 19-PiK Ma: 24 Li 15-AK
Me: 0 Le 43-DK Ju (R): 11 Sg 45-PK Ve: 15 Cn 30-MK Sa: 16 Li 07-BK
Ra: 11 Ta 26-AmK Ke: 11 Sc 26 HL: 19 Pi 52 GL: 12 Li 30

5th Lord mercury in sign placement owned by the Sun. 10th lord Saturn aspects the Sun, so the sun has the connection with 5th and 10th. Mars is the 12th lord

Related to 10th,9th lord Saturn and the 3rd lord Moon, which owns the placement sign of the Sun and Venus the ascendant lord and the 6th lord, Mars also connects to the 8th lord Jupiter through the aspect of Saturn, so the 6, 8, 12 have all established a link.

Example 16: Psychiatrist (the 6th house becomes important factor–Rahu influence is seen)

Sun is related to the sign placement lord of the of the 5th, 8th lord Mercury, sun is with 3rd lord 10th and the Sun as 7th lord. Mars has connection with lord of 5th, 5th and 6th as well. Saturn aspects 6th lord as the 12th lord and the 6th house and is in relation with the placement lord of 5th, 8th lord Jupiter thus, the 6th, 8th, 12th lords are linked. Mars is the lord of 3rd and 10th and Aspects the 6th house and Jupiter the sign placement lord of Mercury, the Jupiter. Notice the influence of planets like Rahu, Saturn, sun all on the 6th house. 3rd and 6th lords link is a very important pointer in Psychiatry.

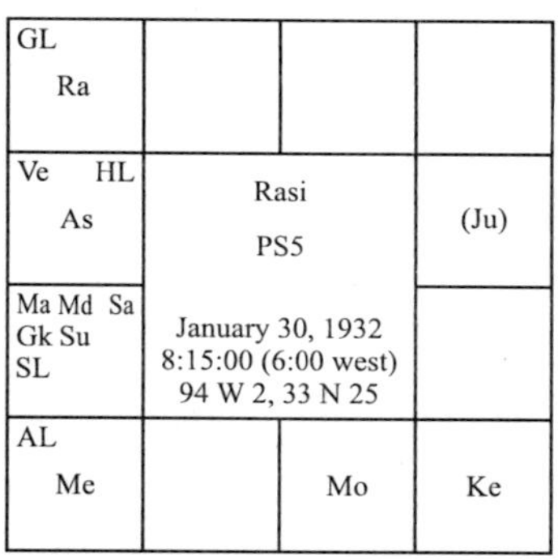

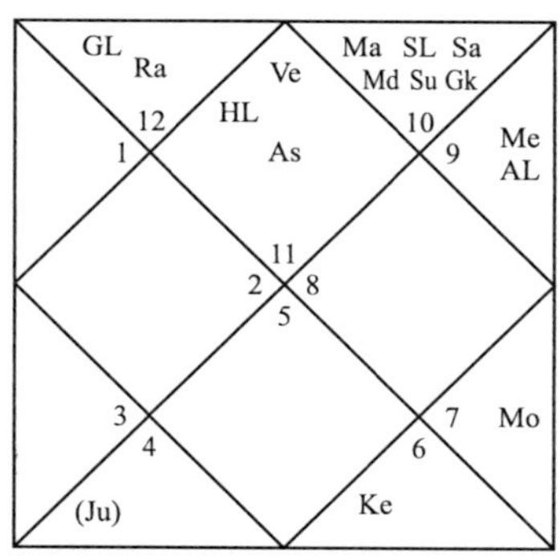

As: 5 Aq 02	Su: 16 Cp 35-GK	Mo: 19 Li 09-PiK	Ma:16 Cp 58-PK
Me: 28 Sg 44-AK	Ju (R): 25 Cn 48-AmK	Ve: 21 Aq 12-MK	Sa: 4 Cp 21-DK
Ra: 4 Pi 25-BK	Ke: 4 Vi 25	HL: 14 Aq 42	GL:26 Pi 54

Example 17: Psychiatrist

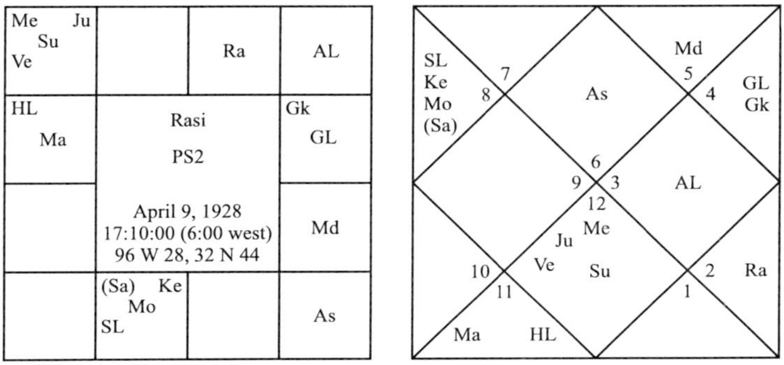

As: 6 Vi 16	Su: 26 Pi 60-AK	Mo: 19 Sc 22-Mk	Ma: 8 Aq 58-PK
Me: 5 Pi 22-GK	Ju: 24 Pi 31-BK	Ve: 5 Pi 12-DK	Sa (R): 26 Sc 10-AmK
Ra: 17 Ta 41-PiK	Ke: 17 Sc 41	HL: 27 Aq 36	GL: 14 Cn 12

Sun is related to the Jupiter, Mercury, Venus because they are in same sign and house. Sun connects to the 5th lord Saturn through the aspect of related planet Jupiter. There is exchange between the 5th, 6th lord Saturn and the 3rd, 8th lord Mars, Mars is 3rd lord in 6th, mars have an exchange with 5th, 6th lord, so the 3rd and 6th link is established. Mercury is lord of 10th with Jupiter, Sun and venus. 6th lord Saturn and 8th lord Mars are related and the lord of 12th Sun has link with Saturn through Jupiter.

Example 18: Psychiatrist

Sun is the 5th lord, Saturn is the 10th, 11th lord and it, aspects the 5th so, sun as 5th lord has a connection with 10th lord. Mars also aspects the 5th and has a mutual aspect relationship with 10th. The sign placement lord of Mars the Venus is in same sign relationship with 3rd, 6th lord Mercury. Mars link with 3rd and 6th is established,

Moreover Mars also connects through trine relationship and Rahu with Mercury and Venus. 12th lord Jupiter is in sign of 8th mars and, while Mars is in trine relationship and under the sign relationship of Venus, which is related to 6th lord Mercury.

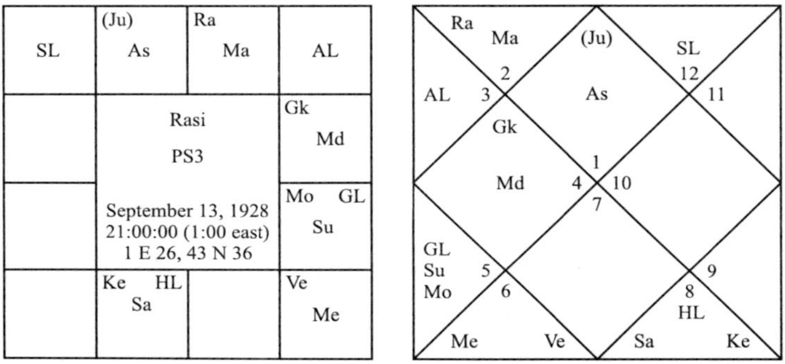

As: 18 Ar 40	Su: 27 Le 54-AmK	Mo: 25 Le 14-BK	Ma: 28 Ta 04-AK
Me: 19 Vi 28-PK	Ju (R): 17 Ar 13-DK	Ve: 18 Vi 06-GK	Sa: 20 Sc 16-MK
Ra: 10 Ta 28-PiK	Ke: 10 Sc 28	HL: 9 Sc 36	GL: 28 Le 00

Example 19: Psychiatrist (Are medical doctors with an additional knowledge of Psychology, the difference between psychologist and Psychiatrist is that only the Psychiatrist can prescribe medicines while psychologist can counsel only)

Sun is with placement sign lord of Saturn who is the 5th, 6th lord placed in sign of mercury, this mercury is in same sign relation to Sun, so Sun has a link with 5th and 6th lord Saturn. Mars the 3rd and 8th lord is in same sign relation with Saturn the 5th, 6th lord. Mars and Saturn are in the 10th and they connect to 6th house through Rahu. Note the high level of impact on 6th.

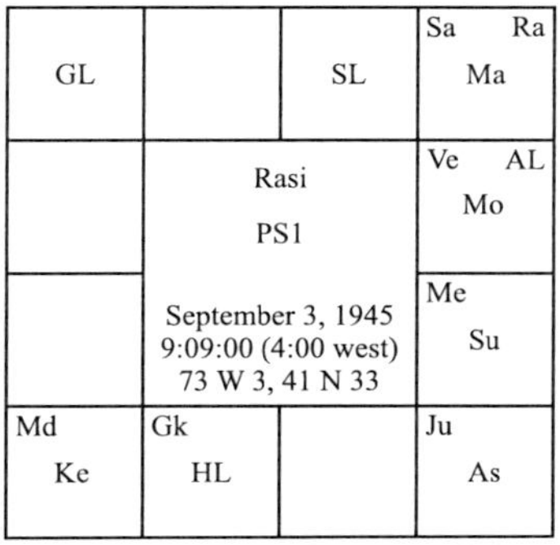

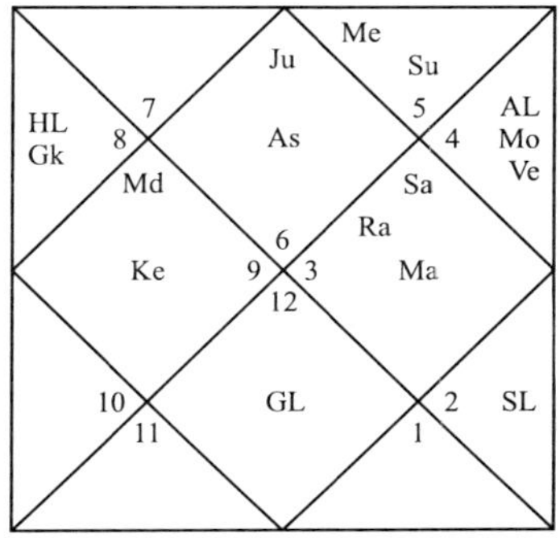

As: 19 Vi 53   Su: 17 Le 34-AmK   Mo: 12 Cn 13-MK   Ma: 4 Ge 19-GK
Me: 0 Le 06-DK   Ju: 8 Vi 49-PK   Ve: 11 Cn 38-PiK   Sa: 28 Ge 19-AK
Ra: 14 Ge 15-BK   Ke: 14 Sg 15   HL: 9 Sc 45   GL: 13 Pi 11

Example 20: Psychiatrist

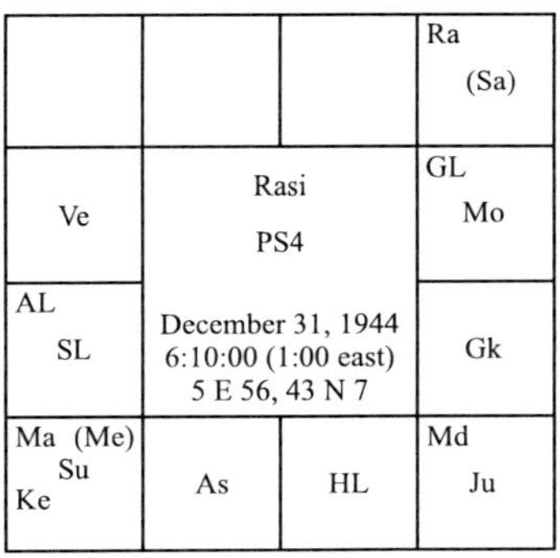

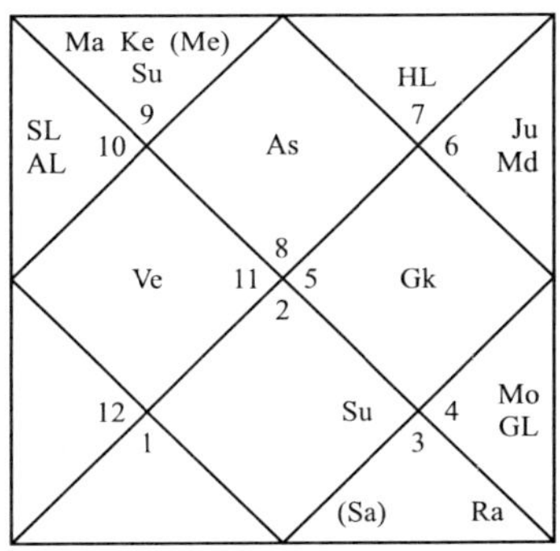

As: 18 Sc 52   Su: 16 Sg 20-AK   Mo: 5 Cn 46-BK   Ma: 2 Sg 46-PK
Me (R): 0 Sg 00-DK   Ju: 4 Vi 11-PiK   Ve: 0 Aq 30-GK   Sa (R): 14 Ge 03-AmK
Ra: 25 Ge 18-MK   Ke: 25 Sg 18   HL: 13 Li 44   GL: 11 Cn 13

Sun in the sign placement of the 2nd and 5th lord Jupiter, Mars is the ascendant & 6th lord with 3rd 4th lord Saturn and 8th and 11th lord mercury. Rahu also connects to 5th and 6th lords. Sun is the 10th lord. 6th lord mars, 8th mercury and 12th Venus are linked, Mercury and Mars are related while Venus is in the sign placement of related lord Saturn.

Example 21: Psychologist (the impact influence now shifts to 6th and 3rd house instead of 5th in Medical profession)

The 10th house has multiple impact of planets, through the Mars to the 10th house, Saturn also aspects the 10th and the 10th lord is placed in its sign. Mars and Mercury are related (Logic Intellect). Mars is in 3rd related to 3rd lord Jupiter and 6th lord Mercury, Mars also aspects the 6th tasking along the influence of Jupiter, Mercury, Sun, Ketu to the 6th. Rahu also aspects the 3rd and 6th lords, Saturn also has a 3rd aspect on the them. The 6th is Mercury,8th is Sun and the Jupiter is the 12th.

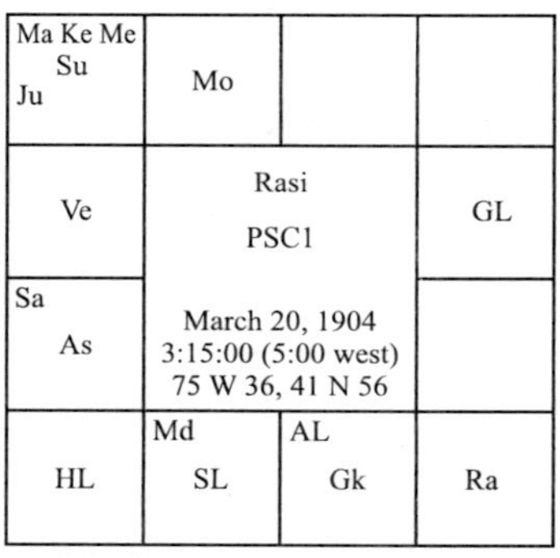

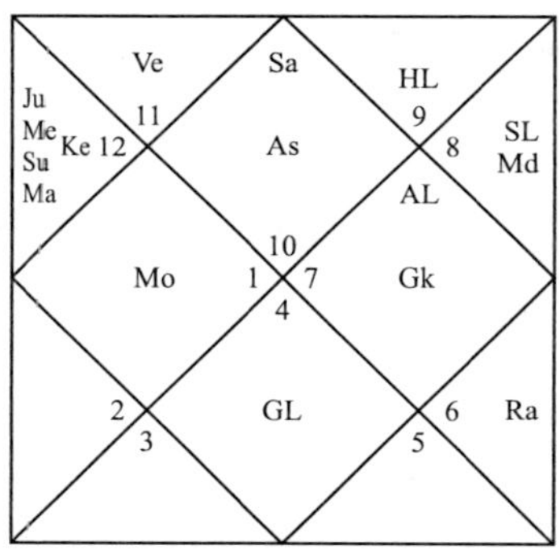

As: 0 Cp 31 Su: 6 Pi 48-GK Mo: 11 Ar 41-PiK Ma: 24 Pi 27-BK
Me: 0 Pi 28-DK Ju: 12 Pi 05-MK Ve: 8 Aq 19-PK Sa: 24 Cp 33AmK
Ra: 4 Vi 58-AK Ke: 4 Pi 58 HL: 7 Sg 06 GL: 23 Cn 52

Example 22: Psychologist

Mars is 8th lord in 3rd and aspects 6th, Mars also aspects the 10th house, Venus the 2nd and 9th is in 10th, Jupiter the 4th and 7th also aspects the 10th and the lord mercury, Saturn is in Kendra to the 10th, while Mars is

Kendra to 10th lord Mercury. Rahu is with the 8th lord Mars in 3rd lending an aspect to 5th, 6th Lord Saturn. The 10th lord mercury also aspects the 6th.

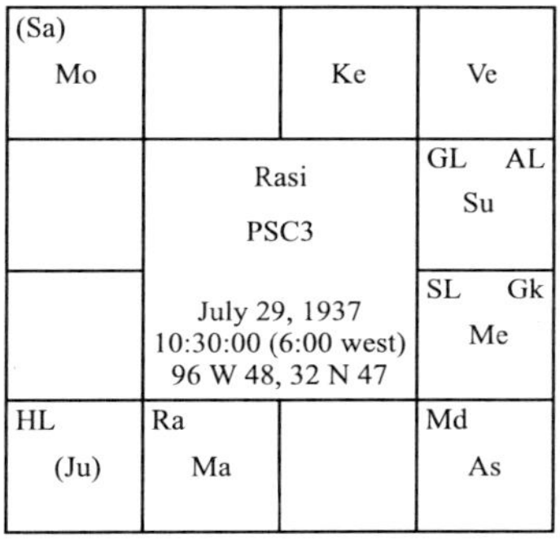

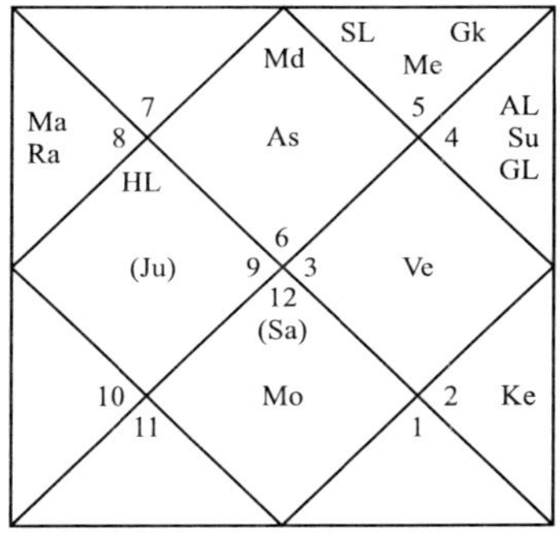

As: 13 Vi 30 Su: 13 Cn 07-BK Mo: 28 Pi 53-AK Ma: 2 Sc 53-GK
Me: 3 Le 33-PK Ju (R): 27 Sg 37-AmK Ve: 0 Ge 11-DK Sa (R): 12 Pi 01-MK
Ra: 20 Sc 42-PiK Ke: 20 Ta 42 HL: 6 Sg 29 GL: 11 Cn 48

The 3rd, 6th, 8th connection of mars is a common observable factor, along with its connection to 10th.

Example 23: Psychologist Clinical

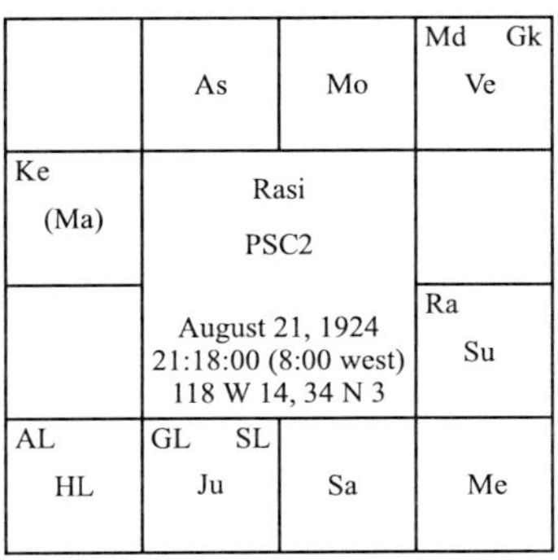

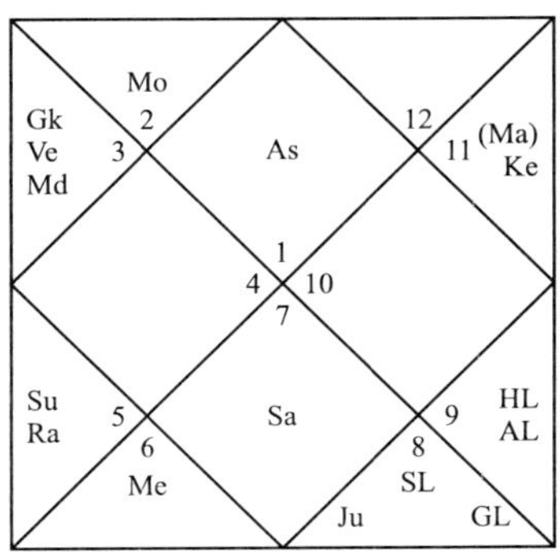

As: 9 Ar 16 Su: 6 Le 01-PiK Mo: 4 Ta 14-GK Ma (R): 7 Aq 51-MK
Me: 2 Vi 05-DK Ju: 17 Sc 36-BK Ve: 21 Ge 45-AmK Sa: 5 Li 07-PK
Ra: 0 Le 09-AK Ke: 0 Aq 09 HL: 3 Sg 02 GL: 29 Sc 31

Mars in sign placement of 10th, 11th lord Saturn, Aspects 5th and 6th along with 5th lord Sun and 3rd.

6th lord Mercury, Mars has a placement relation with Jupiter the 9th and 12th lord. Mars and mercury have a link, Rahu connects to 3rd and 6th through Mars. Sun in 5th indicates the nature and work of psychologist to be clinical.

6th lord Mercury ,8th lord Mars and 12th lord Jupiter has a connection. These three houses have a connection with hospitals and mental agitations etc.

Example 24: Psychologist

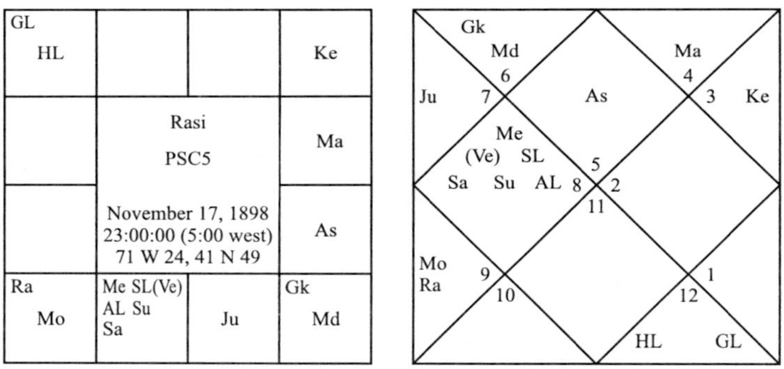

As:	3 Le 03	Su:	3 Sc 26-DK	Mo:	29 Sg 54-AK	Ma:	13 Cn 24-PiK
Me:	19 Sc 49-MK	Ju:	5 Li 42-GK	Ve (R):	23 Sc 48-AmK	Sa:	20 Sc 07-BK
Ra:	16 Sg 55-PK	Ke:	16 Ge 55	HL:	11 Pi 17	GL:	24 Pi 05

Mars Has a connection with 10th lord as it is Located in its Sign, Mars Aspects the 3rd, 6th and the 8th lord, there is an exchange between Mars and Mercury, therefore mars relates with Saturn 6th, 7th, Sun the ascendant lord, Venus the 10th and 3rd lord, Mercury the 2nd and 11th, Mars connects to 5th house and Rahu through its sign lord placement Moon. Connection link between 6th, 8th and 12th is there through sign placement lords of the planets.

Example 25: Psychoanalyst

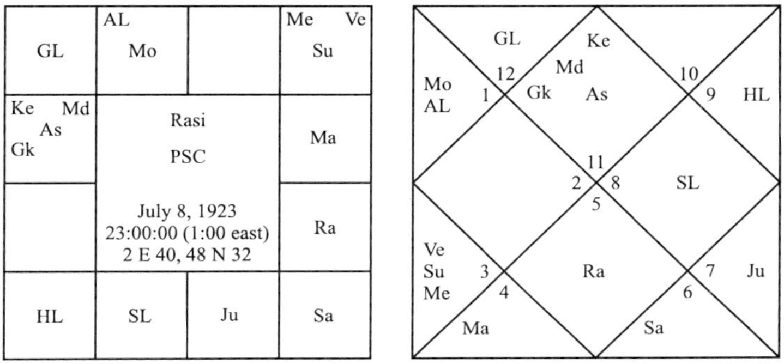

As: 13 Aq 14	Su: 22 Ge 54-AmK	Mo: 23 Ar 51-AK	Ma: 2 Cn 38-DK
Me: 7 Ge 56-PK	Ju: 16 Li 17-MK	Ve: 5 Ge 40-GK	Sa: 20 Vi 58-BK
Ra: 20 Le 34-PiK	Ke:20 Aq 34	HL: 21 Sg 24	GL: 20 Pi 12

Mars in 6th and is the lord of 10th and 3rd in exchange with lord of 6th, Jupiter is in mutual aspect relationship with Moon, therefore is related to Mars as well, the Jupiter aspects the planets Sun the 7th lord. Mercury the 8th and 5th and Venus the 9th and 4th, Saturn is in 8th aspects the 10th, 2nd and 5th house it is placed in sign of Mercury, Saturn is lord of 12th and ascendant. Rahu connects to the 6th lord moon through an aspect or being in trine to it.

Example 26: Dentist, Saturn represents teeth, 2nd house also does the same

Sun, is with 10th lord and in mutual aspect relation with Saturn the 5th, 6th lord. Saturn is also related to 3rd and 8th lord due to Sign exchange, Jupiter is with 2nd lord Venus which is in exchange Mercury the 10th and ascendant lord, this relates Saturn to the 2nd lord as well other than its aspect on 2nd house. Mars and Jupiter also get linked with 2nd and 10th lords. Since dentist is also a medical related field we find influence of Sun on 5th and 10th here.

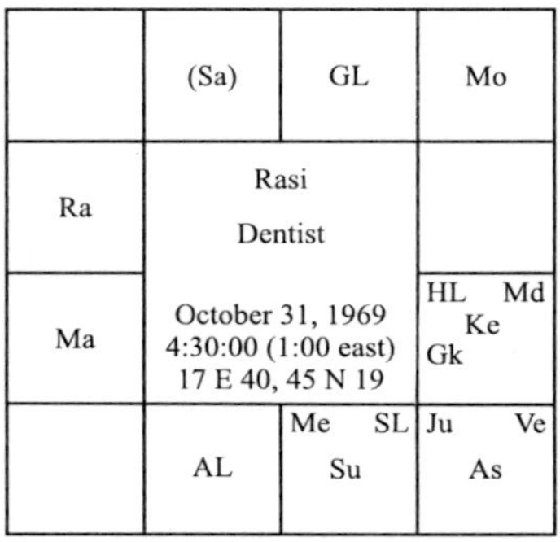

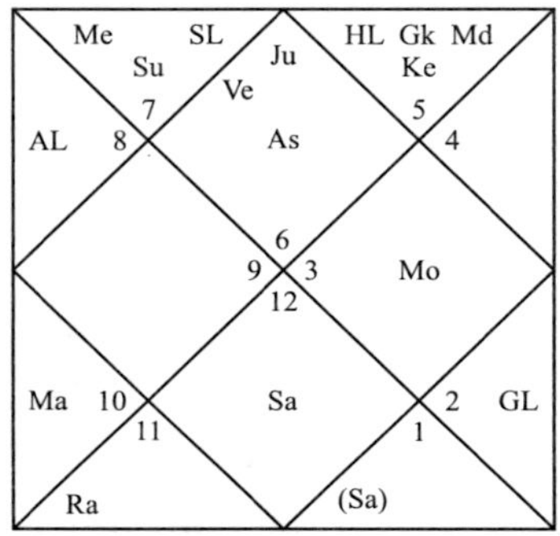

As: 21 Vi 16	Su: 14 Li 06-MK	Mo: 20 Ge 43-BK	Ma: 3 Cp 15-DK
Me: 3 Li 60-PK	Ju: 27 Vi 34-AK	Ve: 23 Vi 24-AmK	Sa (R): 11 Ar 51-PiK
Ra: 26 Aq 27-GK	Ke: 26 Le 27	HL: 13 Le 02	GL: 12 Ta 48

Example 27: Dentist

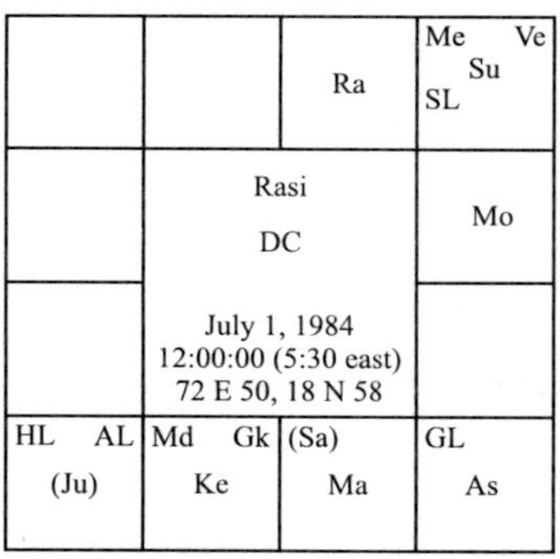

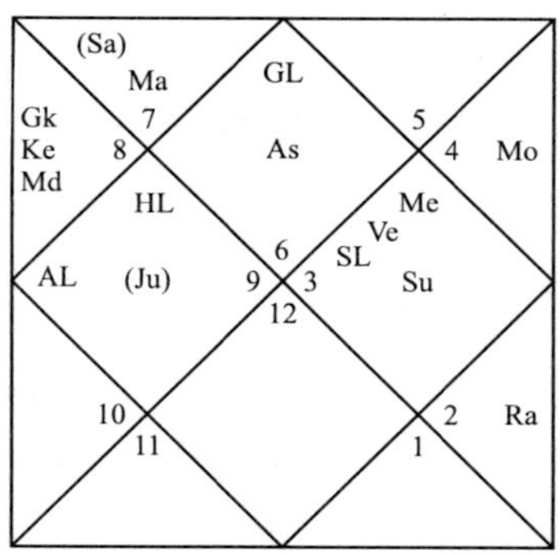

As: 6 Vi 12	Su: 15 Ge 58-PK	Mo: 14 Cn 08-DK	Ma: 18 Li 56-BK
Me: 25 Ge 36-AK	Ju (R): 14 Sg 14-GK	Ve: 20 Ge 11-AmK	Sa (R): 16 Li 11-PiK
Ra: 12 Ta 35-MK	Ke: 12 Sc 35	HL: 11 Sg 23	GL: 4 Vi 51

Saturn is the 5th and 6th lord in 2nd, with 8th and 3rd Saturn, they are both placed in Sign of 2nd lord Venus, which is placed in 10th with ascendant, 10th lord

Mercury,12th lord Sun. Jupiter the 4th and 7th is also related to 2nd and 10th lords. Sun connects to the 5th lord through Venus, which is the placement sign lord of 5th, 6th lord Saturn and 8th, 3rd Mars.

Example 28: Dentist

Sun is in the 2nd related to Sign placement lord of the Saturn, the 5th, 6th lord so Sun has link to 5th and Mars the placement sign lord of the 2nd lord is also with Mercury the sign that houses Saturn, there is an exchange between Mars and Venus here. Jupiter also connects to the 10th through Sun as it is placed in the its Sign and the Sun is with 10th lord .The 6th, 8th and 12th are also linked.

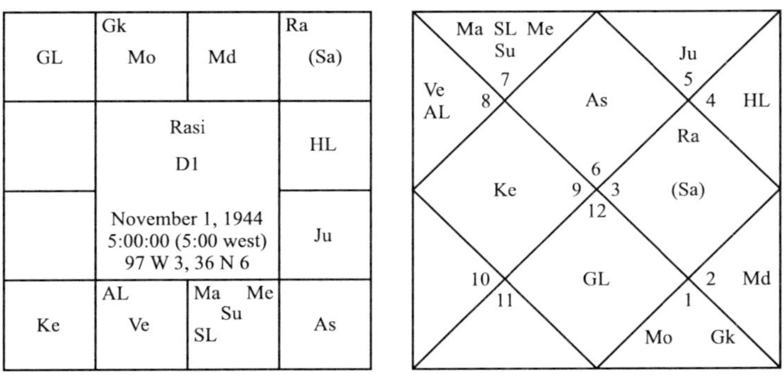

As: 9 Vi 49	Su: 15 Li 47-GK	Mo: 27 Ar 32-AK	Ma: 19 Li 53-MK
Me: 22 Li 58-BK	Ju: 27 Le 18-AmK	Ve: 18 Sc 47-PiK	Sa (R): 17 Ge 38-PK
Ra: 28 Ge 09-DK	Ke: 28 Sg 09	HL: 17 Cn 42	GL: 6 Pi 53

Example 29: Dental surgeon

Sun is related to 5th and 10th, Saturn is the 6th, 7th lord in exchange with 2nd and 11th lord Mercury. Mars aspects the 10th house and the 2nd lord mercury, Saturn aspects mars so mars have the link with 6th a requirement for surgeon. There is a clear-cut link of 6th, 8th and 12th house lords. Jupiter is in 2nd and related to 10th lord Venus as well.

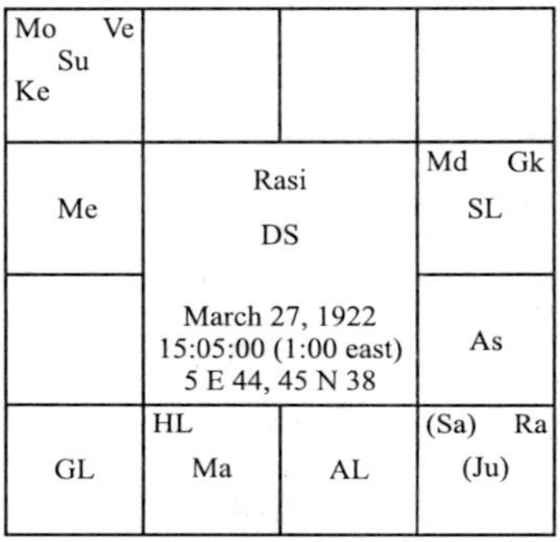

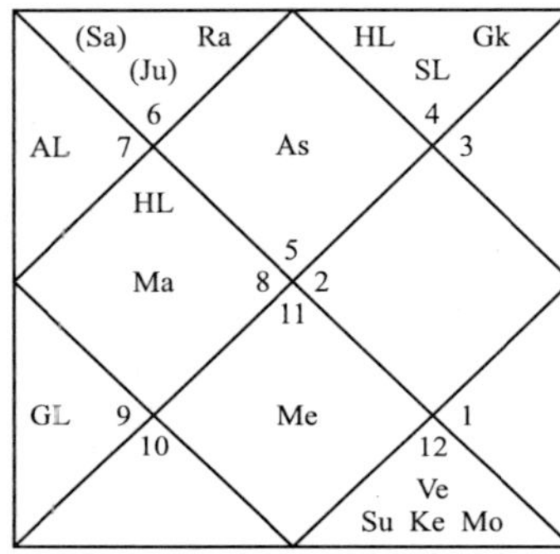

As: 0 Le 35	Su: 13 Pi 21-PK	Mo: 2 Pi 54-DK	Ma: 23 Sc 46-AmK
Me: 19 Aq 48-MK	Ju (R): 22 Vi 15-BK	Ve: 24 Pi-46-AK	Sa (R): 11 Vi 20-GK
Ra: 15 Vi 58-PiK	Ke: 15 Pi 58	HL: 28 Sc 48	GL: 22 Sg 29

Example 30: Dental college professor

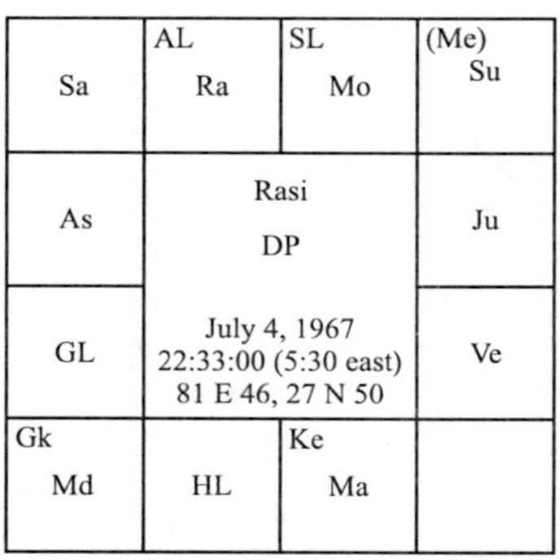

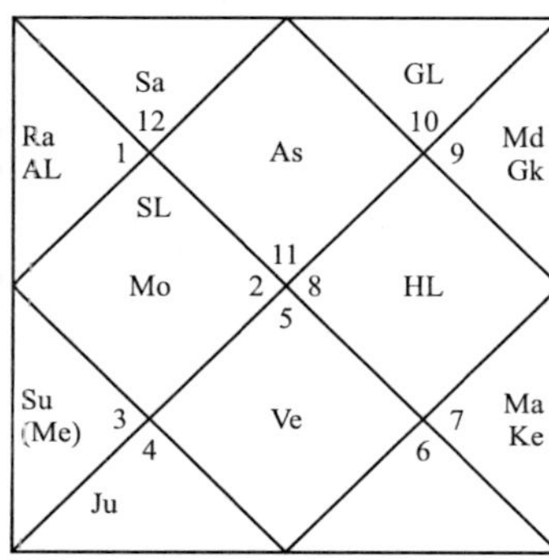

As: 21 Aq 53	Su: 18 Ge 38-MK	Mo: 12 Ta 58-PK	Ma: 0 Li 01-DK
Me(R): 26 Ge 06-AK	Ju: 14 Cn 33-PiK	Ve: 3 Le 13-GK	Sa: 18 Pi 43-AmK
Ra: 11 Ar 22-BK	Ke: 11 Li 22	HL: 26 Sc 46	GL: 25 Cp 00

Saturn in 2nd, related to planet Jupiter placed in 6th in the sign of 6th lord moon, Jupiter aspects own sign and Saturn in 2nd therefore is related, it also aspects the 10th house and the 12th house, its placement sign lord Moon also aspects the 10th, Sun is in 5th with the lord of 5th and 8th, 10th lord Mars and planet moon the 6th lord are in signs owned by Venus therefore linked through Venus, which is in sign owned by Sun therefore it links with Sun the 7th and Mercury 5th and 8th. Saturn in 2nd also aspects the 6th lord as well. 6th and 12th have a connection through aspect while, 8th connects through dispositor.

VETERINARY DOCTORS

Planet Sun represents animals mostly the four legged and Saturn represents some of domesticated animals. 4th house, 6th house and 12th house also represents animals.

Example 31

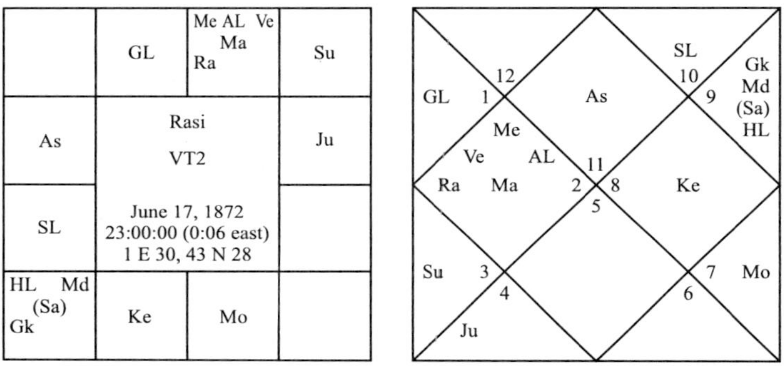

As: 5 Aq 08	Su: 4 Ge 53-DK	Mo: 19 Li 26-PiK	Ma: 26 Ta 48-BK
Me: 26 Ta 27-MK	Ju: 9 Cn 06-GK	Ve: 27 Ta 07-AmK	Sa (R): 27 Sg 27-AK
Ra: 20 Ta 30-PK	Ke: 20 Sc 30	HL: 22 Sg 17	GL: 19 Ar 28

Mars is the 10th lord in 4th, Sun is in 5th in the Sign of mercury and is related to Saturn vide mutual aspect, the 6th lord Moon and 10th lord Mars, the 5th, 8th lord Mercury all have the same sign placement lord Venus, Lord of 4th and 9th. So, the link of Sun, Saturn with 10th, 6th, 4th is established other than that Mars also aspects Saturn. Saturn is in the sign of Jupiter. While Jupiter in 6th lords Sign therefore it too has link with 10th Mars, 4th Venus and 5th, 8th Mercury.

Example 32: Veterinary Doctor

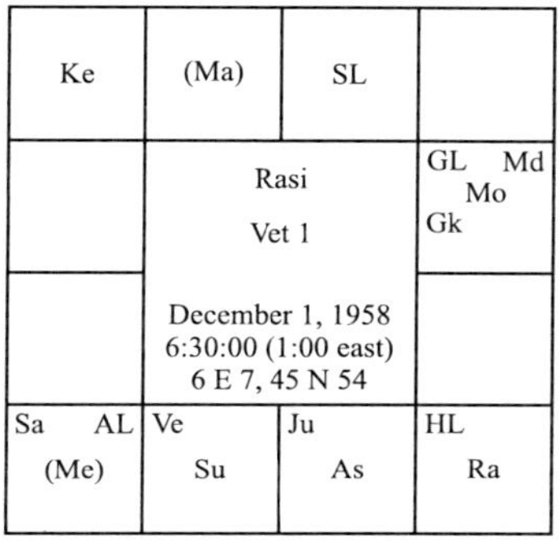

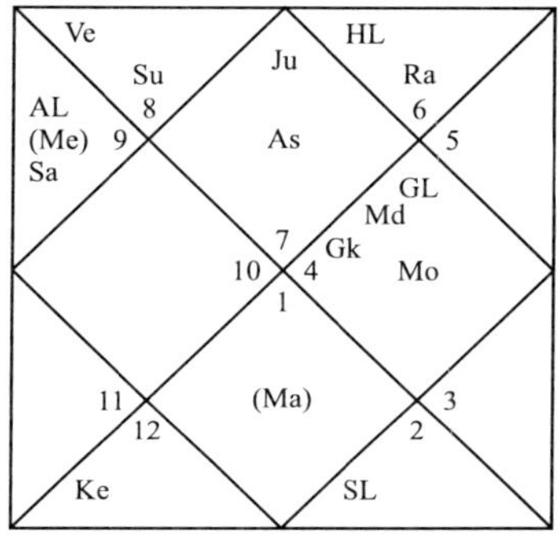

As: 27 Li 44	Su: 15 Sc 14-MK	Mo: 10 Cn 24-PiK	Ma (R): 25 Ar 46-AK
Me (R): 2 Sg 21-GK	Ju: 24 Li 32-AmK	Ve: 20 Sc 06-BK	Sa: 2 Sg 35-PK
Ra: 27 Vi 48-DK	Ke: 27 Pi 48	HL: 29 Vi 05	GL: 21 Cn 16

Saturn and Sun are linked because their Sign placement lords are related, So the 4th and 5th lord Saturn is connected to 3rd and 6th Jupiter, while it is in relation with 9th and 12th mercury. Mars the 2nd and 7th has relationship with 11th lord Sun and ascendant and 8th lord Venus.

Example 33: Veterinary Doctor

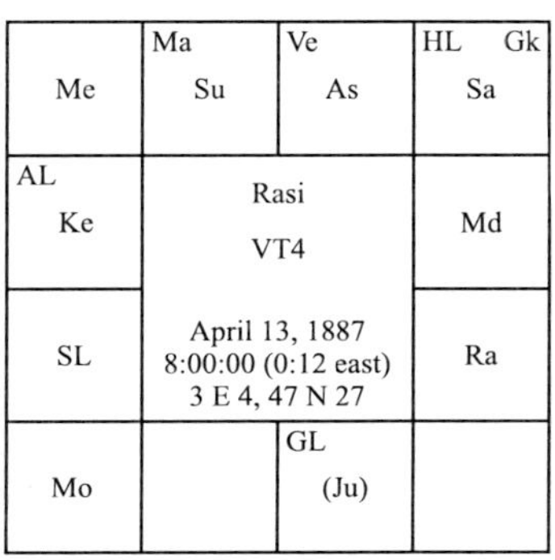

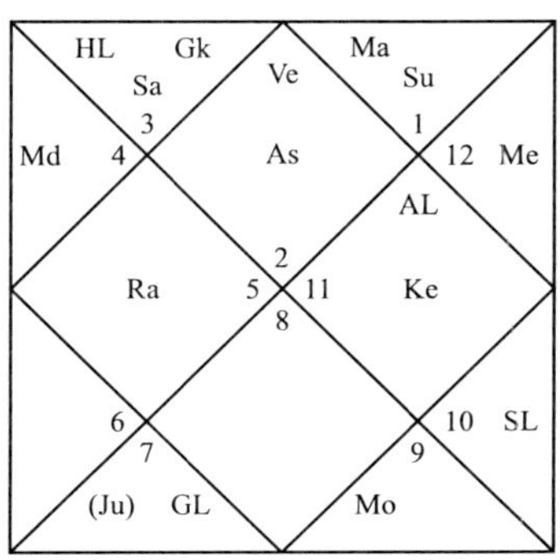

As: 27 Ta 25	Su: 0 Ar 47-DK	Mo: 8 Sg 56-MK	Ma: 3 Ar 27-PK
Me: 4 Pi 19-PiK	Ju (R): 9 Li 45-BK	Ve: 1 Ta 46-GK	Sa: 23 Ge 56-AmK
Ra: 4 Le 02-AK	Ke: 4 Aq 02	HL: 20 Ge 04	GL: 19 Li 08

Mars, Sun, Jupiter are related because of Mutual aspects, Jupiter aspects the 9th, 10th lord Saturn so it will carry forward the energy of Sun the 4th, Mars the 12th and 7th lords to Saturn. The 6th lord Venus is the sign placement lord of Jupiter, therefore will link with planets related to Jupiter as well, Mercury the 5th lord is under aspect by Saturn and in Kendra relation to it as well, the Sign placement lord of Mercury is Jupiter, so the 5th lord also connects to Sun, Mars through Jupiter. 10th lord Saturn aspects the 4th, 8th and 11th houses and lords of 3rd and 5th.

Example 34: Veterinary Doctor

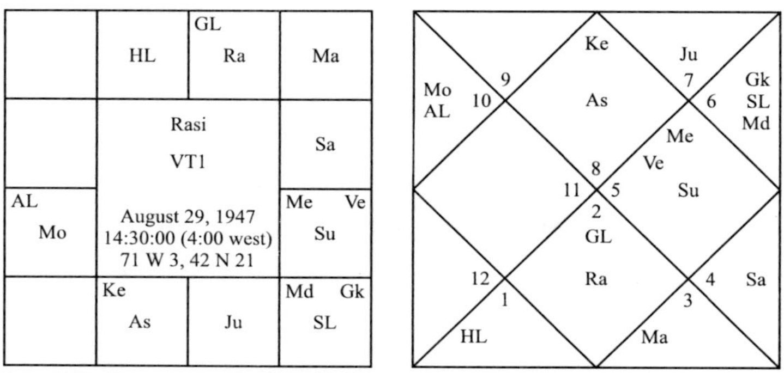

As: 19 Sc 50	Su: 12 Le 27-GK	Mo: 20 Cp 56-MK	Ma: 17 Ge 10-PiK
Me: 13 Le 05-PK	Ju: 27 Li 26-AK	Ve: 11 Le 08-DK	Sa: 22 Cn 22-BK
Ra: 4 Ta 13-AmK	Ke: 4 Sc 13	HL: 22 Ar 09	GL: 7 Ta 13

Sun is the 10th lord in 10th with Venus, the 12th, 2nd, Mercury the 8th and 11th, Jupiter is in sign of the Venus and Mars is in the sign of mercury. So, the 5th lord Jupiter has link with Sun. Saturn and Jupiter in the Kendra to each other thus related as per Phal Deepika.

Saturn is related to moon; the Moon is also in Kendra to Jupiter.

Example 35: Nurse

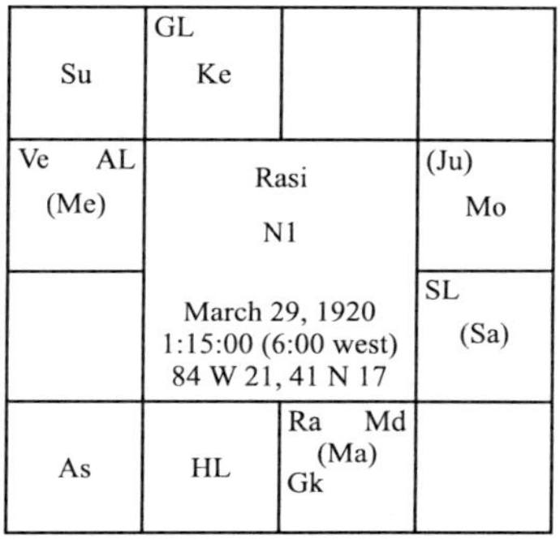

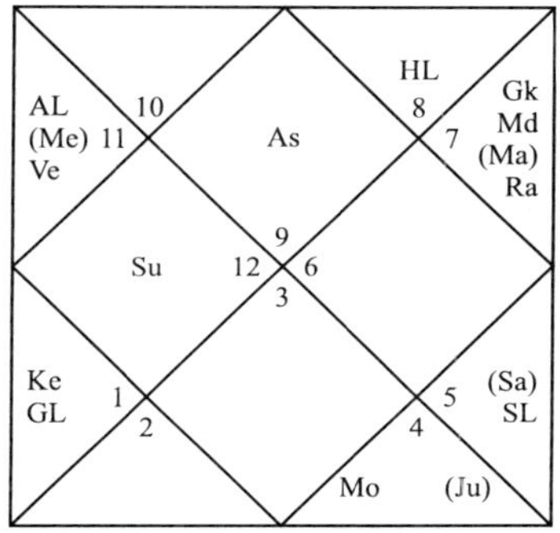

As: 15 Sg 13	Su: 15 Pi 34-BK	Mo: 11 Cn 50-GK	Ma (R): 15 Li 05-PiK
Me (R): 29 Aq 55-AK	Ju (R): 15 Cn 25-MK	Ve: 20 Aq 21-AmK	Sa (R): 13 Le 19-PK
Ra: 23 Li 32-DK	Ke: 23 Ar 32	HL: 6 Sc 09	GL: 23 Ar 16

Saturn and mars are linked, Saturn aspects Mars. Saturn is related to 6th and 11th lord Venus, 10th, 7th lord Mercury, Sun is related to Jupiter and aspects the 10th. Mars connects to 10th as 5th, 12th lord through Rahu.

Example 36: Nurse

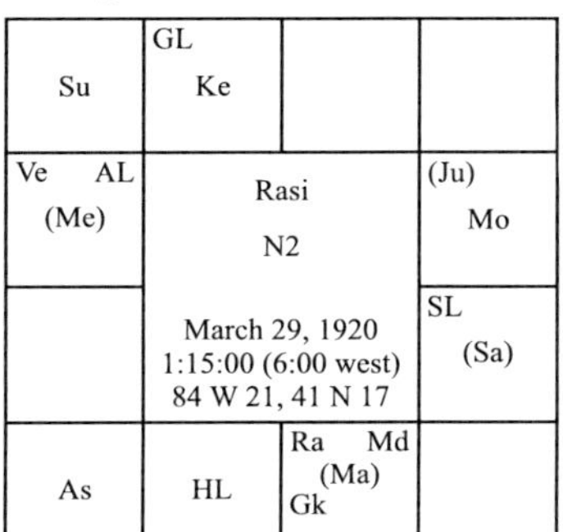

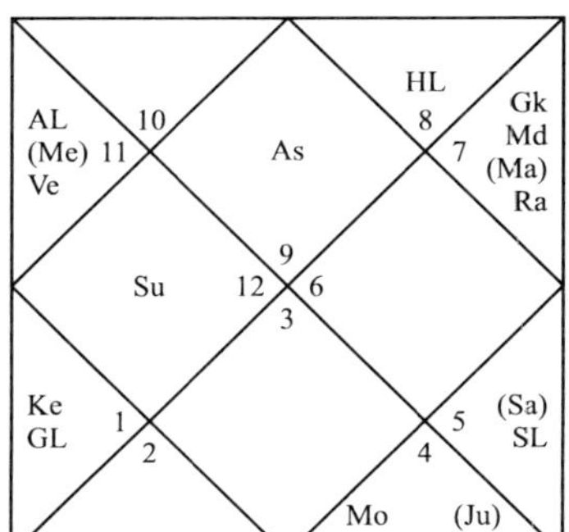

As: 15 Sg 13	Su: 15 Pi 34-BK	Mo: 11 Cn 50-GK	Ma (R): 15 Li 05-PiK
Me (R): 29 Aq 55-AK	Ju (R): 15 Cn 25-MK	Ve: 20 Aq 21-AmK	Sa (R): 13 Le 19-PK
Ra: 23 Li 32-DK	Ke: 23 Ar 32	HL: 6 Sc 09	GL: 23 Ar 16

5th lord Saturn aspects the 10th lord Mercury and Sun further it is placed in the sign owned by sun. Saturn and mars have a link as their sign lords are in relationship, Jupiter is related to Saturn (Mutual aspect) While it, aspects Saturn, its Sign placement lord is also Saturn. Sun is related to 10th lords and connects to Saturn, Mars and Jupiter through sign placement lords. There is a connection of 6th, 8th and 12th lords as well.

Example 37: Nurse

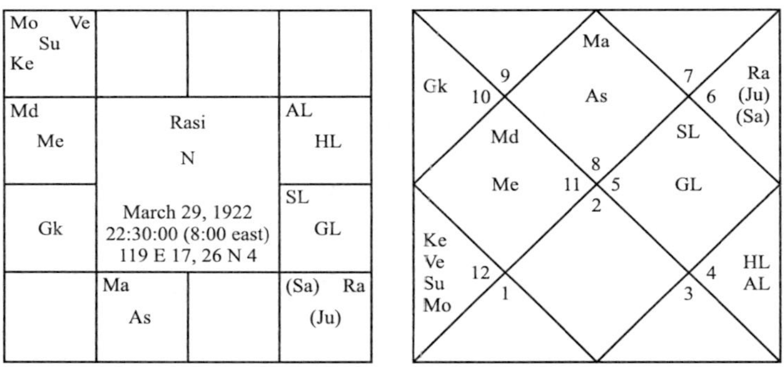

As: 11 Sc 24	Su: 15 Pi 21-PK	Mo: 27 Pi 02-AmK	Ma: 24 Sc 30-BK
Me: 22 Aq 50-MK	Ju (R): 21 Vi 60-PiK	Ve: 27 Pi 16-AK	Sa (R): 11 Vi 10-DK
Ra: 15 Vi 58-GK	Ke: 15 Pi 58	HL: 28 Cn 31	GL: 19 Le 17

Sun is in 5th as a 10th lord, connected to Jupiter Saturn, Venus, moon Through relationship, either of being in same house or Mutual aspect or dispositor aspects own house. Saturn aspects Mars transferring the energy of all related planets, further Mars is in Trikona relationship with Sun, Venus, Moon. Mars also aspects mercury, mercury is placed in the Sign of Saturn, further there is an exchange between Mercury and Saturn, So the 6th, 8th and 12th link is there.

Example 38: Medical Technician ECG (mars and Saturn link are evident)

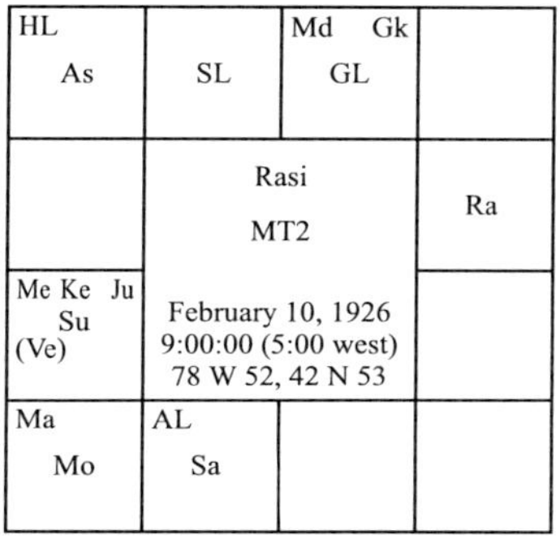

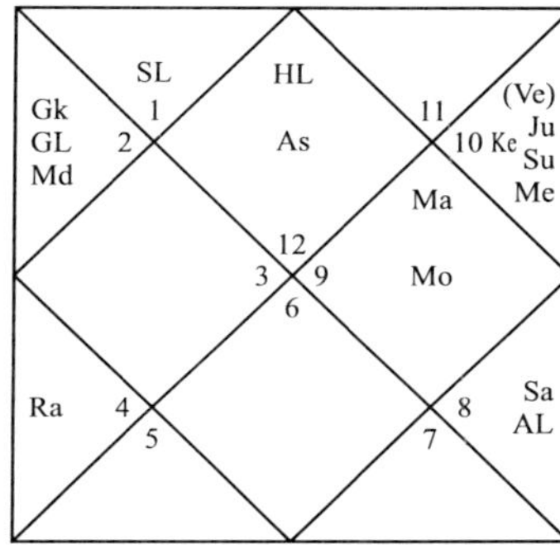

As: 9 Pi 01	Su: 28 Cp 17-AK	Mo: 28 Sg 03-AmK	Ma: 8 Sg 12-GK
Me: 24 Cp 08-MK	Ju: 15 Cp 33-PK	Ve (R): 23 Cp 28-PiK	Sa: 2 Sc 47-DK
Ra: 2 Cn 35-BK	Ke: 2 Cp 35	HL: 15 Pi 28	GL: 26 Ta 21

Sun aspects the 5th and is with 10th lord Jupiter, the 5th lord is in 10th with 2nd and 9th lord, the sign placement lord of 5th is Jupiter which is related to Saturn the 11th,12th lord. Saturn is related to Sign placement Lord of Mars, while Saturn is in the sign owned by Mars. The link of 6th, 8th and 12th is also there as required for medical fields other than Sun's influence on 5th.

Example 39: Medical technician (mars and Saturn link are evident)

Exchange between 5th Lord moon and 4th, 7th mercury. Saturn and Sun are in sign owned by mercury, so is the 5th lord moon, Sun connects with 5th house lord through Mercury the joint Sign owner. 10th lord Jupiter in Relation with Mercury and is placed in sign of Saturn, Saturn and Sun aspect the 10th house, mars also connect with the 10th lord through Saturn, as Saturn aspects

Mars. 6th and 12th lords Sun and Saturn connect with 8th through Mercury and Jupiter.

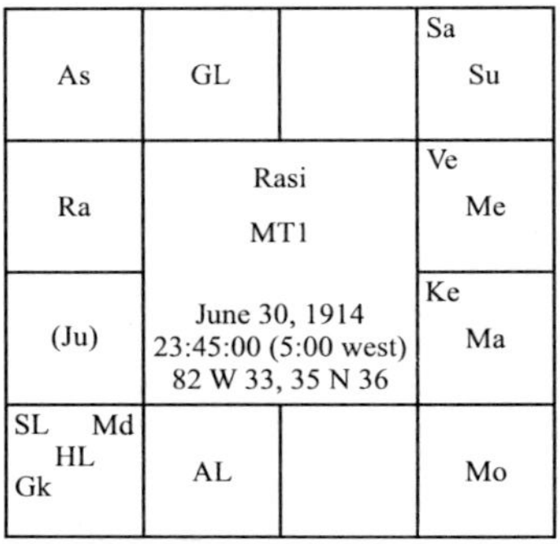

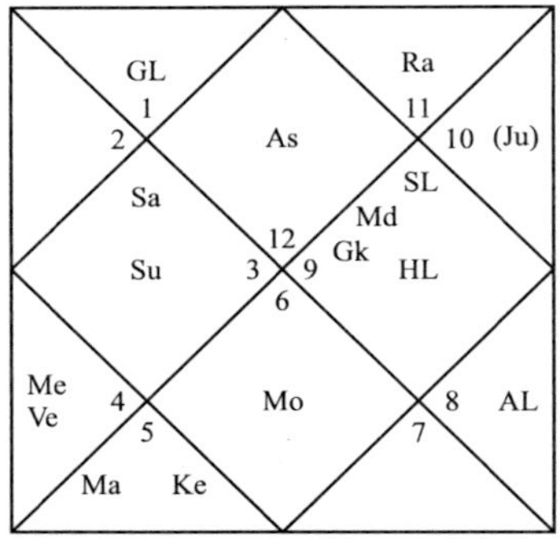

As: 2 Pi 45	Su: 15 Ge 50-MK	Mo: 20 Vi 58-AmK	Ma: 10 Le 16-PK
Me: 6 Cn 17-GK	Ju (R): 29 Cp 00-AK	Ve: 20 Cn 26-BK	Sa: 1 Ge 19-DK
Ra: 14 Aq 59-PiK	Ke: 14 Le 59	HL: 26 Sg 38	GL: 13 Ar 55

Example 40: Medical technician (mars and Saturn link)

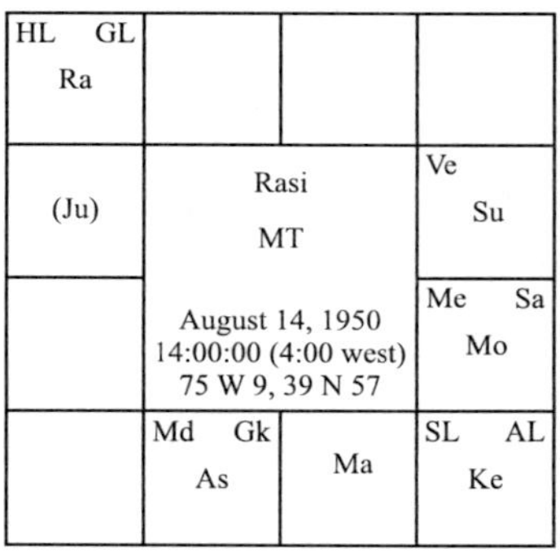

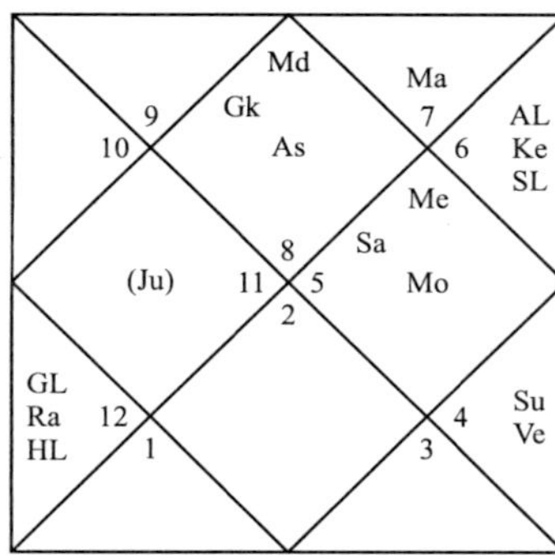

As: 0 Sc 14	Su: 28 Cn 12-AK	Mo: 11 Le 19-PiK	Ma: 9 Li 17-GK
Me: 24 Le 41-BK	Ju (R): 10 Aq 49-PK	Ve: 4 Cn 36-DK	Sa: 25 Le 35-AmK
Ra: 5 Pi 35-MK	Ke: 5 Vi 35	HL: 20 Pi 11	GL: 8 Pi 38

Exchange relationship between Sun the 10th and Moon the 9th, Due to this the 5th lord Jupiter connects with Sun. Saturn aspects Mars, The Saturn is also related to Jupiter the 5th, 2nd Mercury the 8th, 11th, moon the 9th, Sun the 10th and Venus the 12th and 7th.

ACTORS

Prominent Venus, houses 2nd ,3rd and 4th connection to the 10th.

4th is about the masses and emotions ,3rd hidden talents, Second portrays the face, speech and expressions therefrom. Venus represents- the arts of theater and singing etc.

Example 1: Actor Al Pacino

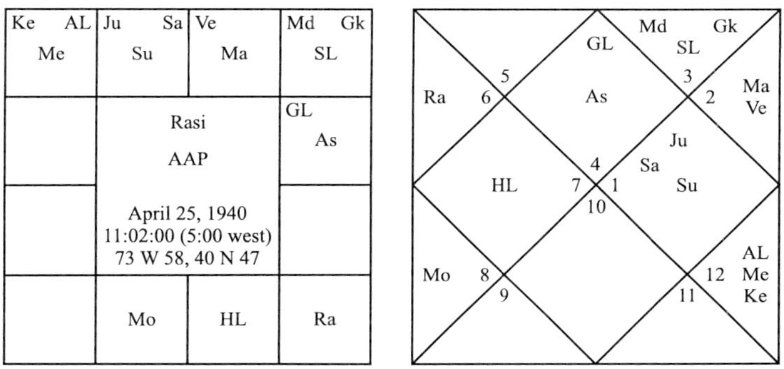

As: 11 Cn 58	Su: 12 Ar 16-PiK	Mo: 28 Sc 39-AK	Ma: 22 Ta 43-BK
Me: 18 Pi 22-MK	Ju: 2 Ar 08-DK	Ve: 27 Ta 37-AmK	Sa: 11 Ar 29-PK
Ra: 26 Vi 55-GK	Ke: 26 Pi 55	HL: 9 Li 28	GL: 5 Cn 37

Mars is the sign placement lord of 2nd the sun, Mars is also the 5th, 10th lord with Venus the lord of 4th, 11th. Third lord mercury is in Sign owned by Jupiter, While Jupiter happens to in 10th in sign owned by Mars, related to Sun and Saturn. So, the third also connects through Jupiter with Venus and Mars. Moon is also related to the Mars and Venus here.

Example 2: Actor Charles Bronson

SL AL Ke			
HL	Rasi ACB		
	November 3, 1921 11:00:00 (5:00 west) 78 W 49, 41 N 21		GL
Mo As	Gk Md	(Me) Su	Ju Ra Ve Ma Sa

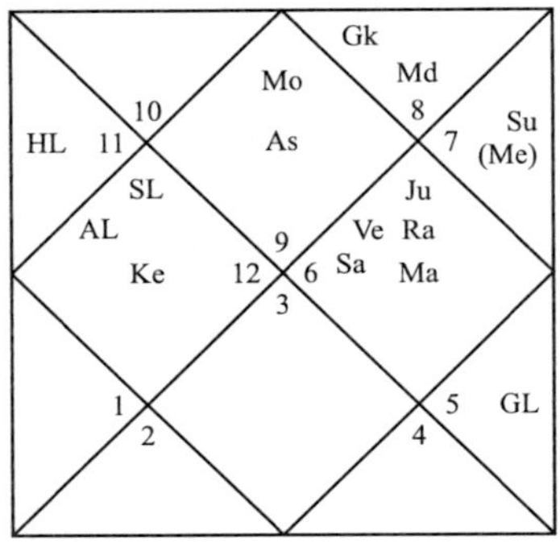

As: 8 Sg 15	Su: 17 Li 57-AmK	Mo: 3 Sg 13-DK	Ma: 5 Vi 23-PK
Me (R): 10 Li 49-MK	Ju: 15 Vi 22-BK	Ve: 24 Vi 31-AK	Sa: 10 Vi 21-PiK
Ra: 25 Vi 06-GK	Ke: 25 Pi 06	HL: 21 Aq 01	GL: 25 Le 54

Venus with mars in 10th with 2nd, 3rd and 4th lord, 10th lord Mercury is placed in Sign of Venus and in exchange as well therefore the connection of all present planets in 10th with 10th Lord mercury and 9th lord Sun is established through Venus. Planet moon the planet of emotions; state of mind and expressions is Linked to Venus through the 4th aspect from mars and also through Jupiter the 4th lord which houses the sign of Moons Placement.

Example 3: Actor Jim Carrey

Venus connects to 2nd lord Mars through a related planet Jupiter, while 2nd lord mars is Placed in the sign of Jupiter and aspects the 10th house. Planet moon the 10th lord the cosmic reflector is in the sign owned by Venus. Therefore, the planets related with Venus connect through Venus. 3rd, 6th lord Jupiter, 4th, 5th Saturn is also related to Venus. So, Venus connects with 2nd, 3rd, 4th 10th and also the Moon here completing the required equation.

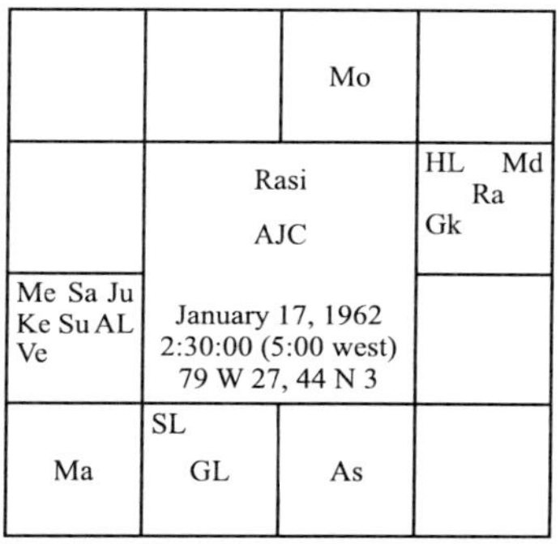

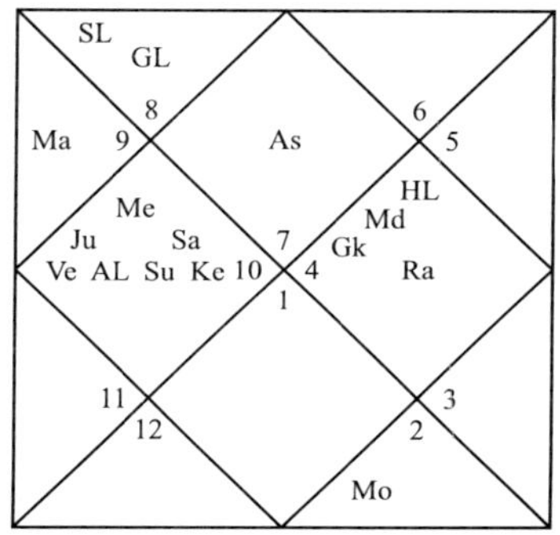

As: 21 Li 53	Su: 3 Cp 24-GK	Mo: 23 Ta 52-AmK	Ma: 24 Sg 36-AK
Me: 21 Cp 25-BK	Ju: 20 Cp 52-MK	Ve: 0 Cp 59-DK	Sa: 8 Cp 16-PiK
Ra: 24 Cn 50-PK	Ke: 24 Cp 50	HL: 20 Cn 18	GL: 16 Sc 51

Example 4: Actor Kirk Douglas

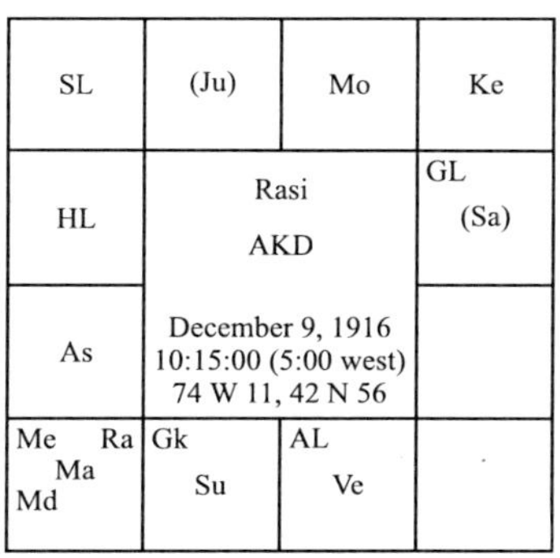

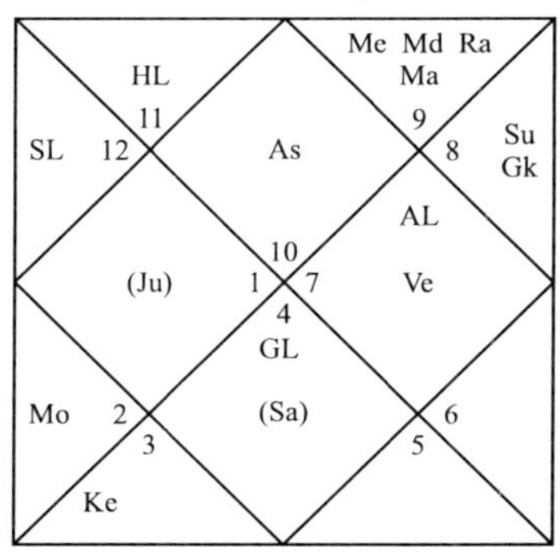

As: 7 Cp 50	Su: 24 Sc 33-AmK	Mo: 25 Ta 44-AK	Ma: 13 Sg 21-MK
Me: 3 Sg 09-PK	Ju (R): 2 Ar 57-GK	Ve: 21 Li 37-BK	Sa (R): 7 Cn 13-PiK
Ra: 27 Sg 23-DK	Ke: 27 Ge 23	HL: 21 Aq 13	GL: 1 Cn 23

Venus is in its MT sign in 10th, creating a Malaya Panch mahapursh yoga. It is related to Jupiter, while is a dispositor of the Moon. Jupiter is related to Mars due to an exchange between Mars and Jupiter, therefore Venus connects with Mars and mercury as well. Mars aspects the Saturn, While Saturn is in Kendra relationship with Venus. Saturn is the lord of ascendant and 2nd, Jupiter the 3rd, 12th and Mars is the 4th lord. So, the Venus connection with house lords 2nd, 3rd, 4th and 10th is established.

Example 5: Actor Marlon Brando

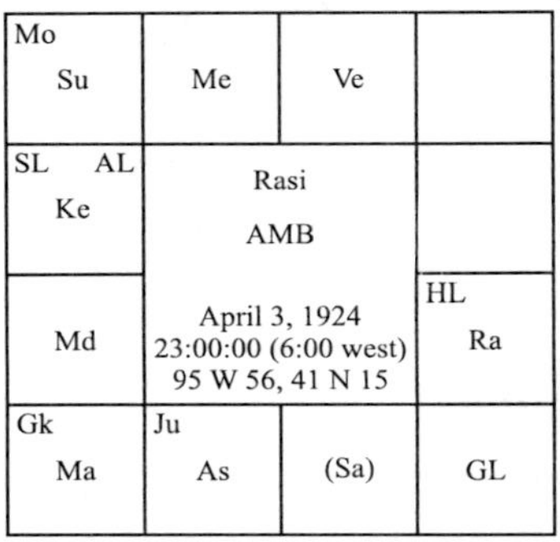

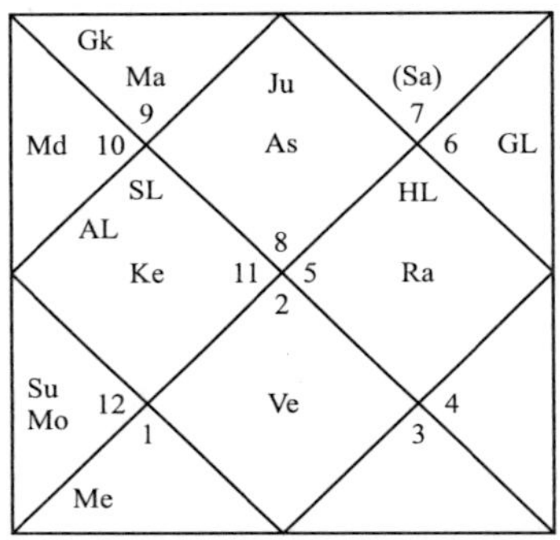

As: 10 Sc 56	Su: 21 Pi 22-BK	Mo: 20 Pi 17-PiK	Ma: 24 Sg 55-AmK
Me: 4 Ar 27-DK	Ju: 27 Sc 06-AK	Ve: 6 Ta 03-GK	Sa (R): 7 Li 21-PK
Ra: 8 Le 46-MK	Ke: 8 Aq 46	HL: 16 Le 28	GL: 25 Vi 09

Jupiter in exchange with Mars, Jupiter is also in Mutual aspect relationship with Venus, Jupiter is also related to the 10th lord Sun and 9th lord Moon as it, aspects the sign of Suns placement and Sun which happen to be its own sign. Venus connects to 3rd, 4th lord Saturn because it is the dispositor of Saturn. So, Venus connects with 2nd, 3rd, 4th and is the lord of 10th itself, While the connection with moon is established through a related planet Jupiter.

Example 6: Actress Cameron Diaz

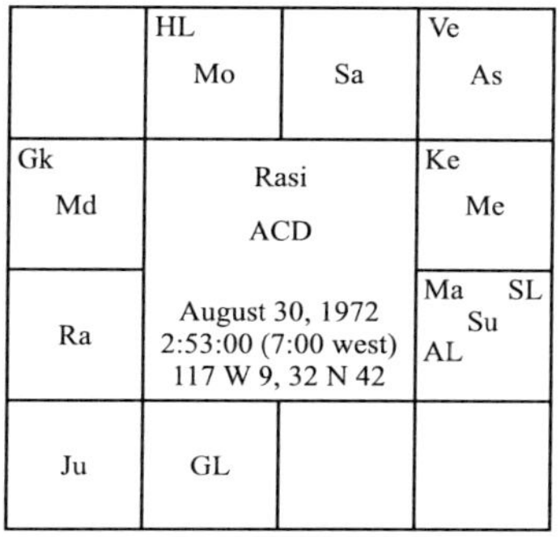

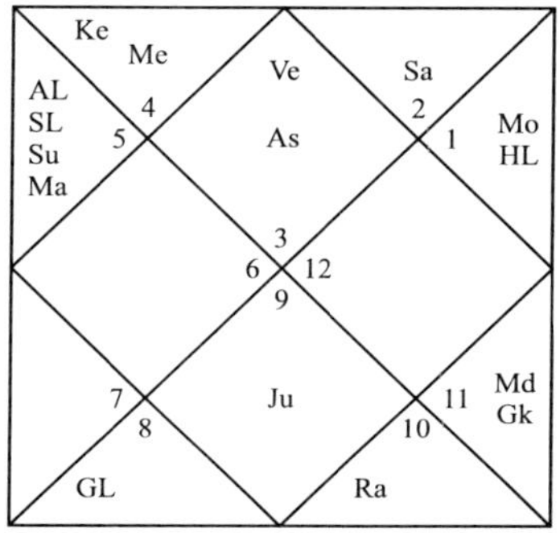

As: 29 Ge 11	Su: 13 Le 38-GK	Mo: 28 Ar 46-AK	Ma: 16 Le 18-PK
Me: 26 Cn 30-MK	Ju: 5 Sg 03-DK	Ve: 27 Ge 51-BK	Sa: 26 Te 08-PiK
Ra: 1 Cp 44-AmK	Ke: 1 Cn 44	HL: 26 Ar 32	GL: 17 Sc 06

Relation between Jupiter and Venus (mutual aspect) Jupiter is lord of 10th, 7th Venus 12th and 5th. Jupiter Aspects Sun the 3rd and Mars 6th, 11th lord, it also aspects the 2nd lord moon. So, Moon the 2nd, Sun the 3rd and mars connect through Jupiter, 4th lord mercury connects with Venus as it is the dispositor of Venus.

Example 7: Actress Halle Barry

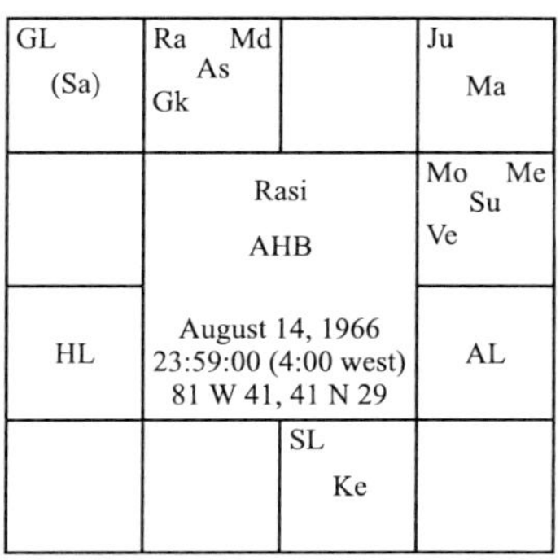

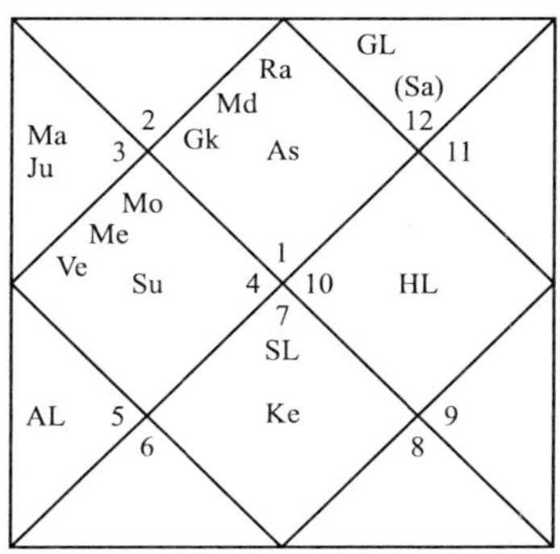

As: 26 Ar 42	Su: 28 Cn 30-BK	Mo: 9 Cn 48-PiK	Ma: 29 Ge 51-AK
Me: 9 Cn 54-MK	Ju: 28 Ge 39-AmK	Ve: 6 Cn 11-PK	Sa (R): 5 Pi 20-GK
Ra: 27 Ar 22-DK	Ke: 27 Li 22	HL: 7 Cp 53	GL: 7 Pi 60

Venus is the 2nd, 7th lord, Related to Mercury 3rd, 6th, Moon 4th and Sun 5th. Mars aspects the 10th house, so do the Planets in 4th. Venus connects to Mars and Jupiter through Mercury, While the 10th lord is in Trikona (trine) to Venus and related planets, while it is in Kendra to Mars and Jupiter. (Saturn aspects Mars and Jupiter by three quarter or 75% aspect) while it, aspects planets in 4th by 50% or half aspect). Phal Deepika recognizes the Kendra and Trikona positions from planets to be a relationship.

Example 8: Actress Ingrid Bergman

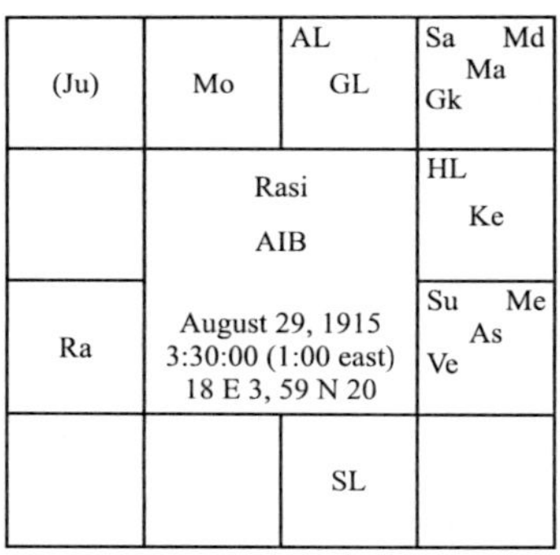

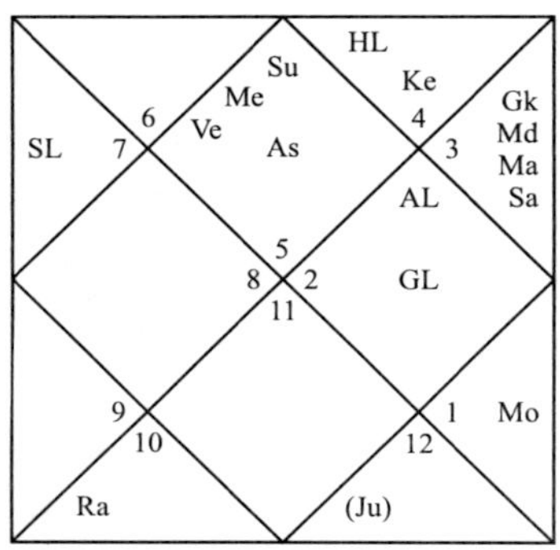

As: 0 Le 57	Su: 11 Le 60-MK	Mo: 2 Ar 52-DK	Ma: 13 Ge 34-BK
Me: 25 Le 25-AK	Ju (R): 3 Pi 17-GK	Ve: 8 Le 01-PiK	Sa: 20 Ge 34-AmK
Ra: 24 Cp 32-PK	Ke: 24 Cn 32	HL: 6 Cn 29	GL: 14 Ta 36

10th, 3rd lord Venus related to 2nd, 11th lord Mercury and ascendant lord Sun. Mercury becomes the dispositor of Saturn the 6th, 7th lord and Mars 4th and 9th lord. Mars the 4th also connects with the Venus through the 3rd aspect of Saturn on the first house and planets therein. Moon is in the sign owned by Mars and in trine position from Venus, Sun and Mercury.

Example 9: Actress Marilyn Monroe

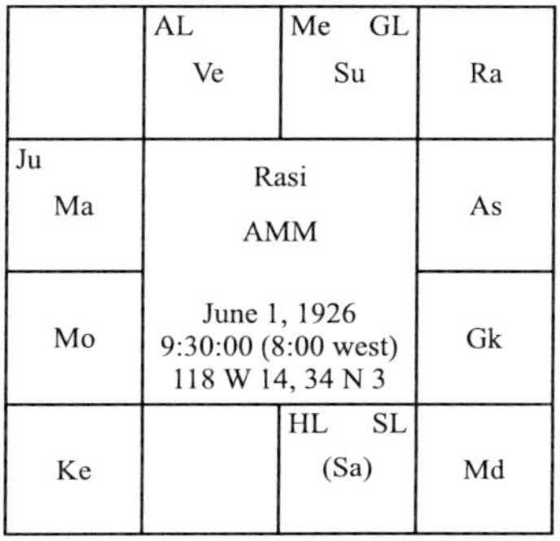

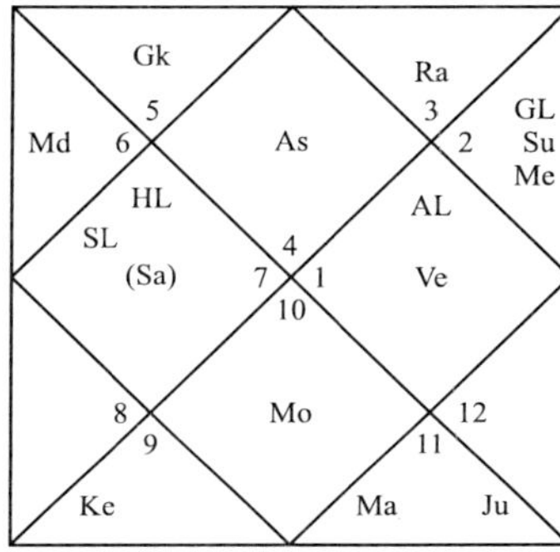

As: 20 Cn 15	Su: 17 Ta 38-MK	Mo: 26 Cp 16-BK	Ma: 27 Aq 55-AmK
Me: 13 Ta 58-PiK	Ju: 4 Aq 00-DK	Ve: 5 Ar 56-PK	Sa (R): 28 Li 37-AK
Ra: 24 Ge 04-GK	Ke: 24 Sg 04	HL: 8 Li 50	GL: 10 Ta 57

10th Lord Mars in 8th in Saturn's Sign with Jupiter. Saturn is related to Venus Mutual aspect and dispositor aspects own sign. So, Mars and Jupiter connect through Saturn, With Venus, further Jupiter also aspects the saturn, 2nd lord Sun and 3rd Lord Mercury are in the Sign owned by Venus the 4th and 11th lord. Planet moon is in Kendra to both Saturn the Dispositor and Venus therefore linked.

Example 10: Actress, vocalist, pop singer Christina Aguilera

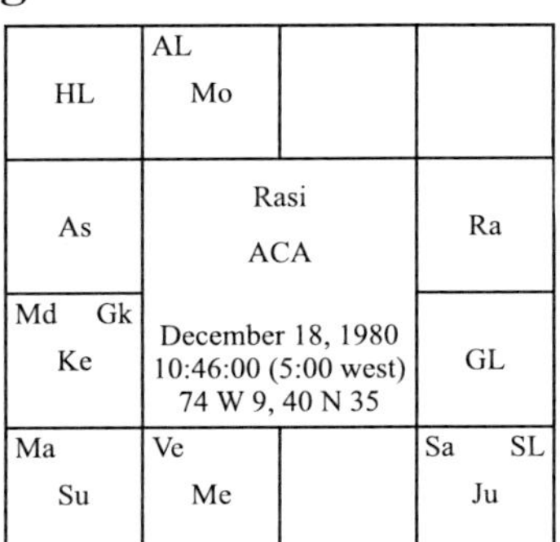

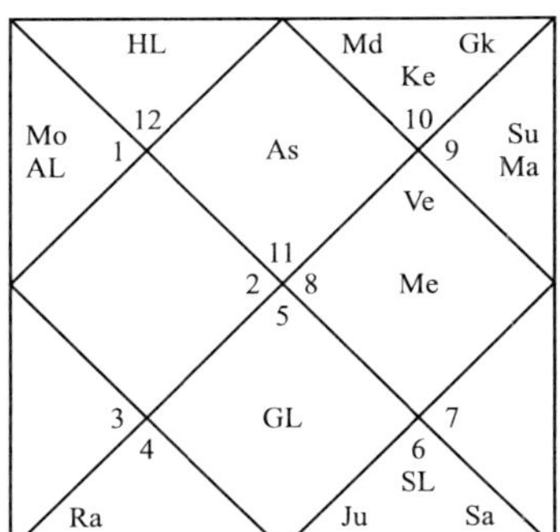

As: 2 Aq 46	Su: 3 Sg 19-DK	Mo: 21 Ar 09-BK	Ma: 26 Sg 50-AK
Me: 26 Sc 11-AmK	Ju: 14 Vi 43-PiK	Ve: 6 Sc 55-GK	Sa: 15 Vi 21-MK
Ra: 18 Cn 16-PK	Ke: 18 Cp 16	HL: 15 Pi 57	GL: 20 Le 06

Sun and Mars are in same sign that belongs to Jupiter, While Jupiter and Saturn are in same sign that belongs to Mercury, Venus and mercury are in same sign that belongs to mars, Moon is in Sign of Mars, so Venus, Mercury and Moon share common dispositor. 2nd lord Jupiter is inn the sign of Mercury related to Venus, 3rd, 10th lord mars is the Sign placement owner of 4th, 9th lord Venus. So, the 2nd, 3rd, 4th and 10th are all connected to Venus.

Example 11: Singer John Lennon of Beatles group

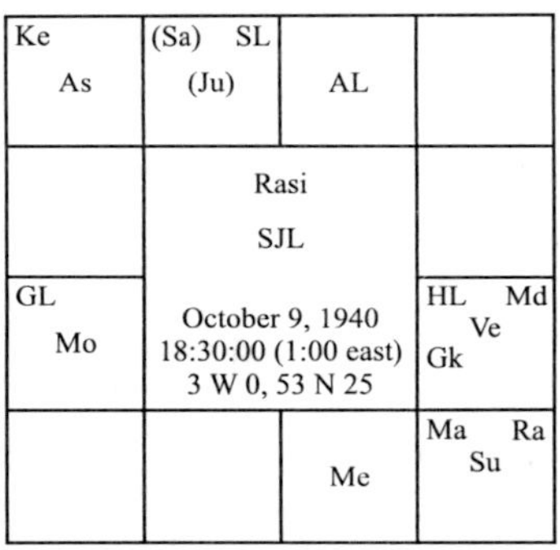

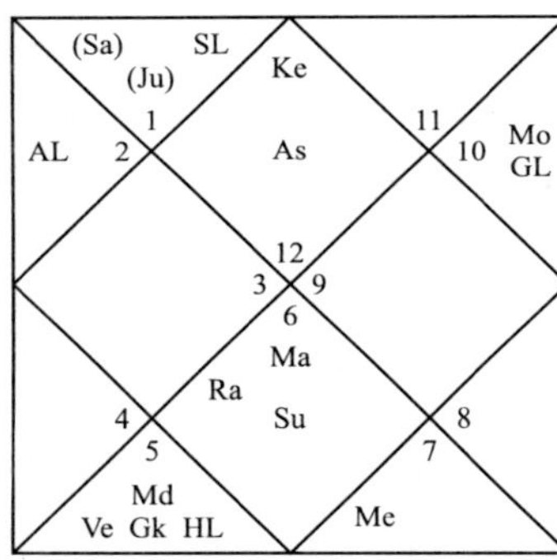

As: 26 Pi 40	Su: 23 Vi 15-AK	Mo: 10 Cp 31-PK	Ma: 9 Vi 39-DK
Me: 15 Li 32-MK	Ju (R): 20 Ar 40-AmK	Ve: 10 Le 11-GK	Sa (R): 20 Ar 11-BK
Ra: 17 Vi 60-PiK	Ke: 17 Pi 60	HL: 21 Le 11	GL: 3 Cp 46

Saturn the 11th, 12th, Jupiter the 10th and Ascendant are related (same house) to Mercury the lord of 4th, 7th due to mutual aspect. Mars the 2nd, 9th is related to Saturn due to aspectual relationship (Dispositor), Mars is also related to Sun the 6th, it also connects to Venus through Jupiter as related planet it aspects the 3rd, 8th lord Venus and through Sun as the dispositor of Venus is Sun the related planet again. Moon is in the sign of Saturn and in relationship with Saturn, Jupiter (dispositor aspects the sign). So once again Venus connects with Mars the 2nd, Mercury the 4th and is the 3rd lord. Mercury is in sign of Venus and related to Jupiter and Saturn.

Example 12: Dancer and actress (12th house also comes to picture now). Sudha Chandran–Indian Bharatanatyam dancer and film and television actress.

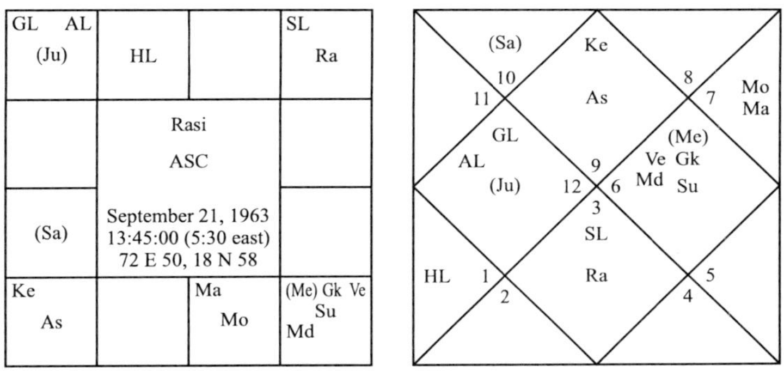

As:	13 Sg 36	Su:	4 Vi 17-GK	Mo:	13 Li 10-BK	Ma:	12 Li 41-MK
Me (R):	1 Vi 58-DK	Ju (R):	23 Pi 19-AmK	Ve:	10 Vi 19-PiK	Sa (R):	23 Cp 51-AK
Ra:	24 Ge 12-PK	Ke:	24 Sg 12	HL:	11 Ar 09	GL:	6 Pi 53

Saturn is the lord of 2nd and 3rd in aspectual relationship with Mars, which happens to have Venus as dispositor, Mars is in same sign with moon, Mars is the lord of 12th and 5th, Moon the 8th, Venus is in relationship with Mercury, the 7th, 10, Sun the 9th and Jupiter the ascendant and 4th lord, Saturn aspects the 4th house and lord as well. Here also the Venus link with 2nd, 3rd, 4th lords plus the 12th lord as the legs play an important part in dancing is established.

Example 13: Dancer and actress–Malaika Arora

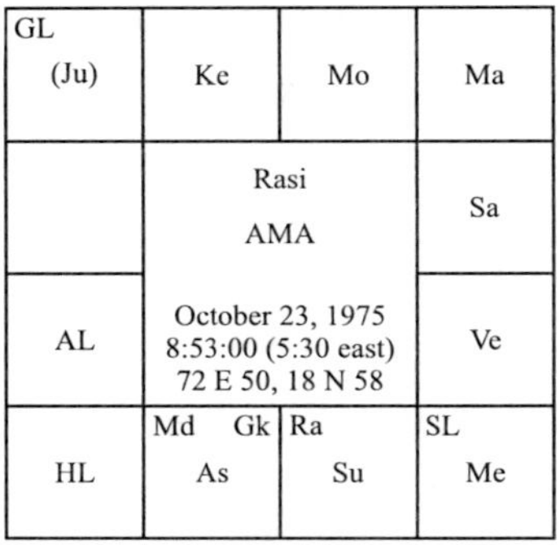

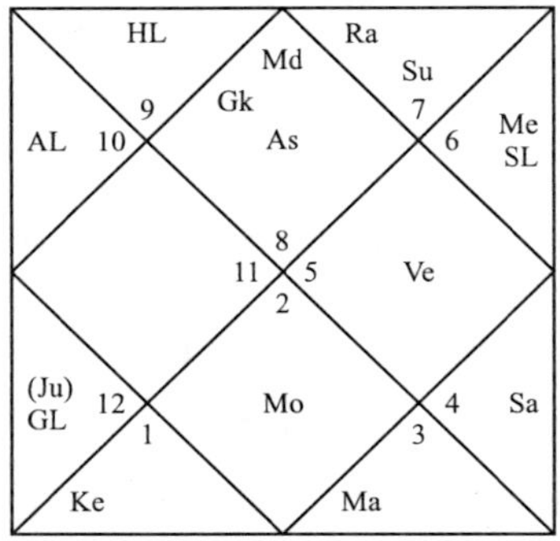

As: 5 Sc 59	Su: 5 Li 35-GK	Mo: 8 Ta 18-PiK	Ma: 7 Ge 45-PK
Me: 17 Vi 29-BK	Ju (R): 24 Pi 52-AK	Ve: 19 Le 56-AmK	Sa: 8 Cn 59-MK
Ra: 28 Li 17-DK	Ke: 28 Ar 17	HL: 12 Sg 39	GL: 23 Pi 22

Sun and Venus in exchange, Sun is the 10th lord, Venus the 7th and 12th, Jupiter the 2nd aspects 2nd, 3rd lord Saturn and is in relationship with Mercury the 8th, 11th, Venus is the sign placement lord of Moon, while moon is the dispositor of 2nd, 3rd lord Saturn. Here also the link of Venus with Moon and lords 2nd, 3rd, 4th, 12th and 10th is established, Mars is in Kendra relationship with both Jupiter and mercury and in Trikona relation to the 10th lord Sun which is in exchange relation with Venus.

Example 14: Dancer modern and ballet

The relationship of Venus with 2nd, 3rd, 4th houses and lords along with 10th and 12th lords is established here in this chart, Saturn is in joint relationship with planets in 3rd, while it is in dispositor relationship with moon the 10th lord, Jupiter becomes the main joint dispositor of all the planets on 3rd. Venus has the mars and moon connection as well.

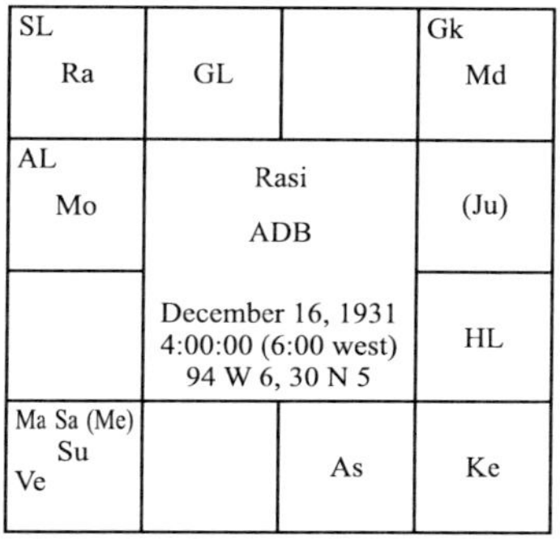

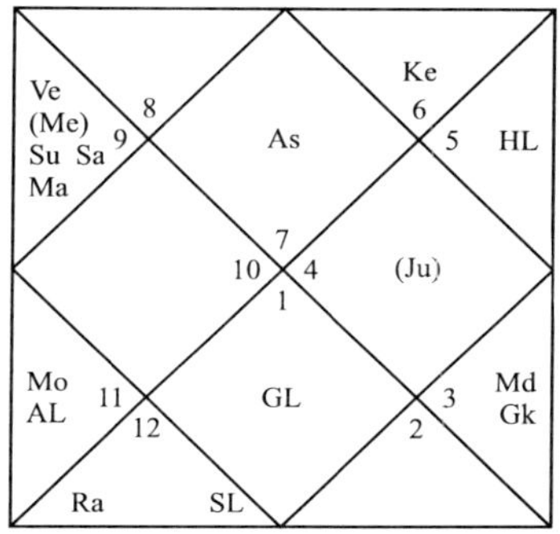

As: 20 Li 07	Su: 0 Sg 35-DK	Mo: 24 Aq 49-MK	Ma: 11 Sg 53-PK
Me (R): 11 Sg 34-GK	Ju (R): 29 Cn 39-AK	Ve: 25 Sg 25-BK	Sa: 29 Sg 06-AmK
Ra: 8 Pi 37-PiK	Ke: 8 Vi 37	HL: 25 Le 14	GL: 3 Ar 30

Example 15: Choreographer and dancer

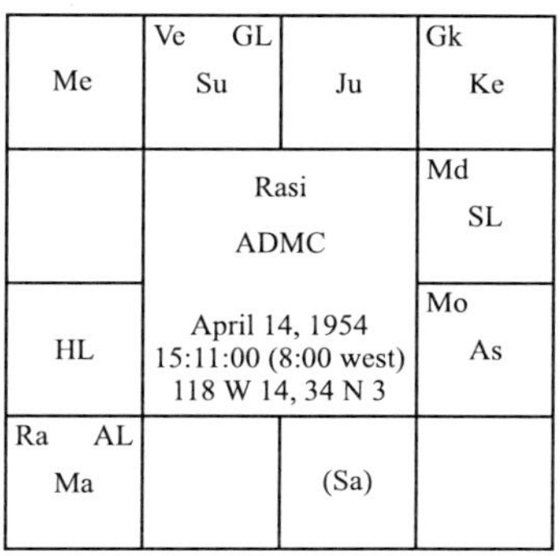

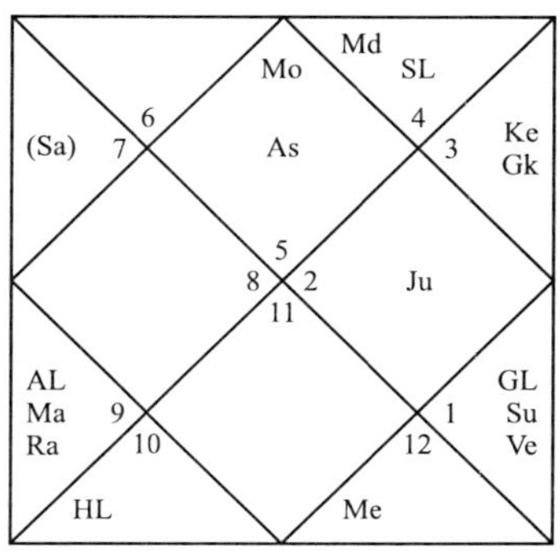

As: 21 Le 43	Su: 1 Ar 14-DK	Mo: 25 Le 26-AmK	Ma: 7 Sg 36-PK
Me: 9 Pi 05-PiK	Ju: 29 Ta 09-AK	Ve: 19 Ar 41-BK	Sa (R): 13 Li 42-MK
Ra: 25 Sg 53-GK	Ke: 25 Ge 53	HL: 22 Cp 25	GL: 9 Ar 47

Venus is the lord of 3rd, 10th in relationship with ascendant lord Sun and 6th, 7th lord Saturn ,The dispositor of Venus is Mars, so the 4th house connection is there, Mars aspects the 2nd lord mercury, both Mercury and Mars have a joint dispositor Jupiter, the Dispositor of

Jupiter is Venus ,While moon is linked to Venus, through the trine relationship and because Sun is the dispositor of Moon and it is related to Venus, because the two are in same sign. Venus link to 2nd, 3rd, 4th, 10th, 12th and Mars is established.

DIRECTORS

Rahu is the Hardware, mercury the software. Since Film directors stay behind the camera the influence of Rahu on Venus becomes important.

Example 16: Actor and Director Kevin Costner

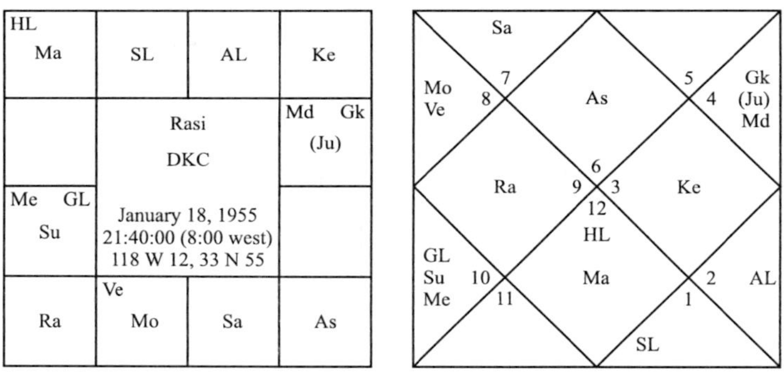

As:	2 Vi 15	Su:	5 Cp 09-GK	Mo:	11 Sc 02-PiK	Ma:	9 Pi 40-PK
Me:	20 Cp 22-AmK	Ju (R):	1 Cn 13-DK	Ve:	18 Sc 28-BK	Sa:	26 Li 32-AK
Ra:	12 Sg 12-MK	Ke:	12 Ge 12	HL:	23 Pi 35	GL:	22 Cp 11

Venus is the 2nd, in 3rd lord Mars Sign and is Related to Moon (same sign), Jupiter the 4th, 7th aspects the moon, Venus combination. Jupiter is also related to Sun and Mercury (mutual aspect) Mercury is the 10th and ascendant lord, Sun is 12th lord. Jupiter also relates with Mars as a dispositor aspects own sign with 8th, 3rd lord Mars in it.

Saturn is in the sign of Venus, Rahu and Mars have a joint dispositor Jupiter. So, the combination of Venus with 2nd, 3rd, 4th, 10th is established, The Rahu also connects to Venus, it is represented more clearly in the Bhava Chalit as following. He directed and acted in Dancing With the wolves.

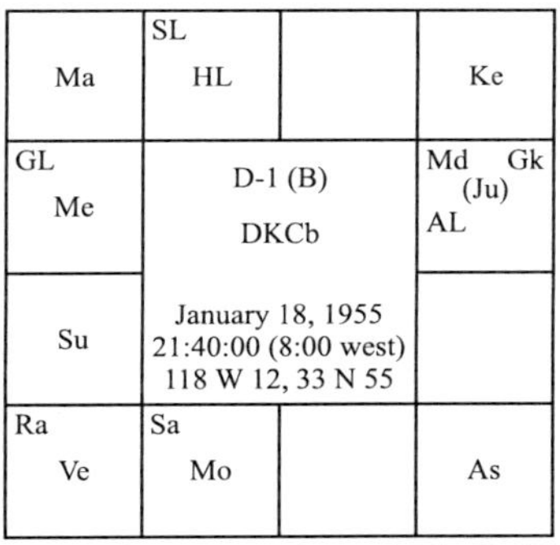

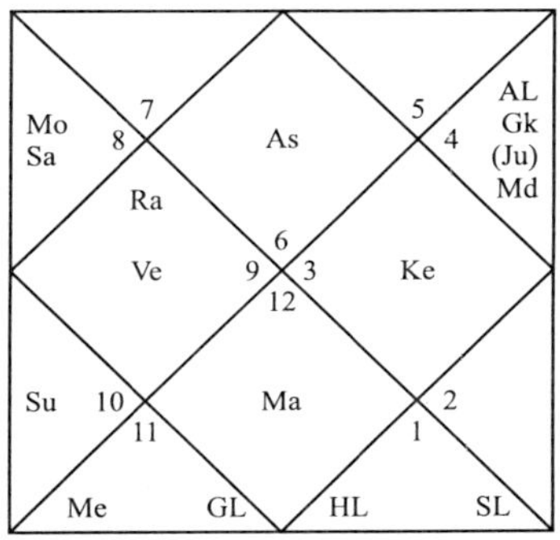

As: 20 Vi 13	Su: 16 Cp 18-GK	Mo: 9 Sc 18-PiK	Ma: 27 Pi 03-PK
Me: 3 Aq 18-AmK	Ju (R): 11 Cn 55-DK	Ve: 16 Sg 14-BK	Sa: 28 Sc 50-AK
Ra: 19 Sg 48-Mk	Ke: 19 Ge 48	HL: 2 Ar 17	GL: 19 Aq 93

Example 17: Director

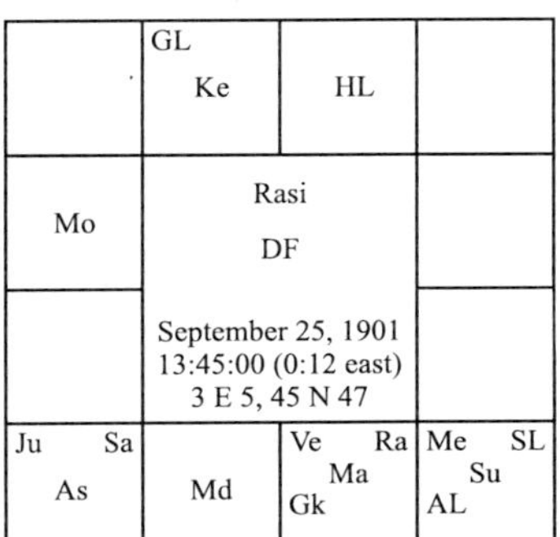

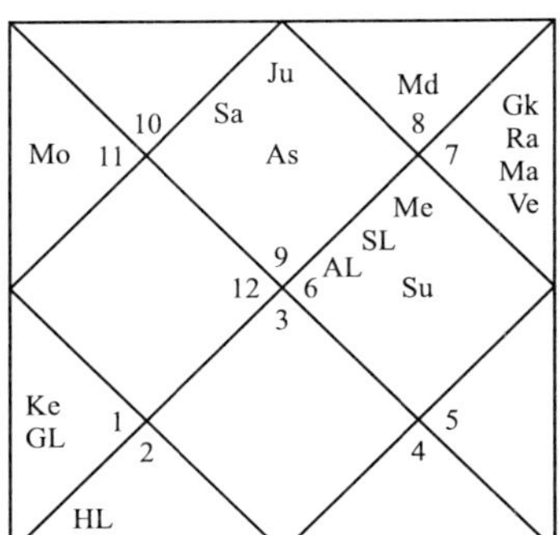

As: 10 Sg 44	Su: 9 Vi 17-PK	Mo: 3 Aq 19-DK	Ma: 24 Li 12-AmK
Me: 29 Vi 45-AK	Ju: 11 Sg 46-PiK	Ve: 17 Li 10-MK	Sa: 17 Sg 24-BK
Ra: 21 Li 54-GK	Ke: 21 Ar 54	HL: 4 Ta 18	GL: 27 Ar 17

Saturn is related to Jupiter and Moon, Rahu,Venus and Mars are altogether in same sign, Saturn aspects the 10th lord mercury and 9th lord Sun. Rahu is in trine to Moon the 8th lord So the Mars and Venus connect through Rahu aspect and also because of trine relationship. So the link of Venus, Rahu/Venus, Mars/Venus, Moon is established, Mars aspects the 2nd, Rahu the 3rd, Saturn is associated with 4th and 10th, Venus associates through Moon.

Example 18: Director Steven Spielberg

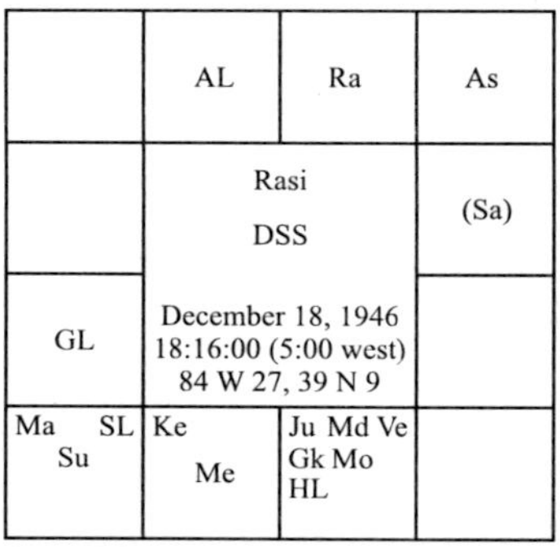

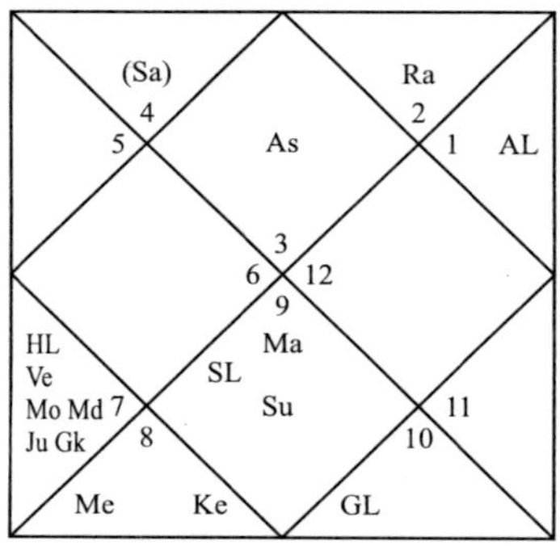

As: 17 Ge 40	Su: 3 Sg 21-DK	Mo: 13 Li 44-PiK	Ma: 8 Sg 03-GK
Me: 14 Sc 42-MK	Ju: 24 Li 50-AmK	Ve: 26 Li 08-AK	Sa (R): 15 Cn 03-BK
Ra: 18 Ta 38-PK	Ke: 18 Sc 38	HL: 12 Li 29	GL: 26 Cp 51

Venus, is with 2nd lord and 10th lord, Venus connects to Rahu because its in the Sign of Venus. The joint dispositor for 3rd lord Sun and the 6th, 11th Mars is Jupiter, which is related, meanwhile the fourth lord mercury is in the Sign of Mars, whose dispositor Jupiter is in same sign relationship with Venus. Influence / connection of 2nd and 10th plays an important role in cinema and related arts.

Example 19: Director actor Raj Kapoor (source Astro sage)

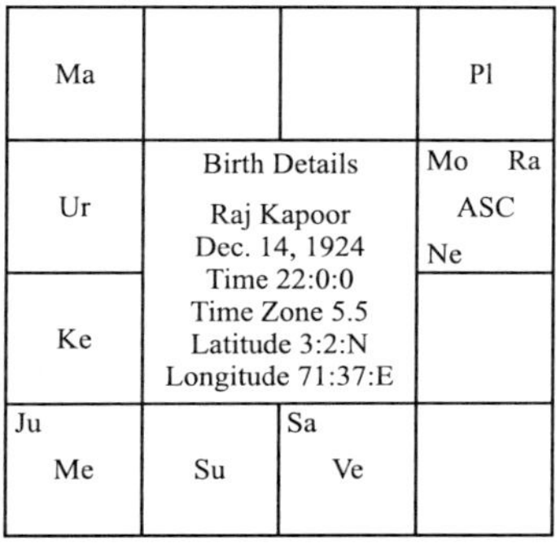

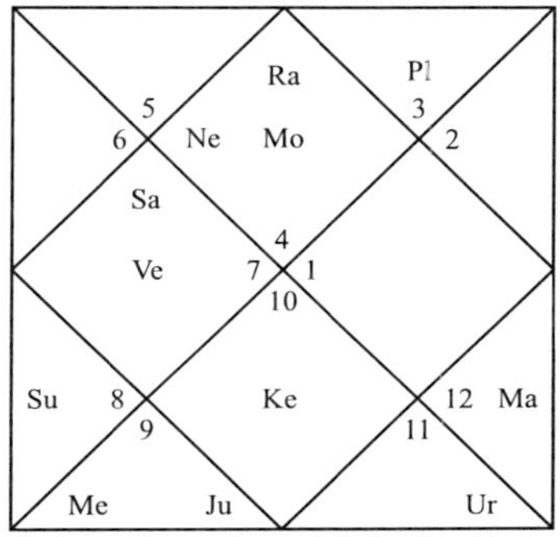

Mars the 10th is linked to 2nd lord Sun as Sun is in the sign of Mars the 5th and 10th lord, Mars Aspects the Saturn, Venus combine. Rahu/Moon linked to Venus through the aspect of Saturn, moreover there is a Kendra relationship as well. Mars is in the sign owned by Jupiter and in Kendra to Jupiter and Mercury combine. Saturn aspects the 3rd lord mercury and Jupiter combine, creating the link for Venus as well. Venus, Rahu/ Venus, Mars /Venus, Moon is linked, 2nd, 3rd, 4th and 10th all are linked to Venus.

Example 20: Director Producer

Venus is the 4th and 11th lord in 11th, With 10th lord Mars. Rahu is also in trine to Venus and Mars. Sun is 2nd lord in sign of the mercury. Moon and Saturn are related and Mercury is in the sign of moon. Sun the 2nd lord and Jupiter the 6th and 9th lord is both in signs of mercury, Jupiter aspects Mars and Venus, therefore it links Mercury and Sun to the Venus. Saturn, moon are in Kendra relationship with Venus and Mars and in trine relation with Sun the 2nd lord.

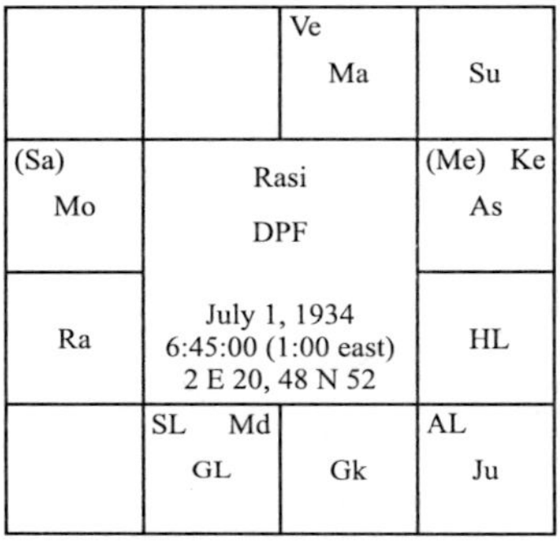

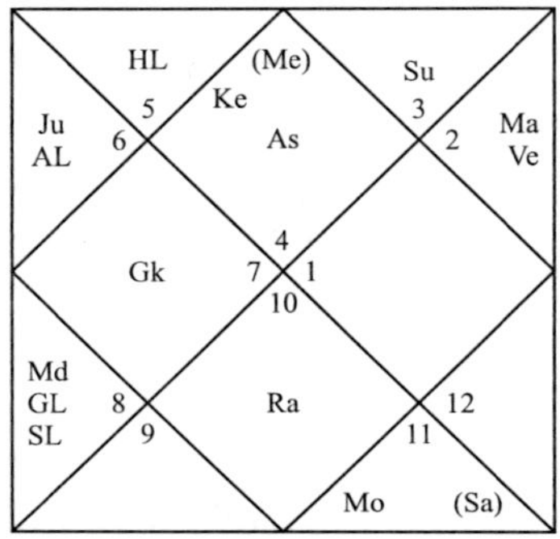

As: 6 Cn 57
Me (R): 0 Cn 42-DK
Ra: 17 Cp 39-MK
Su: 15 Ge 45-BK
Ju: 20 Vi 58-AmK
Ke: 17 Cn 39
Mo: 11 Aq 57-PiK
Ve: 10 Ta 23-PK
HL: 9 Le 46
Ma: 27 Ta 04-AK
Sa (R): 4 Aq 50-GK
GL: 0 Sc 54

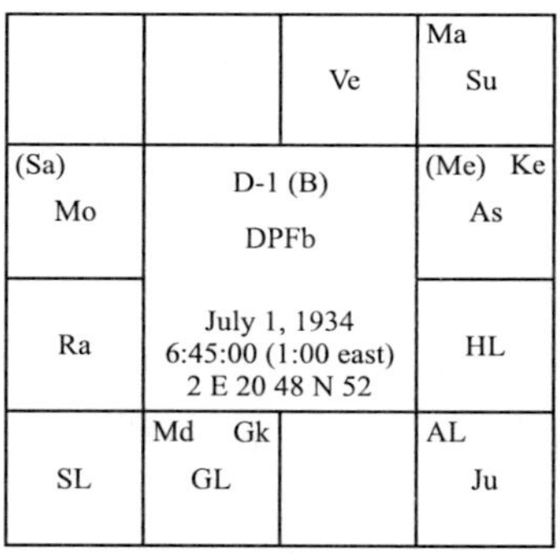

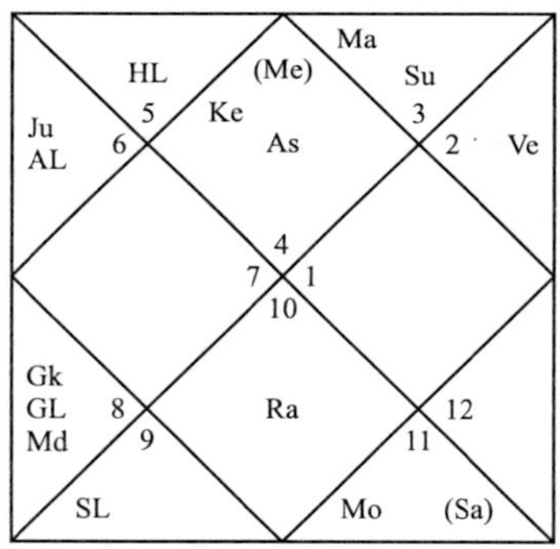

As: 2 Cn 31
Me (R): 6 Cn 22-DK
Ra: 8 Cp 49-ML
Su: 21 Ge 49-BK
Ju: 8 Vi 39-AmK
Ke: 8 Cn 49
Mo: 17 Aq 30-PiK
Ve: 3 Ta 30-PK
HL: 27 Le 57
Ma: 3 Ge37-AK
Sa (R): 13 Aq 28-GK
GL: 8 Sc 08

The Bhava Chalit Chart of the above native, shows the 2nd and 10th connection more precisely.

ARTISTS

Fine Arts Drawing, Painting and Sculpting

Talents and dexterity of hands is obtained from 3rd and mercury, obviously when we talk about the 3rd we have to consider Mars because it is the significator of 3rd and how can we leave the planet of beauty and expression Venus and Moon the emotions and state of mind.

Example 21: Artist, Writer (fine arts)

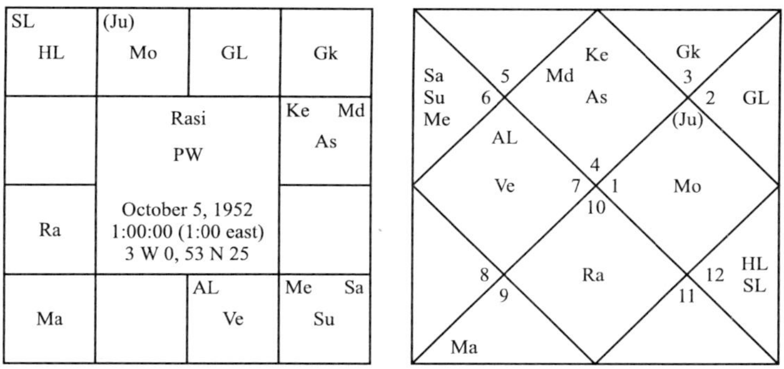

As: 12 Cn 27	Su: 18 Vi 30-MK	Mo: 8 Ar 31-PK	Ma: 1 Sg 44-DK
Me: 26 Vi 16-AmK	Ju (R): 26 Ar 44-AK	Ve: 15 Li 44-PiK	Sa: 23 Vi 59-BK
Ra: 27 Cp 06-GK	Ke: 27 Cn 06	HL: 5 Pi 37	GL: 17 Ta 24

5th,10th lord Mars in exchange with 6th, 9th Jupiter. Jupiter is related to moon and Venus, so the link with Mars is also established, Venus is the 4th lord and moon the ascendant lord and significator of 4th. Venus represents the arts and fine arts. Mercury the 3rd, 12th, Sun the 2nd and Saturn the 7th and 8th are all related in 3rd house for being in the same house, they also are in Kendra relationship and have a three-quarter aspect on Mars. So, the Link of 2nd, 3rd, 4th, 10th is established with

Venus, the 2nd and 3rd through Mars. Venus, mercury is also there due to mars.

Example 22: Artist of surreal paintings Sofia Bassi

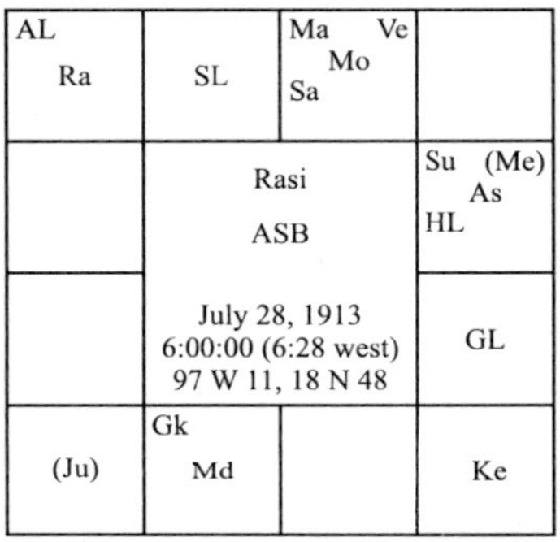

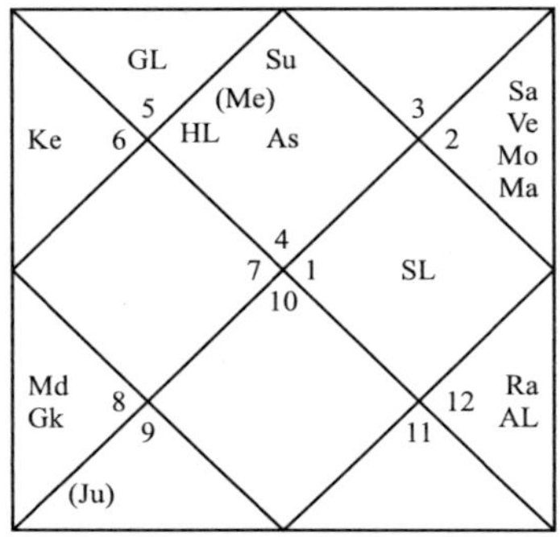

As:	16 Cn 47	Su:	12 Cn 09-PK	Mo:	6 Ta 33-DK	Ma:	6 Ta 44-GK
Me (R):	23 Cn 40-BK	Ju (R):	17 Sg 31-PiK	Ve:	28 Ta 08-AK	Sa:	22 Ta 03-MK
Ra:	2 Pi 48-AmK	Ke:	2 Vi 48	HL:	22 Cn 29	GL:	8 Le 01

Venus, the 4th, Saturn the 7th, 8th, Mars the 5th, 10th, Moon the ascendant lord are all related and in same sign. Saturn aspects Sun the 5th and 3rd lord mercury which are in the sign of related planet moon. So, the link of Venus with 2nd, 3rd, 4th, 10th is established, since painting is expression through hands the role of 3rd and 11th houses and lords is also prominent.

Example 23: French Artist award winner

2nd Lord Sun and Mars 10th, 5th lord together with mercury in the 3rd, the 4th, 11th lord Venus in sign owned by Sun. Jupiter is related to planets in 3rd vide the mutual aspect, Moon is in the sign owned by Mercury. Saturn is in the sign of 10th lord and aspects the Venus. Connection of Venus and mercury with 2nd, 3rd, 4th, 10th and 11th is established.

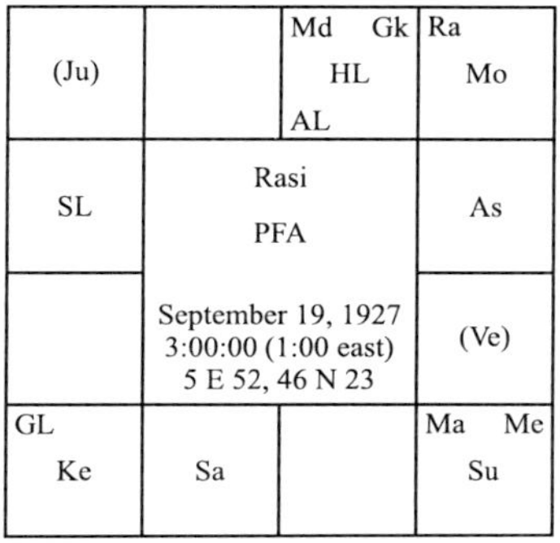

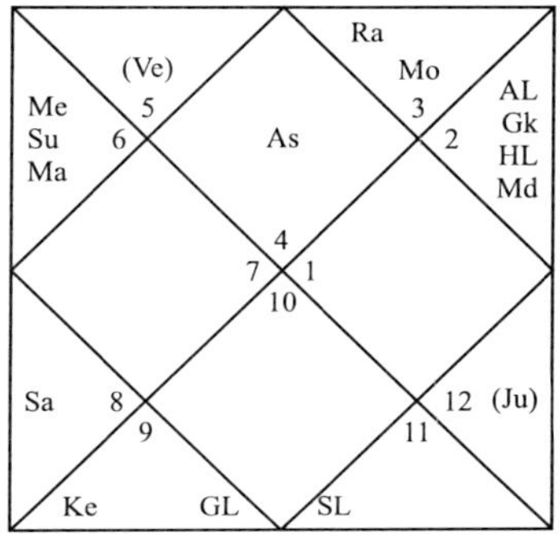

As:	24 Cn 36	Su:	2 Vi 18-DK	Mo:	13 Ge 53-MK	Ma:	12 Vi 41-PiK
Me:	15 Vi 33-BK	Ju (R):	6 Pi 07-GK	Ve (R):	19 Le 21-AmK	Sa:	9 Sc 43-PK
Ra:	0 Ge 31-AK	Ke:	0 Sg 31	HL:	20 Ta 40	GL:	19 Sg 29

Example 24: A French artist

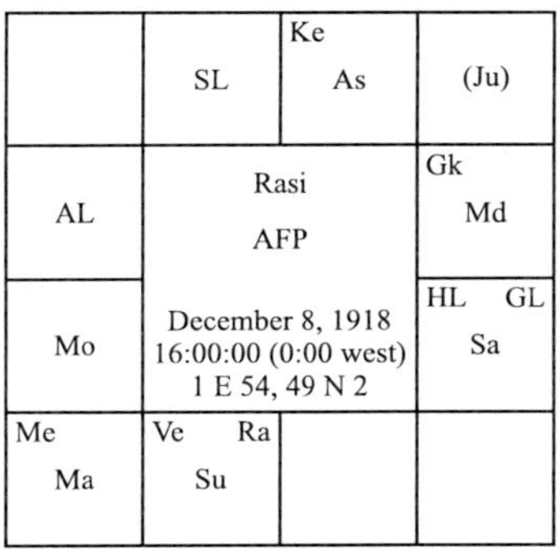

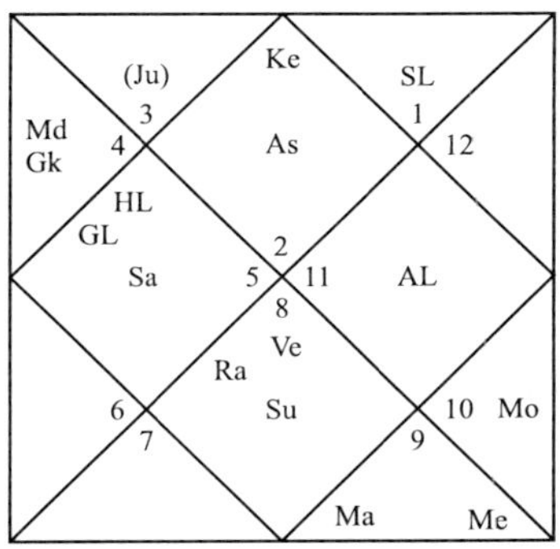

As:	25 Ta 59	Su:	23 Sc 03-BK	Mo:	22 Cp 13-MK	Ma:	28 Sg 09-AK
Me:	11 Sg 06-PK	Ju (R):	21 Ge 07-PiK	Ve:	26 Sc 37-AmK	Sa:	5 Le 31-DK
Ra:	20 Sc 18-GK	Ke:	20 Ta 18	HL:	3 Le 11	GL:	18 Le 56

Mars and 2nd lord mercury are related. Jupiter is in mutual aspect relation with both. 4th lord Sun and ascendant lord are in the sign of Scorpio, Sun is the dispositor of Saturn, while moon is in the sign of Saturn, Saturn is the 9th and 10th lord. Sun, Venus and Saturn are in Kendra relationship. The connection of Mars, Mercury, Venus, Saturn, moon is established.

Example 25: French Painter artist

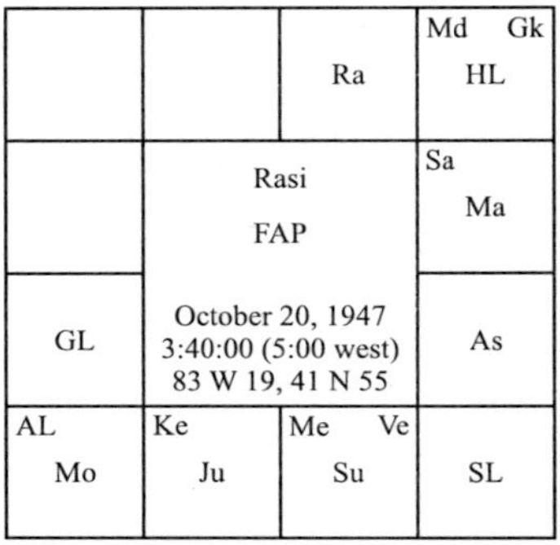

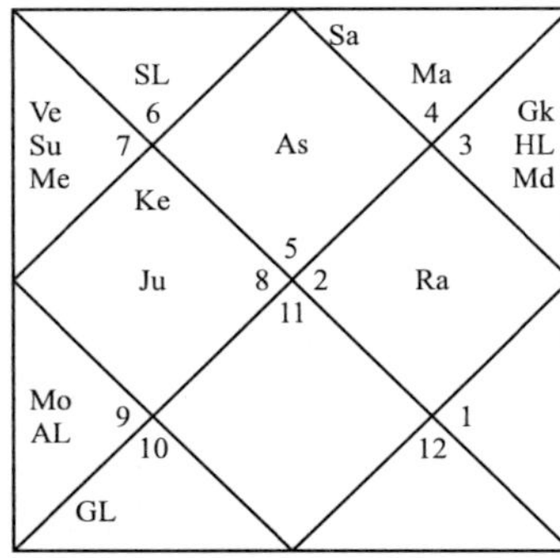

As: 24 Le 50	Su: 2 Li 60-DK	Mo: 14 Sg 36-PK	Ma: 17 Cn 38-MK
Me : 26 Li 39-BK	Ju: 6 Sc 07-GK	Ve: 15 Li 21-PiK	Sa: 27 Cn 44-AmK
Ra: 0 Ta 35-AK	Ke: 0 Sc 35	HL: 25 Ge 05	GL: 29 Cp 31

Mars aspects Venus and Mercury, Venus is the 3rd and 10th lord, mercury is the 2nd and 11th lord here, sun is the ascendant lord, Mars is the dispositor of Jupiter, while moon is the dispositor of Saturn and Mars. So, the 2nd, 3rd, 4th and 10th, 11th lords have a link with Venus, Venus, mercury link is there, Venus, Mars, Venus, moon is also there.

Example 26: Sculptor and a painter

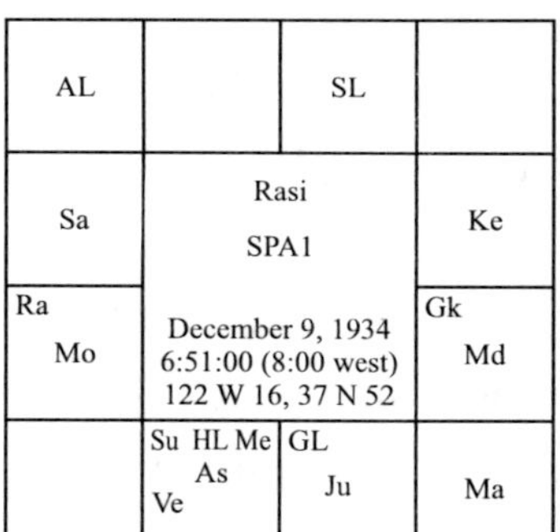

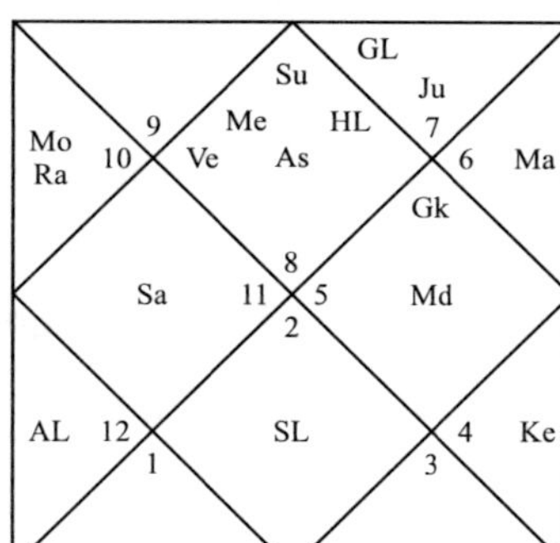

As: 18 Sc 18	Su: 23 Sc 55-AmK	Mo: 2 Cp 59-GK	Ma: 6 Vi 09-PK
Me: 12 Sc 10-PiK	Ju: 19 Li 45-MK	Ve: 28 Sc 57-AK	Sa: 0 Aq 09-DK
Ra: 8 Cp 55-BK	Ke: 8 Cn 55	HL: 9 Sc 58	GL: 20 Li 33

Venus connects to Jupiter the 2nd, 5th as Jupiter is placed in the sign of Venus, Mercury the 8th, 11th is in exchange with 1st, 6th lord Mars, Saturn is the lord of 3rd and 4th in aspect to the Sun the 10th, Mercury 8th, 11th, Venus 7th, 12th, Moon is in the sign owned by Saturn. Venus connects to 2nd, 3rd, 4th, 10th, 11th, Venus establishes link with Mercury, Mars, moon as well.

Example 27: Sculptor/Painter

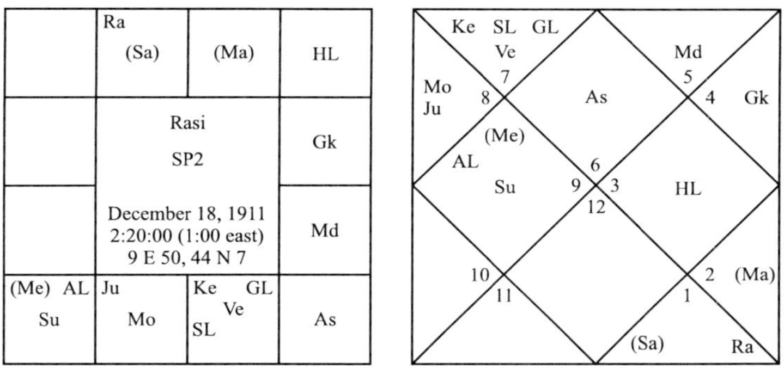

As:	26 Vi 48	Su:	2 Sg 23-DK	Mo:	3 Sc 58-PK	Ma (R):	2 Ta 36-GK
Me (R):	17 Sg 33-BK	Ju :	9 Sc 01-PiK	Ve:	16 Li 59-MK	Sa (R):	21 Ar 26-AmK
Ra:	7 Ar 02-AK	Ke:	7 Li 02	HL:	13 Ge 58	GL:	2 Li 31

2nd, 9th lord Venus is in libra, while its other sign the Taurus houses Mars, the third lord, Third and 8th lord mars aspects the 4th house, the lord of 4th Jupiter and lord of 10th, ascendant Mercury. Mars is related to Moon and Jupiter on account of mutual aspect relationship. Saturn is in the sign of Mars and in relation with Venus. Venus connects to 3rd, 4th, 10th, 11th lords through Mars.

Bhava Chalit chart is here under for better understanding.

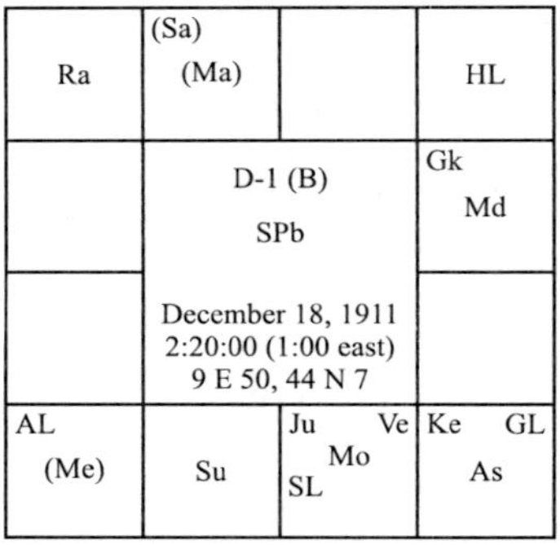

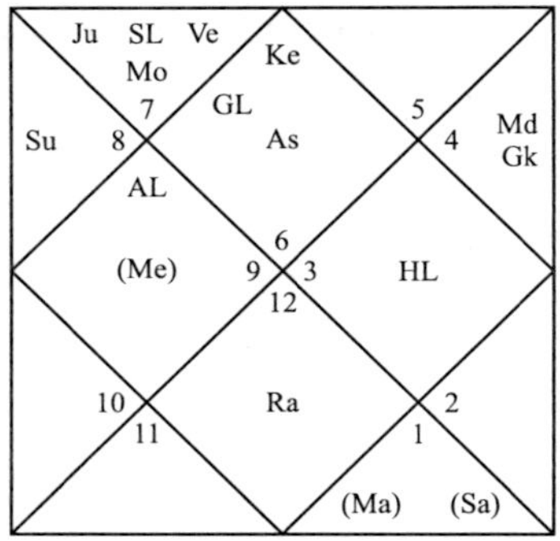

As:	1 Vi 15	Su:	21 Sc 31-DK
Me (R):	8 Sg 01-BK	Ju:	21 Li 08-PiK
Ra:	3 Pi 21-AK	Ke:	3 Vi 21

Mo:	5 Li 38-PK	Ma (R):	23 Ar 23-PK
Ve:	2 Li 53-MK	Sa (R) :	12 Ar 53-AmK
HL:	5 Ge 45	GL:	22 Vi 38

SPORTS PERSONALITIES

A career in sports

Third and eleventh represent arms, 11th, 12th the legs, competing with others 6th, 5th represents insignia or medal, 4th is the kingdom, 9th being honored by the state, 10th the career and rewards from government. 2nd and 12th eyes eye coordination with limbs is must in sports.

Example 1: Muhammad Ali

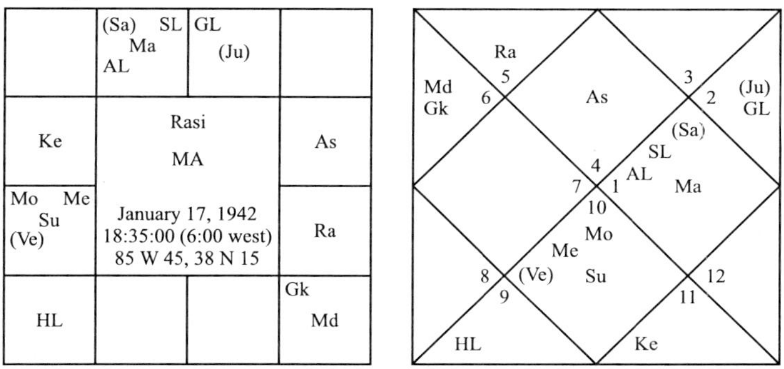

As: 26 Cn 29	Su: 4 Cp 15-DK	Mo: 19 Cp 23-MK	Ma: 10 Ar 01-PK
Me: 20 Cp 29-BK	Ju (R): 18 Ta 54-PiK	Ve (R): 27 Cp 37-AmK	Sa (R): 28 Ar 37-PK
Ra: 21 Le 13-GK	Ke: 21 Aq 13	HL: 19 Sg 50	GL: 28 Ta 56

3rd and 11th lord is related, the 6th lord Jupiter aspects the 3rd, 11, ascendant, 2nd, Saturn is related to planets in 7th as it, aspects the house and planets as sign lord. Saturn is related to the 10th lord as they are in same sign.

Example 2: Steffi graph

2nd lord moon is related to Mars, while 12th lord in the sign owned by Mars.

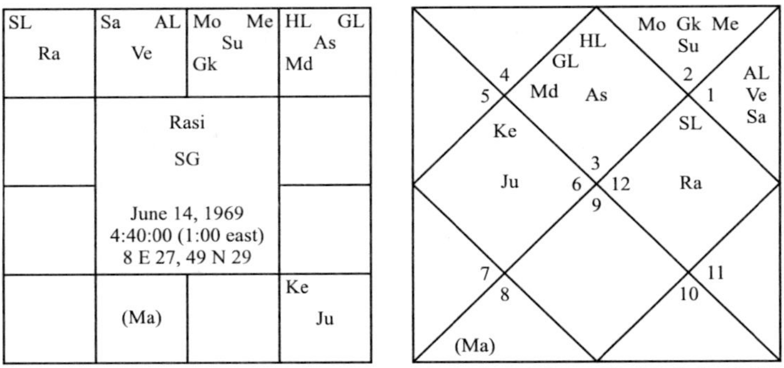

As: 3 Ge 01	Su: 29 Ta 29-AK	Mo: 20 Ta 33-BK	Ma (R): 12 Sc 08-PiK
Me: 10 Ta 27-GK	Ju: 3 Vi 23-DK	Ve: 13 Ar 48-MK	Sa: 11 Ar 49-PK
Ra: 2 Pi 41-AmK	Ke: 2 Vi 41	HL: 6 Ge 43	GL: 17 Ge 34

Mars is the 6th and 11th lord related to 3rd Sun, ascendant, 4th lord Mercury, moon the 2nd lord. Mars is also related to the dispositor of the 10th lord Jupiter, Saturn the 8th, 9th and Venus lord of 12th and 5th Venus are related and have a common dispositor Mars. The 2nd, 3rd, 5th, 6th, 8th, 10th, 11th and 12th are linked to mars the planet of action.

Example 3: World record weight lifter

Mars aspects the 12th lord while 2nd and 12th are in exchange .

Mars is the lord of 3rd in relation with lord of 5th and 6th Saturn, while mars is placed in the sign of Moon in 11th, the dispositor of Mars is exalted. Mars also aspects the Lord of 12th sun and ascendant and 10th lord Mercury. There is an exchange between Sun and Venus so planets in 12th are related to planets in 2nd. Mars the planet of action again establishes a link with 3rd, 5th, 6th, 10th, 11th and 12th.

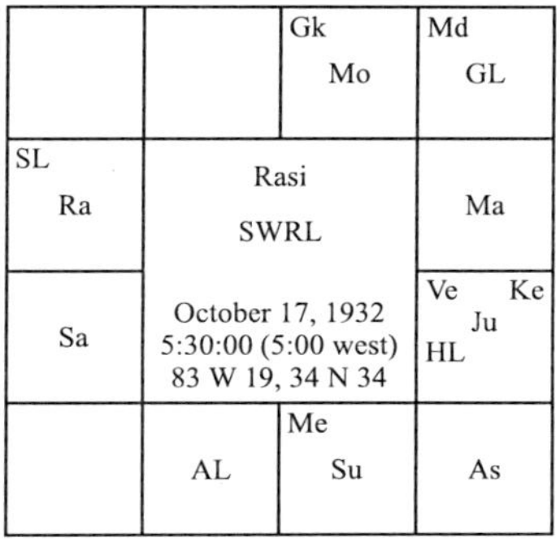

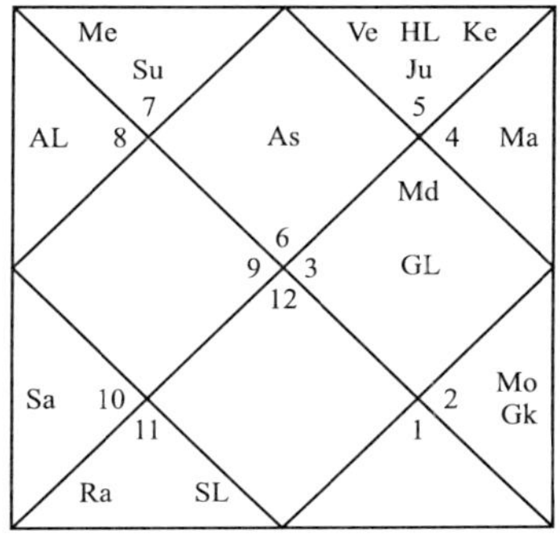

As: 15 Vi 22	Su: 0 Li 56-DK	Mo: 2 Ta 22-GK	Ma: 22 Cn 39-AK
Me : 13 Li 02-MK	Ju: 21 Le 13-AmK	Ve: 18 Le 40-BK	Sa: 5 Cp 23-PK
Ra: 23 Aq 37-PiK	Ke: 23 Le 37	HL: 23 Le 05	GL: 27 Ge 44

Example 4: Footballer par excellence, Pele of Brazil

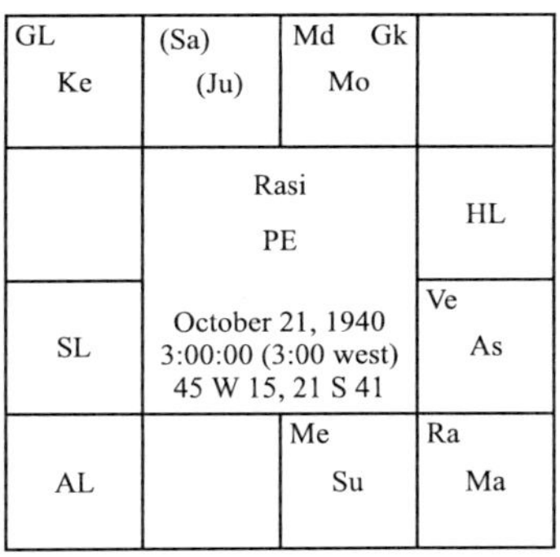

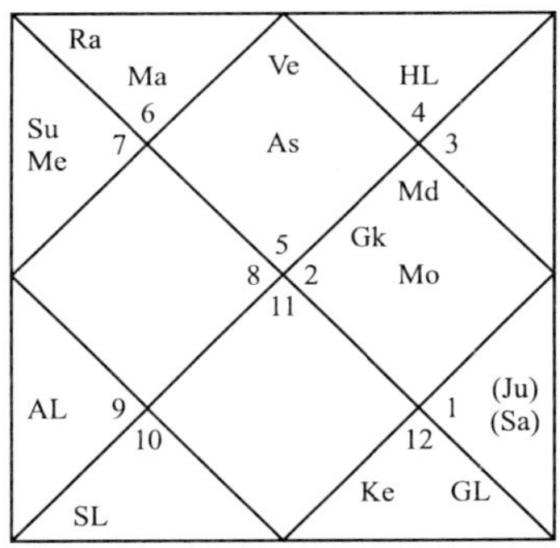

As: 16 Le 29	Su: 4 Li 40-DK	Mo: 28 Ta 59-AmK	Ma: 17 Vi 05-PK
Me: 28 Li 59-AK	Ju (R): 19 Ar 18-PiK	Ve : 23 Le 27-BK	Sa (R): 19 Ar 21-MK
Ra: 17 Vi 54-GK	Ke: 17 Pi 54	HL: 19 Cn 09	GL: 27 Pi 12

Mars is related to 6th lord Saturn and Jupiter the 8th, 5th. Jupiter and Saturn are related to Sun and Mercury (mutual Aspect), Mercury is dispositor of Mars. There is an exchange relationship between Sun and Venus. Mars connects to third through its dispositor mercury. So, Mars connects to 2nd, 3rd, 5th, 6th, 8th, 10th, 12th (through Rahu). Mars aspects 5th, 8th, 9th, 6th through Rahu, 10th through Rahu.

Example 5: Olympian Wrestler

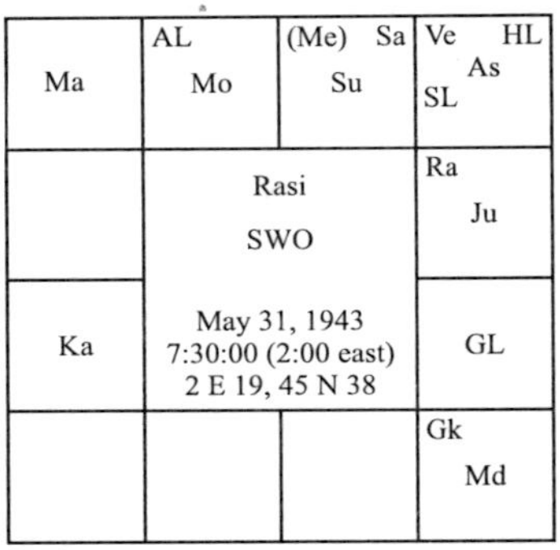

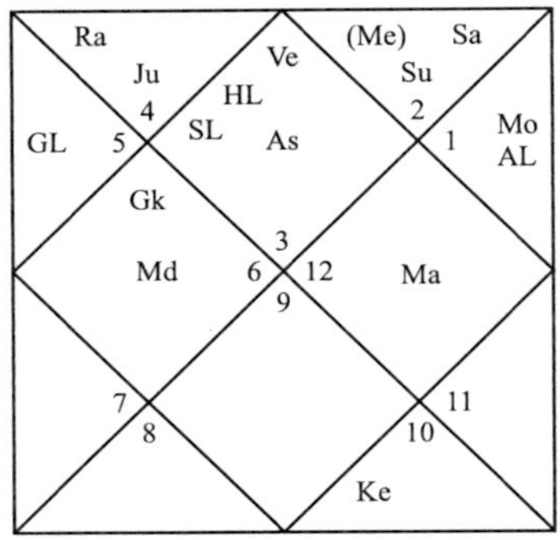

As: 5 Ge 60	Su: 15 Ta 51-AK	Mo: 14 Ar 02-MK	Ma: 9 Pi 47-PiK
Me (R): 4 Ta 47-PK	Ju: 0 Cn 45-DK	Ve: 29 Ge 04-AK	Sa: 21 Ta 59-AmK
Ra: 25 Cn 39-GK	Ke: 25 Cp 39	HL: 24 Ge 57	GL: 23 le 41

Mars aspects the 5th as lord of 6th and 11th, while it is placed in 10th, 10th, 7th lord Jupiter is related to Mars as Jupiter aspects mars being its dispositor, Mars aspects the 12th, 5th lord as well. There is an exchange between Venus and Mercury that relates 3rd lord Sun, ascendant and 4th lord Mercury, 5th, 12 Venus. Mars is linked to 3rd, 5th, 6th, 10th, 11th and 12 houses, as required for a distinguished sports career.

Example 6: Cricketer Vivian Richards

Mars is the lord of 5th and 12th is in 11th in the sign of 6th lord Venus and also in Kendra relationship with Venus. Jupiter the ascendant lord is in relationship with 10th lord Mercury and 2nd 3rd lord Saturn. Saturn is related to 10th lord and is dispositor of 6th, 11th Venus and 9th Sun. Mars connects to lords of 3rd Saturn and 10th Mercury through Venus/Saturn. Venus is in Kona relationship to

Venus as well. Mara again connects to 3rd, 5th, 6th, 10th, 11th and 12th.

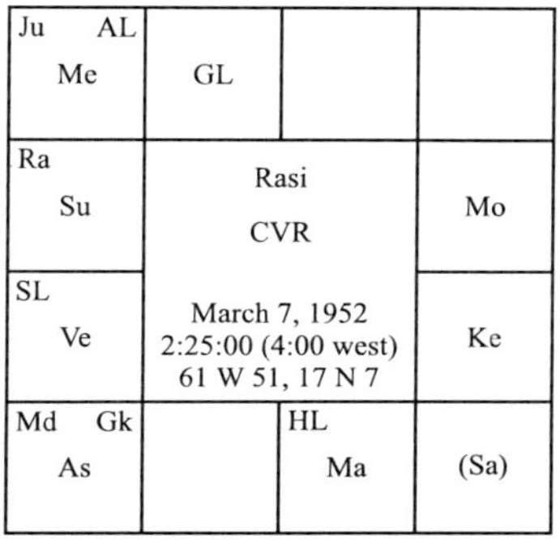

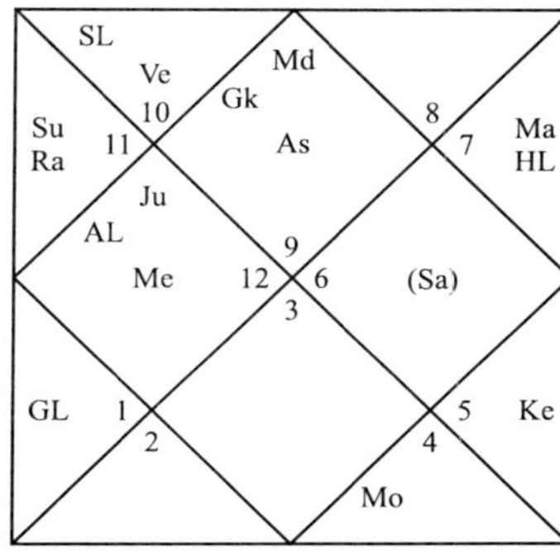

As:	17 Sg 40	Su:	23 Aq 27-BK	Mo:	3 Cn 49-DK	Ma:	23 Li 25-MK
Me :	6 Pi 60-GK	Ju:	24 Pi 22-AmK	Ve:	25 Cp 21-AK	Sa (R) :	20 Vi 17-PK
Ra:	7 Aq 22-PiK	Ke:	7 Le 22	HL:	22 Li 16	GL:	21 Ar 44

Example 7: famed Tennis player, Martina Navratilova

Exchange Between ascendant Saturn, 12th and 3rd, 10th Mars, Mars aspects the 5th, 8th lord Mercury, while it connects to the 6th lord Moon through its related planet Jupiter. Jupiter, Venus and Mars are related due to mutual aspect. Mars is linked to 3rd, 5th, 6th, 8th, 11th and 12th.

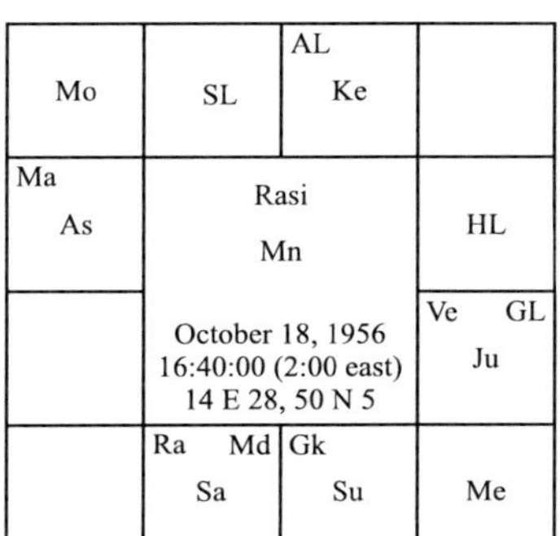

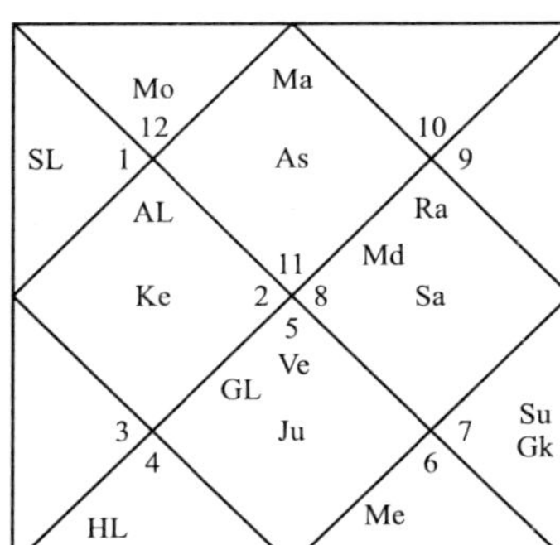

As:	17 Aq 54	Su:	1 Li 57-DK	Mo:	18 Pi 30-PiK	Ma:	20 Aq 20-MK
Me:	15 Vi 56-PK	Ju :	28 Le 04-AK	Ve :	21 Le 08-BK	Sa :	7 Sc 33-GK
Ra:	6 Sc 06-AmK	Ke:	6 Ta 06	HL:	4 Cn 30	GL:	23 Le 54

Example 8: High Jump World Record Holder 1973

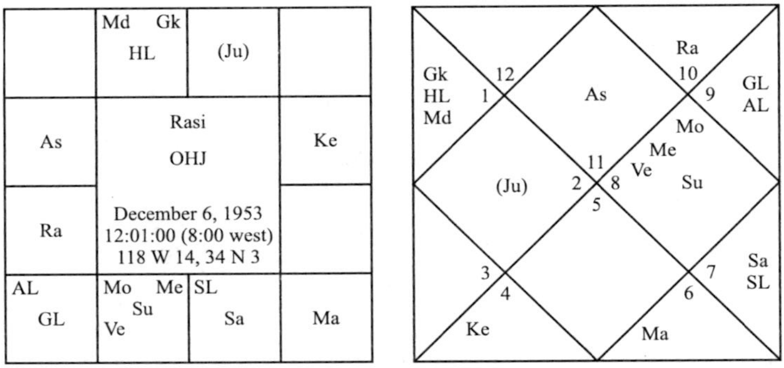

As: 17 Aq 27	Su: 21 Sc 13-PiK	Mo: 25 Sc 44-MK	Ma: 28 Vi 31-BK
Me: 1 Sc 44-DK	Ju (R): 29 Ta 07-AK	Ve: 8 Sc 14-GK	Sa: 11 Li 60-PK
Ra: 1 Cp 16-AmK	Ke: 1 Cn 16	HL: 26 Ar 55	GL: 20 Sg 48

Mars in exchange with Mercury the lord of 5th, 8th, Mars is the lord of 3rd, 10th. Mars aspects the 11th house and has relation to thee 11th lord through an exchange with mercury, Mars is also related to the dispositor of the 12th lord Saturn the Venus in the same way. Mars also connects with 6th lord moon as well. So, mars links with 3rd, 5th, 6th, 8th, 10th, 11th, 12th.

Example 9: Badminton, Saina Nehwal

The dispositor of Mars the Saturn lord of 4th, 5th is related to Jupiter the lord of 3rd, 6th. While Jupiter is also related to the 11th lord Sun and 9th, 12th lord Mercury, due to an exchange with Mercury. 10th lord Moon is the Sign of Mars, while 8th and ascendant lord is related for being in same sign. Mars thus connects with 3rd, 4th, 5th, 6th, 10th, 11th, 12th a requirement for a sports career. (planet of action Mars connection to have coordination of limbs)

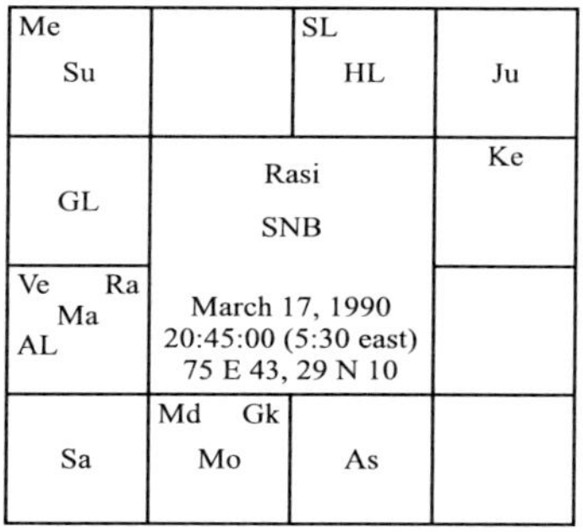

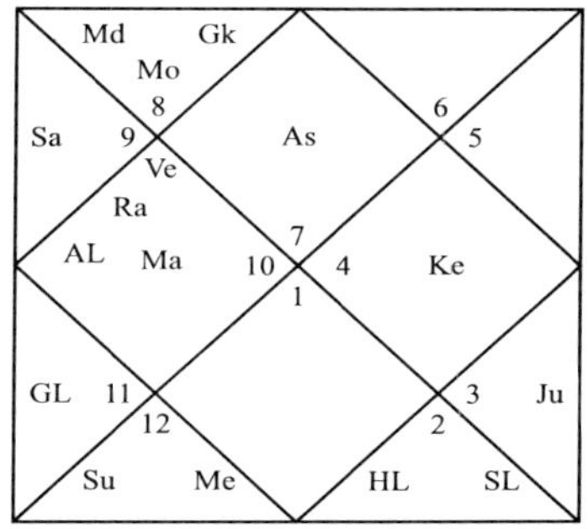

As: 1 Li 57	Su: 3 Pi 03-GK	Mo: 11 Sc 23-BK	Ma: 10 Cp 43-MK
Me : 1 Pi 38-DK	Ju: 7 Ge 48-PK	Ve: 17 Cp 16-AmK	Sa : 29 Sg 47-AK
Ra: 21 Cp 51-PiK	Ke: 21 Cn 51	HL: 5 Ta 25	GL: 9 Aq 50

Example 10: Shooting- Abhinav Bindra

Mars is the lord of 5th, 10th in 3rd, aspects 6th and the lord Jupiter, While Mars is related to lord of 12th, 3rd Mercury and the second lord Sun, 11th, 4th lord Venus is in exchange with ascendant lord Moon, Moon is related to the Saturn lord of 7th, 8th Mars is in trine to Saturn, moon, going by Phal Deepika it's a relation because of Trikona. As per BPHS it's an aspect of 50% between Mars and Saturn, Moon. Mars connects to 3rd, 5th, 6th, 8th, 10th, 11th and 12th, 3rd Lord is in position of strength.

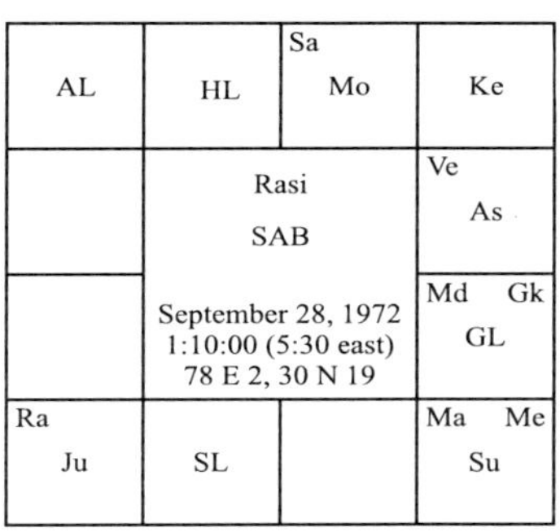

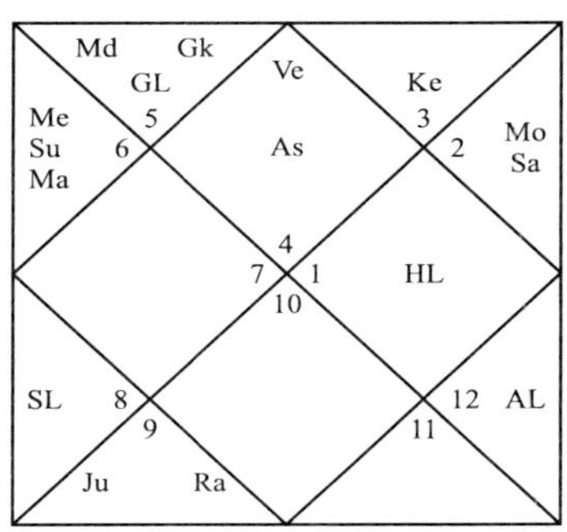

As: 6 Cn 28	Su: 11 Vi 18-PiK	Mo: 15 Ta 14-MK	Ma: 4 Vi 30-GK
Me: 17 Vi 37-BK	Ju : 6 Sg 43-PK	Ve : 27 Cn 59-AK	Sa : 27 Ta 06-AmK
Ra: 29 Sg 38-DK	Ke: 29 Ge 38	HL: 9 Ar 11	GL: 22 Le 09

Example 11: Judo player Olympic medalist

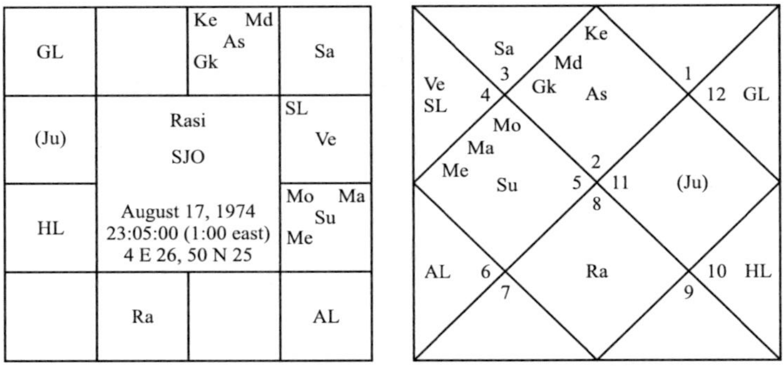

As: 6 Ta 40	Su: 1 Le 06-DK	Mo: 2 Le 55-PK	Ma: 19 Le 56-BK
Me: 1 Le 38-GK	Ju (R): 21 Aq 46-AK	Ve: 10 Cn 05-MK	Sa: 20 Ge 48-AmK
Ra: 23 Sc 30-PiK	Ke: 23 Ta 30	HL: 13 Cp 34	GL: 18 Pi 19

7th and 12th Lord Mars is related to 3rd lord moon, 4th lord Sun, 5th, 2nd lord Mercury and 8th, 11th Jupiter. The dispositor of ascendant and 6th lord Venus, the moon is also related to Mars, the related planet Jupiter aspects the 10th lord Saturn and is in trine to each other a relationship as per Phal Deepika and a 50% aspect as per Parashar. Saturn the 10th lord also aspects the planets in 4th including Mars. So, Mars links with 3rd, 4th, 5th, 6th, 8th, 10th, 11th and 12th.

Example 12: Olympic Swimmer

Mars related with lord of 3rd, 4th Saturn and 8th, 11th Mercury. Mars, is the lord of ascendant and 6th. 12th and 7th lord Venus in mars owned sign therefore linked. Mars aspects the 5th, 2nd Jupiter, Jupiter is also in the related planet Saturn's Sign. 10th lord Sun in Jupiter's Sign, Jupiter also aspects the 10th. Mars links to Sun through Jupiter, Moreover Sun Aspects Mars by 75% aspect or three quarters aspect as well.

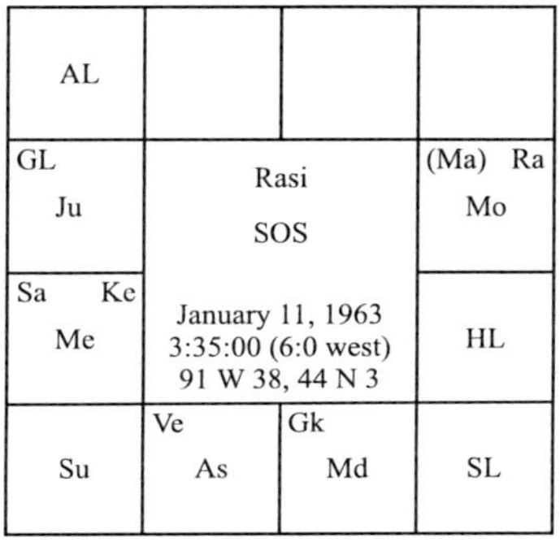

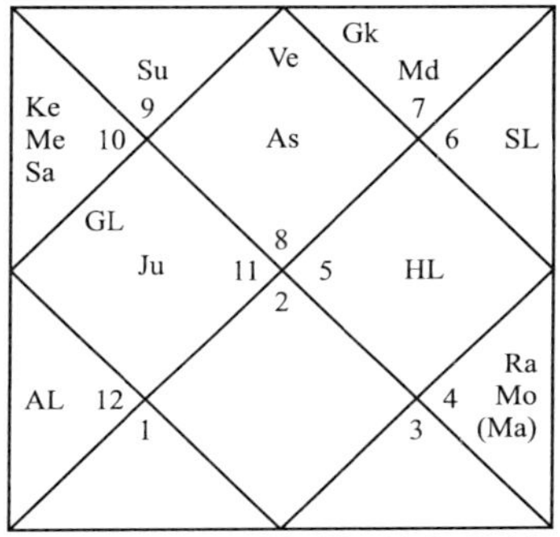

As: 1 Sc 47	Su: 27 Sg 07-AmK	Mo: 14 Cn 37-PK	Ma (R): 29 Cn 43-AK
Me: 13 Cp 22-GK	Ju: 17 Aq 37-PiK	Ve: 10 Sc 50-DK	Sa: 17 Cp 46-MK
Ra: 6 Cn 17-BK	Ke: 6 Cp 17	HL: 20 Le 44	GL: 12 Aq 26

The bhava chart of the above Olympic swimmer's chart explains the links rather more lucidly. The bhava chart as below:

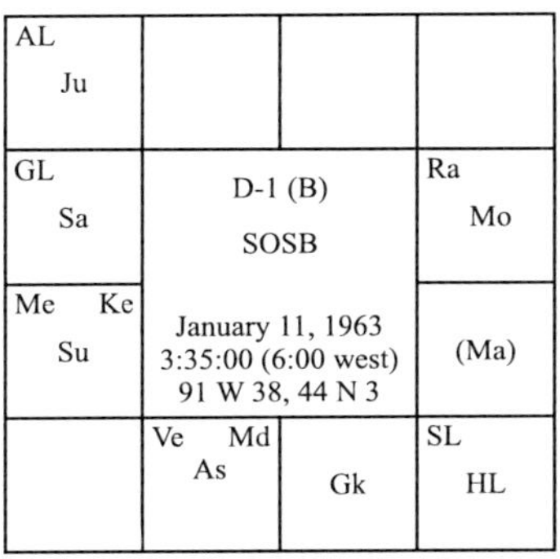

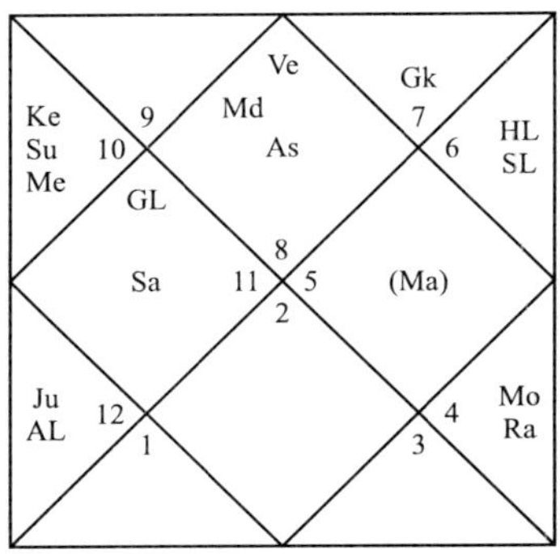

As: 16 Sc 02	Su: 3 Cp 59-AmK	Mo: 11 Cn 31-PK	Ma (R): 27 Le 26-AK
Me: 0 Cp 16-GK	Ju : 8 Pi 33-PiK	Ve : 7 Sc 28-DK	Sa : 9 Aq 55-MK
Ra: 26 Cn 33-BK	Ke: 26 Cp 33	HL: 6 Vi 36	GL: 21 Aq 52

The link of Mars and Sun becomes clearer as Sun becomes the dispositor for Mars. The link of Mars with 3rd Saturn and 5th Jupiter is again established.

The link with 8th and 11th Mercury is established through Sun.

Example 13: Field Hockey Player

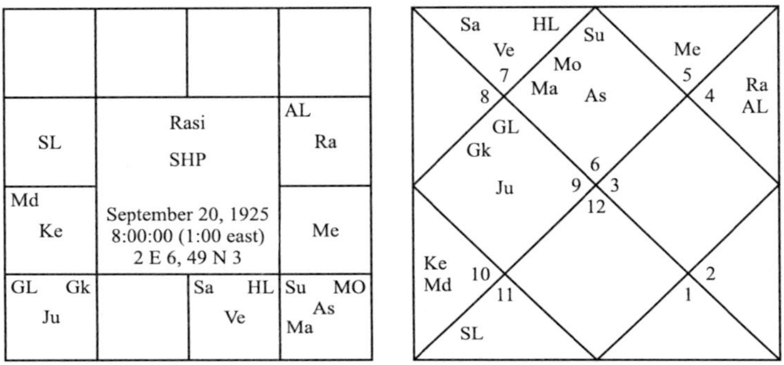

As: 18 Vi 37	Su: 3 Vi 59-GK	Mo: 28 Vi 52-AK	Ma: 1 Vi 43-DK
Me: 20 Le 09-AmK	Ju: 20 Sg 04-BK	Ve: 12 Li 11-PK	Sa: 18 Li 32-PiK
Ra: 10 Cn 26-MK	Ke: 10 Cp 26	HL: 14 Li 17	GL: 14 Sg 49

Mars is the lord of 3rd, 8th in relation with lord of 12th Sun, Lord of 11th moon. The Sun is in exchange with mercury the lord of ascendant and 10th. Mars aspects the 4th lord. Saturn the 5th, 6th lord is in relation with Venus and aspects the Jupiter 4th, 7th lord. Here Mercury aspects the 6th which later forms an exchange relationship with Mars related planet Sun. Mars is in trine to 5th house thereby it has the 50% aspect to it. Here in this horoscope mars do not connect to the 5th and 6th lord Saturn, but completes the other parameters.

Example 14: Athlete a 400 meters Hurdler, Olympic Medalist

The Bhava chart depicts the clearer picture, Mars is related to all concerned house lords the 3rd, 5th, 6th, 8th, 10th, 11th and 12th.

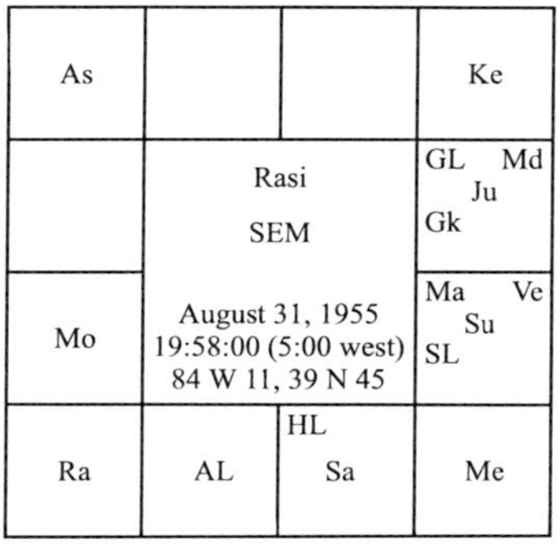

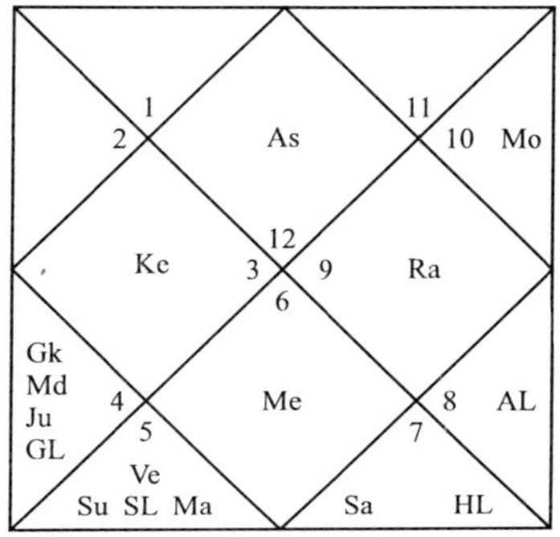

As: 6 Pi 18 Su: 14 Le 36-PiK Mo: 28 Cp 59-AmK Ma: 9 Le 42-GK
Me: 6 Vi 05-DK Ju: 23 Cn 54-BK Ve: 14 Le 31-PK Sa: 22 Li 46-MK
Ra: 0 Sg 18-AK Ke: 0 Ge 18 HL: 9 Li 15 GL: 2 Cn 05

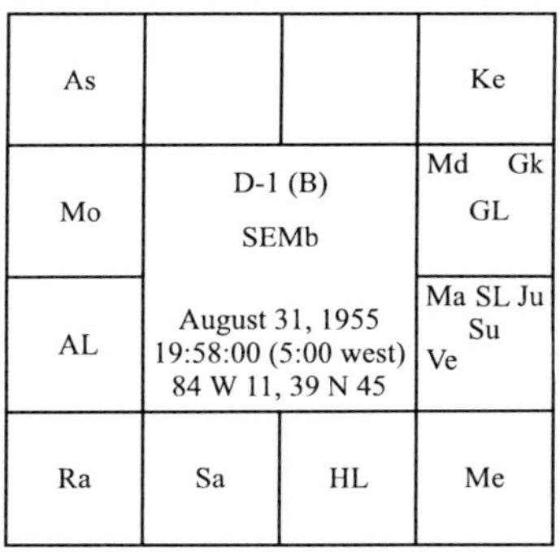

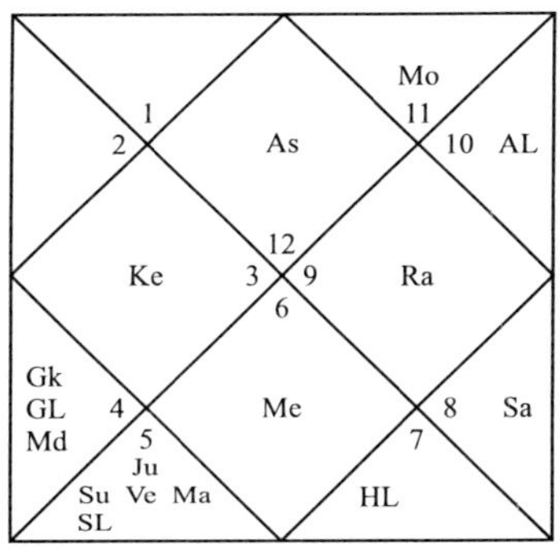

As: 26 Pi 45 Su: 11 Le 21-PiK Mo: 20 Aq 54-AmK Ma: 27 Le 20-GK
Me: 24 Vi 46-DK Ju : 5 Le 06-BK Ve : 10 Le 42-PK Sa : 24 Sc 55-MK
Ra: 2 Sg 44-AK Ke: 2 Ge 44 HL: 23 Li 19 GL: 18 Cn 47

Example 15: Decathlon Champion Olympic 1952

Mars is the lord of ascendant and 6th. Mars ids in trine relationship with planets in the ascendant and it is also the dispositor of all of them. Mars Aspects the 3rd and 4th houses. Jupiter and Saturn are related, the dispositor Jupiter is Mercury. The 3rd and 4th lord Saturn aspects Mars by three quarters aspect or 75 % aspect. Mars in Kendra to the moon the 9th lord. So here mars connect to 10th, 11th, 12th, 6th, 5th (through Mercury). With Saturn the 3rd, 4th the connection is the 75% aspect of Saturn as explained above.

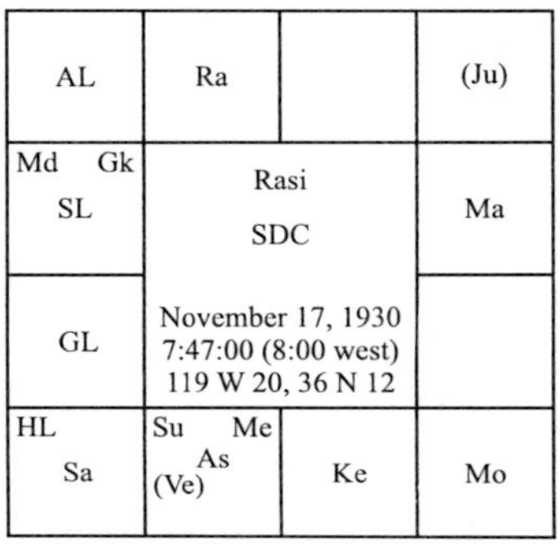

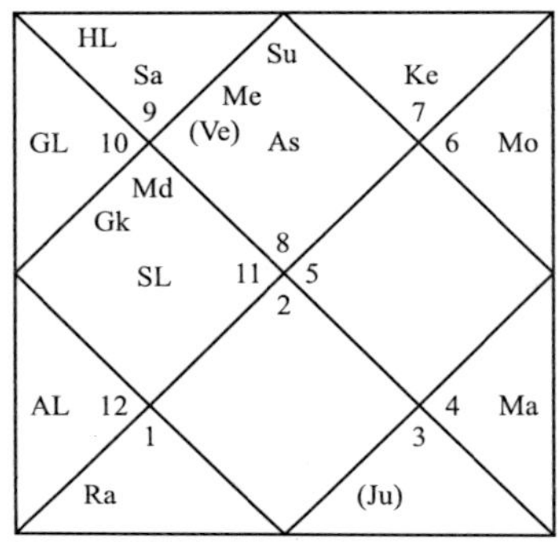

As: 15 Sc 19	Su: 1 Sc 42-DK	Mo: 26 Vi 08-BK	Ma: 18 Cn 32-MK
Me: 7 Sc 47-GK	Ju (R): 27 Ge 28-AmK	Ve (R): 9 Sc 50-PK	Sa: 15 Sg 57-PiK
Ra: 0 Ar 35-AK	Ke: 0 Li 35	HL: 4 Sg 54	GL: 24 Cp 47

ARMY AND POLICE PERSONNEL

An insignia is seen from 5th.

Danger or hidden danger elements from 8th.

6th is servitude.

10th the work sphere.

11th a significant position or post.

4th is the state or kingdom.

Mars is the planet responsible for vocations that require courage and ability to handle dangerous situations.

Sun is the authorities or Government.

For government service there must be a connection of the 5th ,10th and 11th lords.

Sun's connection with 10th or 5th is another common observable factor.

3rd house and the Karak (significator) Mars signify courage.

Example 1: Army officer

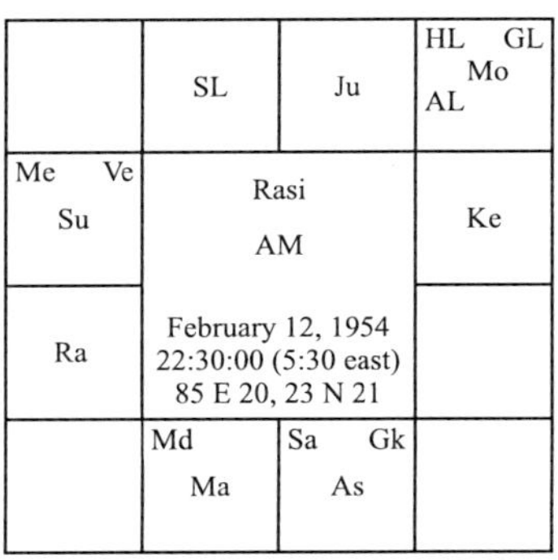

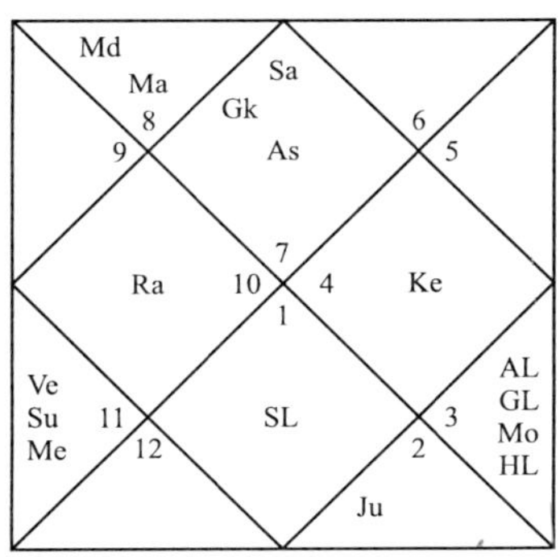

As: 6 Li 26	Su: 0 Aq 15-GK	Mo: 0 Ge 02-DK	Ma: 8 Sc 24-PiK
Me: 18 Aq 19-BK	Ju: 23 Ta 12-AmK	Ve: 3 Aq 33-PK	Sa: 16 Li 07-MK
Ra: 0 Cp 32-AK	Ke: 0 Cn 32	HL: 0 Ge 46	GL: 2 Ge 33

Mars aspects the 5th house and the 8th house. It also aspects the lord of 10th moon and the lord of 11th Sun. It is related to the lord of 6th and 3rd Jupiter. The 5th lord Saturn ,10th lord Moon and the 11th lord Sun are in trine to each other thus related as per Phal Deepika. There is an exchange relationship between Venus and Saturn, Venus is the related planet for Sun as well, while another related planet mercury is the dispositor of 10th lord.

Example 2: Army officer

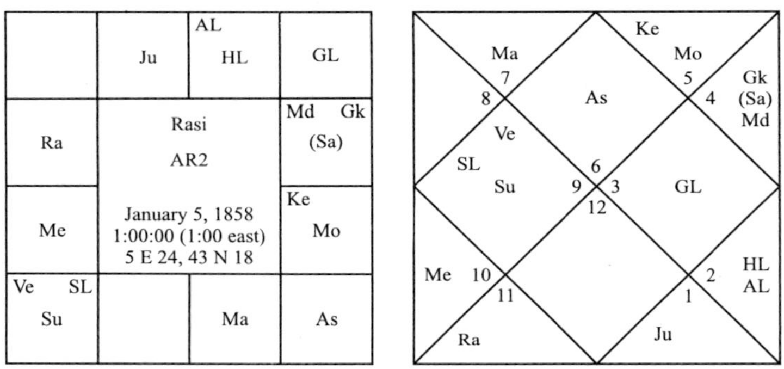

As: 23 Vi 21	Su: 22 Sg 33-AmK	Mo: 29 Le 09-AK	Ma: 6 Li 23-PK
Me: 9 Cp 60-MK	Ju : 14 Ar 09-BK	Ve : 9 Sg 25-PiK	Sa (R): 3 Cn 52-GK
Ra: 28 Aq 15-DK	Ke: 28 Le 15	HL: 13 Ta 30	GL: 15 Ge 58

Mars is the 3rd and 8th lord it, aspects the 5th house, the 10th lord and the 4th ,7th lord Jupiter, it is in fact related to Jupiter, Jupiter in turn is related to Sun and Venus. Jupiter aspects the 11th lord Moon and Sun is its dispositor, Sun is related to Jupiter and Jupiter to Mars.

The 5th and 10th lords are in relation due to mutual aspect, while Moon the 11th lord is the dispositor of 5th lord Saturn. Obviously, it is a government job and related to armed forces.

Example 3: Army currently a Major

	GL	Ra	SL
	Rasi AJAG		
AL Ma	November 17, 1984 4:17:00 (5:30 east) 76 E 11, 30 N 9		HL Md Mo Gk
Ve Ju	Me Ke Su	Sa	As

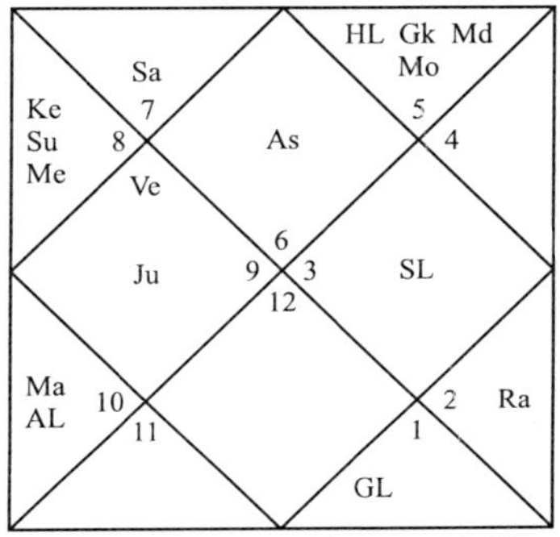

As: 27 Vi 17	Su: 1 Sc 08-DK	Mo: 9 Le 40-PK	Ma: 7 Cp 15-GK
Me: 21 Sc 07-BK	Ju: 18 Sg 04-MK	Ve: 9 Sg 55-PiK	Sa: 26 Li 07-AmK
Ra: 3 Ta 48-AK	Ke: 3 Sc 48	HL: 10 Le 59	GL: 12 Ar 06

Mars in 5th and aspects the 8th, 10th lord mercury in the sign owned by Mars, Mars aspects the 11th house and lord.

Saturn the 5th, 6th lord is dispositor for mars and Mars is the dispositor of 10th lord Mercury and 12th lord Sun, Sun in turn is the dispositor of 11th lord Moon.

The conditions for army service and the government service are fulfilled.

Example 4: Fighter Pilot

AL		Ra	As
	Rasi FPAR		
Ju Ma	December 6, 1980 18:15:00 (1:00 east) 13 E 24, 52 N 31		Md Gk Sa
GL SL Me	(Ve) Ke Su		HL Mo

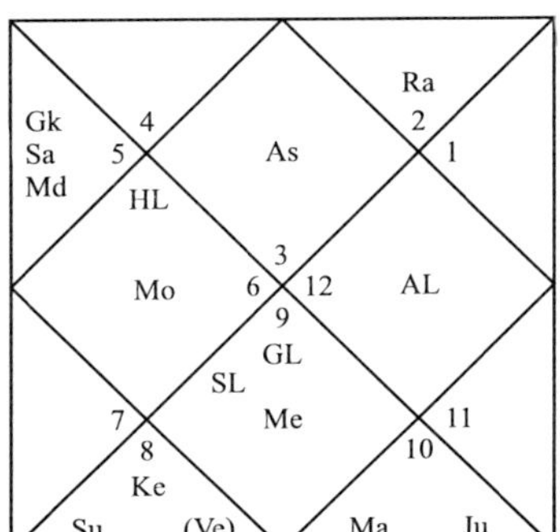

As: 25 Ge 54	Su: 22 Sc 16-BK	Mo: 16 Vi 10-PK	Ma: 29 Cp 58-AK
Me: 3 Sg 01-DK	Ju: 17 Cp 03-PiK	Ve (R): 18 Sc 10-MK	Sa: 24 Le 27-AmK
Ra: 22 Ta 23-GK	Ke: 22 Sc 23	HL: 25 Vi 06	GL: 29 Sg 60

Mars is in 8th, while 5th lord in the sign of Mars. 10th lord Jupiter is with Mars, Mars is the lord of the 6th and 11th.

5th Lord Venus and 3rd lord sun is together in the sign owned by Mars, 10th lord Jupiter is related to the dispositor of the 10th lord.

For pilot (9th Air travel and 10th the sky and work sphere area link) 9th lord Saturn and 10th lord Jupiter are connected.

Example 5: Navy veterans and an astronaut later

8th and 12th represent oceans and seas their link to 10th will represent career in the navy.

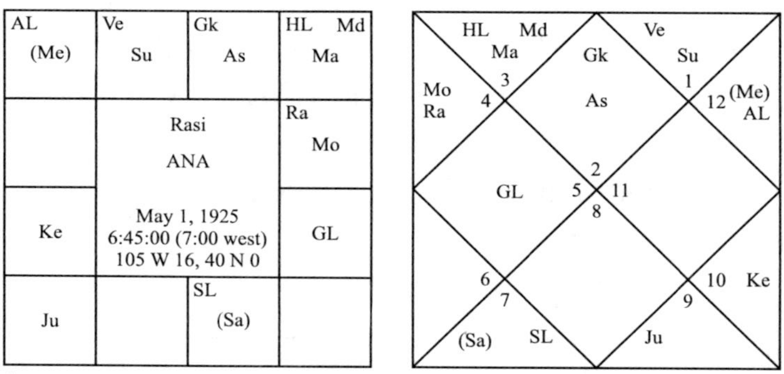

As: 18 Ta 41	Su: 17 Ar 51-PK	Mo: 22 Cn 37-BK	Ma: 1 Ge 53-DK
Me (R): 29 Pi 13-AmK	Ju: 29 Sg 35-AK	Ve: 19 Ar 50-MK	Sa (R): 18 Li 13-PiK
Ra: 16 Cn 13-GK	Ke: 16 Cp 13	HL: 7 Ge 12	GL: 21 Le 19

Mars aspects the 5th and 8th houses and is in relation with Jupiter (mutual aspect). The 5th lord Mercury is placed in the sign owned by Jupiter the 8th. 11th lord Saturn the 9th, 10th is related to Venus and Sun. Venus and Sun have a joint dispositor Mars. So, mars have the connection with 5th, 8th, 10th and 11th.

The lords of 5th, 11th and 10th are linked, Saturn aspects 11th lord, while 5th lord mercury is in the sign of Jupiter.

Example 6: Navy

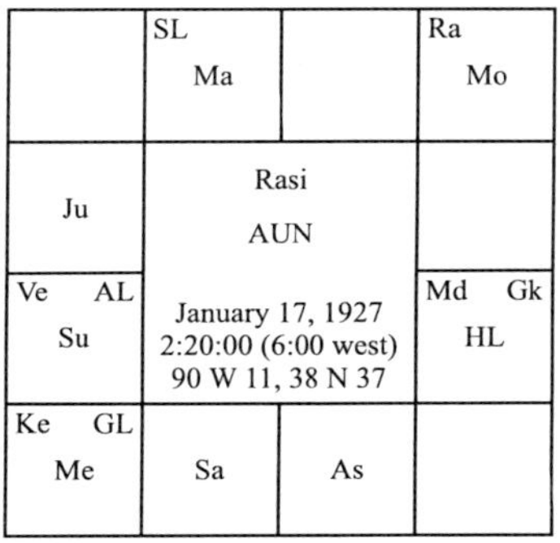

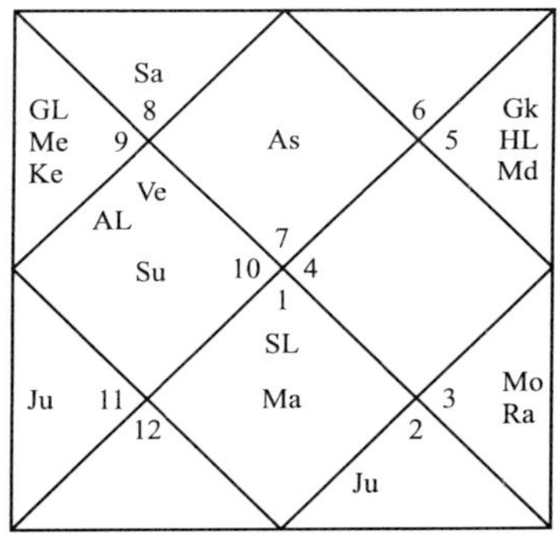

As: 25 Li 43	Su: 3 Cp 24-DK	Mo: 26 Ge 35-AK	Ma: 20 Ar 47-BK
Me: 26 Sg 14-AmK	Ju: 6 Aq 55-GK	Ve: 17 Cp 02-MK	Sa: 12 Sc 01-PK
Ra: 14 Ge 22-PiK	Ke: 14 Sg 22	HL: 1 Le 31	GL: 14 Sg 54

Mars is related to 4th, 5th lord Saturn. Saturn is related to 11th lord Sun and ascendant lord plus the 8th lord Venus. Jupiter casts an aspect to the 10th lord.

The 5th lord Saturn and 11th Sun are related, while the dispositor of Mercury the Jupiter has a link with Saturn as Saturn is the sign owner of Jupiter's placement. This mercury is related to moon the 10th lord, otherwise also Jupiter aspects the 10th lord Moon while in the sign of Saturn.

The bhava chart depicts a more profound clear Picture.

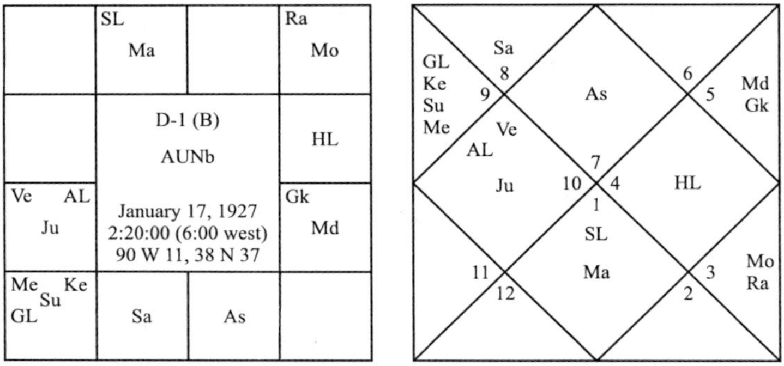

As: 21 Li 31	Su: 0 Sg 38-DK	Mo: 29 Ge 16-AK	Ma: 7 Ar 04-BK
Me: 26 Sg 07-AmK	Ju: 2 Cp 17-GK	Ve: 2 Cp 18-MK	Sa: 18 Sc 05-PK
Ra: 9 Ge 18-PiK	Ke: 9 Sg 18	HL: 13 Cn 40	GL: 14 Sg 04

Here Jupiter connects to Venus, Saturn becomes related to Jupiter and Venus, While Jupiter is dispositor of 11th lord Sun, 12th and 9th lord Mercury, Moon the 10th lord is related to Mercury and Sun. As the dispositor of the Mercury and Venus it connects with the 10th lord moon.

Example7: Navy personnel killed by Gun fire

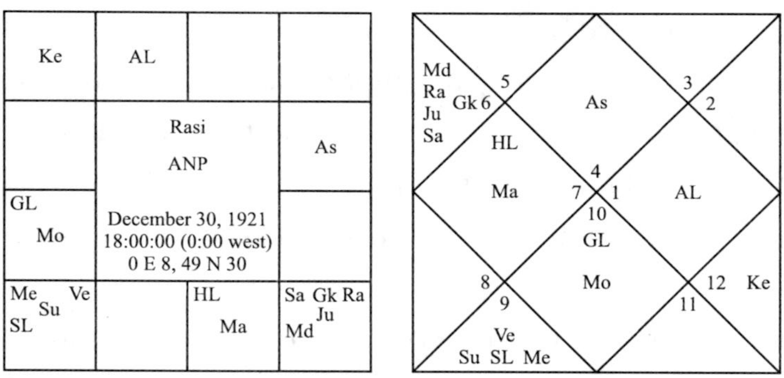

As: 8 Cn 44	Su: 15 Sg 46-BK	Mo: 2 Cp 55-DK	Ma: 9 Li 44-PiK
Me: 17 Sg 35-AmK	Ju: 24 Vi 21-AK	Ve: 6 Sg 04-GK	Sa: 14 Vi 34-MK
Ra: 21 Vi 03-PK	Ke: 21 Pi 03	HL: 14 Li 08	GL: 12 Cp 20

Mars is the 5th and 10th lord in the sign of 11th, 4th lord Venus. There is an exchange between Jupiter and Mercury on account of that planets in 3rd and 6th become related, Mars connects to all these planets through its dispositor Venus.

Navy combination the 8th lord Saturn and 12th lord Mercury are together, along with the dispositor of 5th and 10th lord mars the Venus.

Armed forces combination 5th and 8th lord link of mars here Mars is lord of 5th and 10th it connects to 8th Saturn through Venus a planet related to Saturn as mars is in the sign of Venus. (Mercury And Jupiter exchange Signs here)

Example 8: A naval officer who rose from the ranks

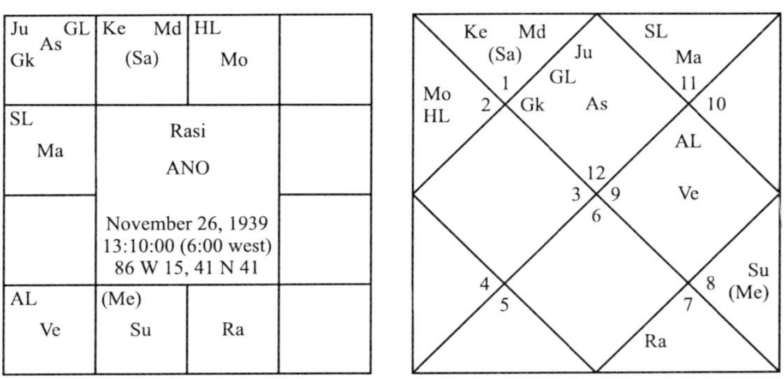

As: 0 Pi 00	Su: 10 Sc 37-MK	Mo: 9 Ta 12-PiK	Ma: 11 Aq 33-BK
Me (R): 15 Sc 08-AmK	Ju: 5 Pi 51-PK	Ve: 1 Sg 30-DK	Sa (R): 2 Ar 16-GK
Ra: 5 Li 58-AK	Ke: 5 Ar 58	HL: 19 Te 39	GL: 3 Pi 36

Mars aspects the 5th lord, the 5th lord is placed in sign of 3rd and 8th lord Venus. Mars and Saturn exchange Signs and are thus related. So, Mars has connection with 5th Moon and 11th, 12th lord Saturn. Jupiter is the 10th lord it is in Kendra from 3rd and 8th lord Venus and it, aspects the 6th lord Sun and 4th, 7th lord mercury. Since Saturn is retrograde we as well take its aspect to previous house, that will connect Saturn to Jupiter and Jupiter the ascendant and 10th lord to Mars.For armed services Mars has to have connection with 5th and 8th or 3rd, 6th or all as listed. Here mars aspects the 5th lord, the 3rd house, 6th house. The related planet Saturn which is in exchange with mars aspects the 8th house. While the sign placement lord of 5th happens to be the 3rd, 8th house lord.

Since armed forces is a government owned service.

Let's check government job combinations, the link of 5th with 10th and 11th. Moon is the 5th lord is under aspect by Mars a planet related to 11th, 12th Saturn. Jupiter the 10th cast an aspect to the 5th house. While retrograde Saturn the 11th connects to previous house placed Jupiter on account of being retrograde.

Checking on navy Connection – The 8th lord Venus is in 10th and 12th lord Saturn establishes a link with 10th lord Jupiter on account of being retrograde.

Overall – This is a very typical and difficult chart to comprehend for careers.

Example 9: Air force – Major general

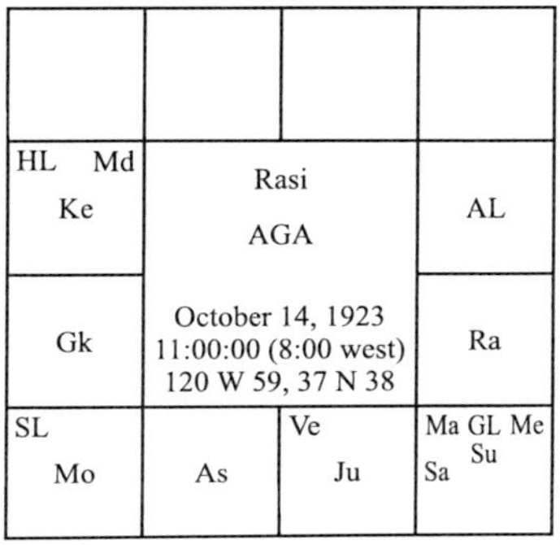

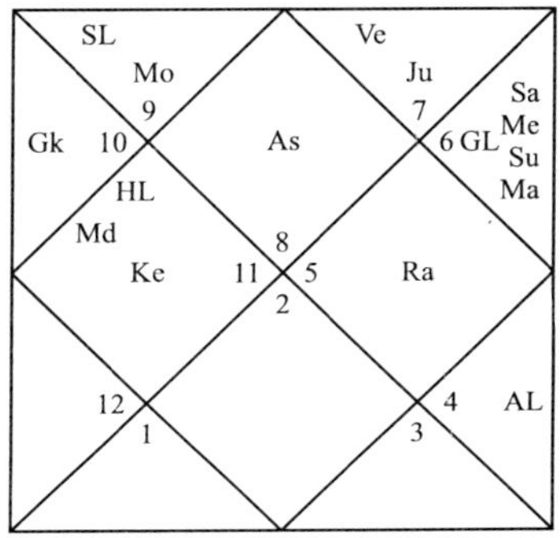

As: 25 Sc 29	Su: 27 Vi 37-BK	Mo: 0 Sg 52-DK	Ma: 5 Vi 04-GK
Me: 9 Vi 35-PiK	Ju: 28 Li 210-AmK	Ve: 6 Li 43-PK	Sa: 29 Vi 56-AK
Ra: 17 Le 59-MK	Ke: 17 Aq 59	HL: 20 Aq 01	GL: 23 Vi 54

Mars aspects the 5th and is related to lord of 8th and 10th and 11th.

Mars casts a aspect to the 9th lord moon, while the 10th and 11th lords are related to Mars.

So, the condition for pilot 9th, 10th, 11th link is fulfilled.

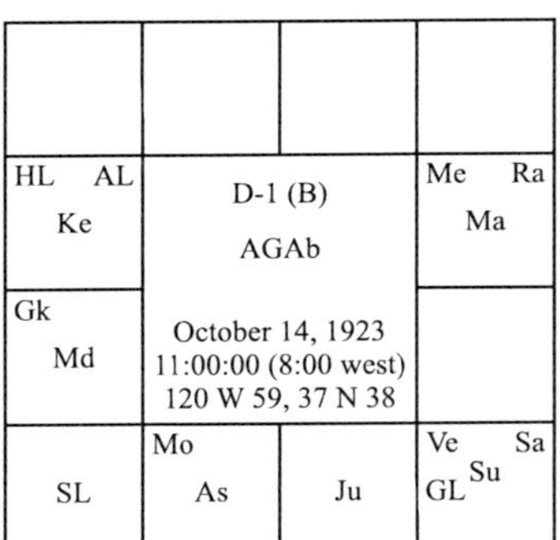

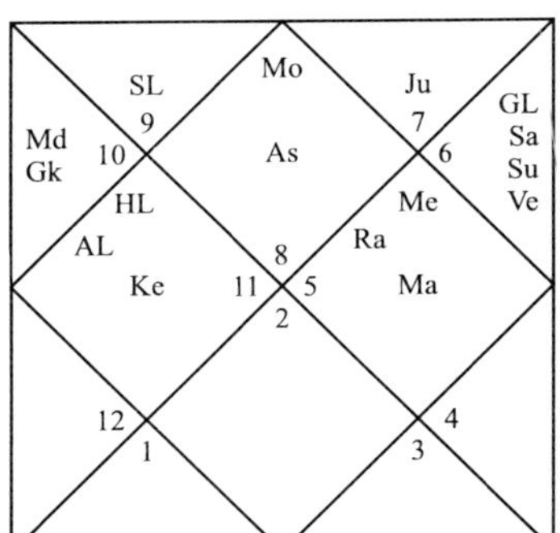

As: 19 Sc 23	Su: 8 Vi 33-BK	Mo: 7 Sc 50-DK	Ma: 15 Le 32-GK
Me: 26 Le 16-PiK	Ju: 15 Li 06-AmK	Ve: 0 Vi 24-PK	Sa: 29 Vi 28-AK
Ra: 11 Le 51-MK	Ke: 11 Aq 51	HL: 0 Aq 06	GL: 5 Vi 05

The connection of 5th, 10th and 11th as required for government service is visible in Bhava chart that follows.

The dispositor of Jupiter is related to 10th lord Sun. While Mercury the 11th lord and Sun exchange places. Therefore, the connection of 5th, 10th and 11th is evident.

Example 10: An ace Fighter Pilot

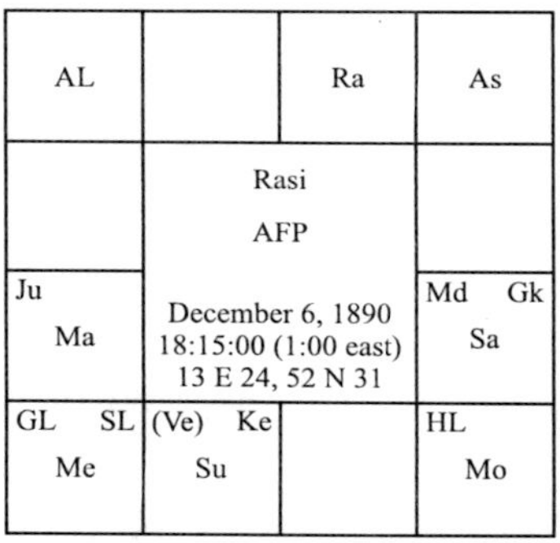

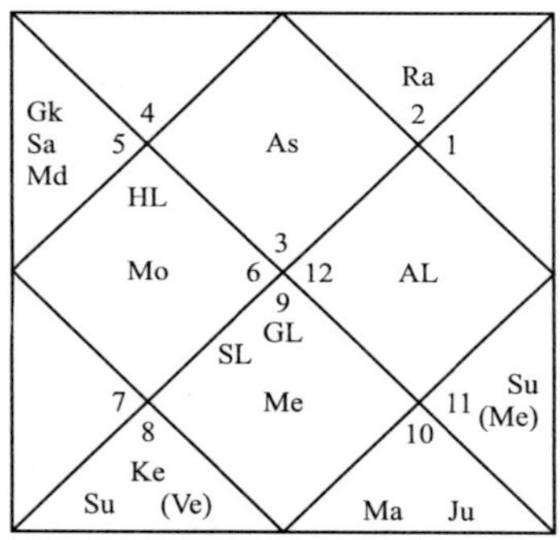

As: 25 Ge 54
Me: 3 Sg 01-DK
Ra: 22 Ta 23-GK
Su: 22 Sc 16-BK
Ju: 17 Cp 03-PiK
Ke: 22 Sc 23
Mo: 16 Vi 10-PK
Ve (R): 18 Sc 10-MK
HL: 25 Vi 06
Ma: 29 Cp 58-AK
Sa: 24 Le 27-AmK
GL: 29 Sg 60

Mars is in 8th, the 5th lord Venus is in sign owned by Mars, Mars also aspects the 8th, 9th lord Saturn. Mars is related to 10th lord Jupiter as well as they both are in 8th in sign of Saturn.

Here the connection of mars to 5th, 6th, 8th, 3rd, 10th and 11th is established.

5th lord Venus and 10th Jupiter link through Mars which happens to be lord of 11th as well, so the government service combination is evident.

9th lord Saturn, 10th Jupiter and 11th mars connect so the pilot, thus air force.

Example 11: Army Col. Indian

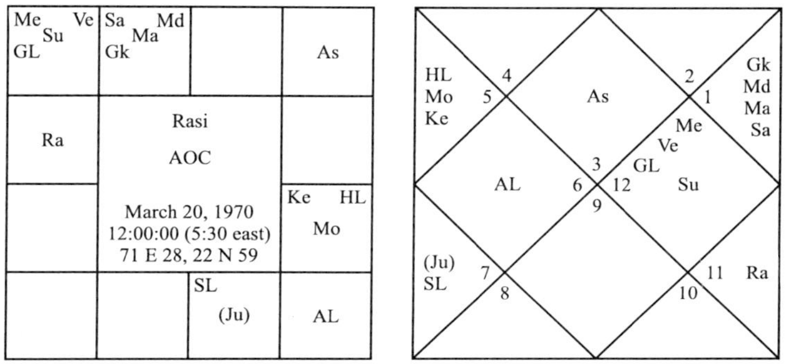

As: 3 Ge 44	Su: 5 Pi 48-PK	Mo: 4 Le 34-GK	Ma: 15 Ar 58-AmK
Me: 2 Pi 32-DK	Ju (R): 11 Li 18-PiK	Ve: 19 Li 03-AK	Sa: 13 Ar 20-BK
Ra: 18 Aq 24-MK	Ke: 18 Le 24	HL: 9 Le 18	GL: 29 Pi 53

Mars is the lord of 6th, 11th aspects 5th house, 10th, 7th lord Jupiter as well. Mars is also with 8th, 9th lord Saturn.

Here Mars connect with 3rd lord through related planet Jupiter, Mars is the 6th and 11th lord its related to 10th lord Jupiter and 8th lord Saturn. So, all conditions related to career in armed forces are fulfilled.

5th lord Venus, 10th lord Jupiter are in exchange, while Mars the 11th is related to Jupiter, the requirement for government job is also fulfilled.

Example 12: Indian army officer

Mars aspects the 5th/Sun the 11th lord and 8th houses and also the 9th house and the lord of the 10th Moon. Mars is the lord of 2nd and 7th houses. Moon the 10th has a Kendra relation with Jupiter the lord of 3rd, 6th. Jupiter is related to Venus the lord of ascendant, 8th and Saturn the lord of 5th, 6th .Jupiter is placed in sign owned by mercury and is in trine relation to Mercury the lord of 9th and 12th.

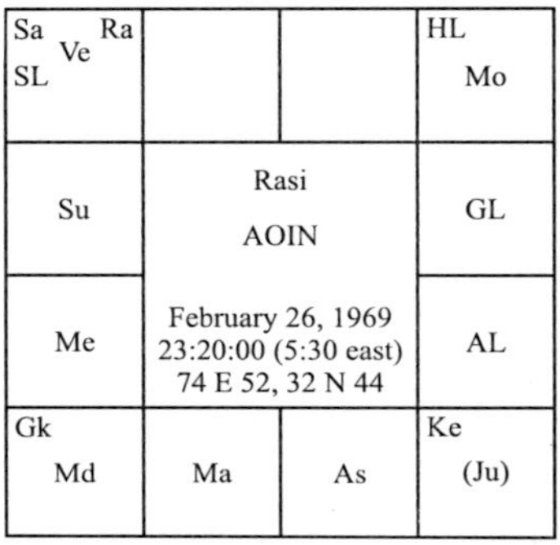

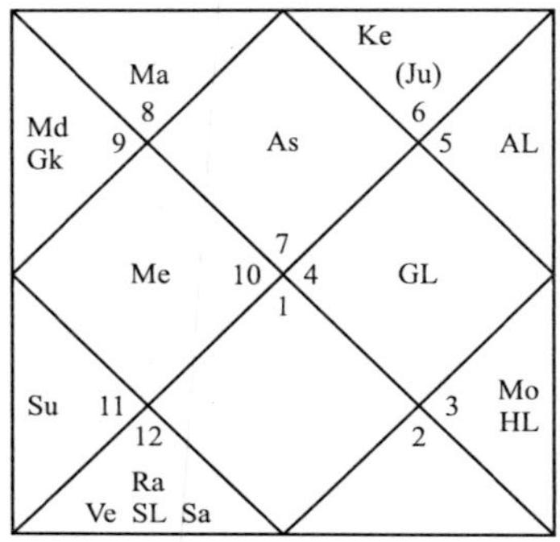

As: 17 Li 43	Su: 14 Aq 33-PiK	Mo: 12 Ge 21-PK	Ma: 7 Sc 15-DK
Me: 18 Cp 03-MK	Ju (R): 10 Vi 32-GK	Ve: 26 Pi 41-AmK	Sa: 29 Pi 05-AK
Ra: 7 Pi 04-BK	Ke: 7 Vi 04	HL: 20 Ge 35	GL: 0 Cn 41

Saturn the 5th lord is in Kendra to the Moon the lord of 10th, while the lord of 11th the Sun is placed in Saturn's Sign in 5th house, so the Government Job requirement of 5th, 10th, 11th lord's link is also established.

Example 13:A naval officer in India

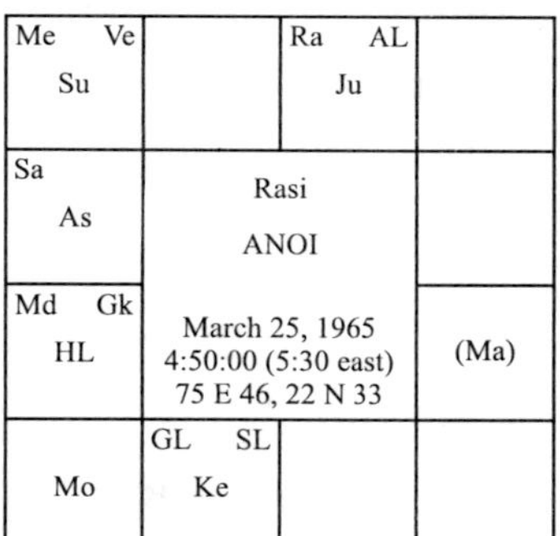

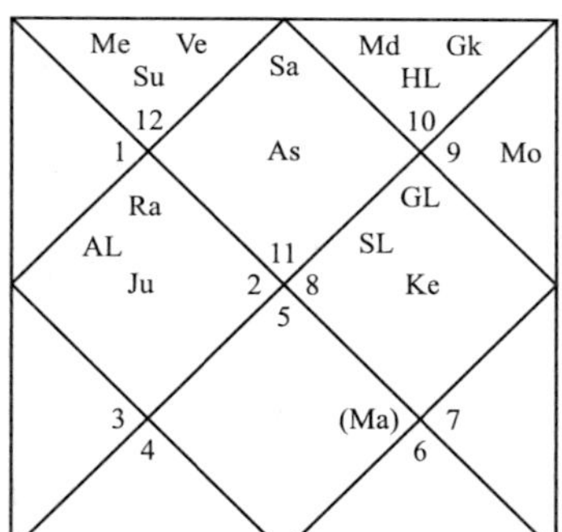

As: 7 Aq 57	Su: 10 Pi 44-MK	Mo: 9 Sg 42-PiK	Ma (R): 19 Le 39-AmK
Me: 28 Pi 32-AK	Ju: 0 Ta 42-DK	Ve: 6 Pi 06-GK	Sa: 17 Aq 25-BK
Ra: 23 Ta 25-PK	Ke: 23 Sc 25	HL: 19 Cp-09	GL: 3 Sc 09

Mars is the lord of 3rd and 10th related to 12th and ascendant lord it, aspects the 5th and 8th lord mercury.

Jupiter and Venus are in exchange, so Sun the 7th, mercury the 5th ,8th, Venus the 4th ,9th get related, Mars connects with these all through Mercury, Sun and Venus as it, aspects these three. The dispositor of 6th lord moon is Jupiter.

Navy – 12th lord Saturn connects with 10th lord Mars, while mars connects with 8th and 5th Mercury. Link of 8th, 10th, and 12th is established.

Example 14: Indian Army officer

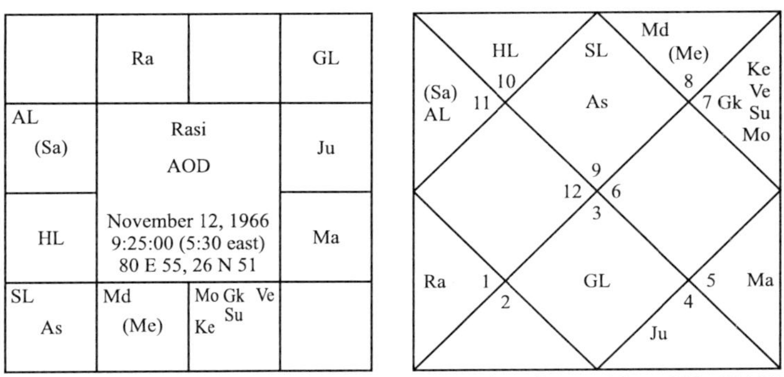

As: 4 Sg 37	Su: 25 Li 56-BK	Mo: 20 Li 01-PiK	Ma: 24 Le 29-MK
Me (R): 7 Sc 32-GK	Ju: 10 Cn 57-PK	Ve: 26 Li 43-AmK	Sa (R): 29 Aq 42-AK
Ra: 22 Ar 48-DK	Ke: 22 Li 48	HL: 24 Cp 41	GL: 7 Ge 59

Mars is the 5th and 12th lord in relationship with lord of 10th ,7th Mercury, Mars is also related to 2nd,3rd lord Saturn, the dispositor of Mars Sun is related to 6th ,11th Venus, the 8th Moon.

Mars link with 3rd, 5th, 6th, 8th, 10th, and 11th is established.

The 5th lord Mars is related to 10th mercury and with 11th Venus through Sun. (So, the Government job)

Example 15: A young Army officer

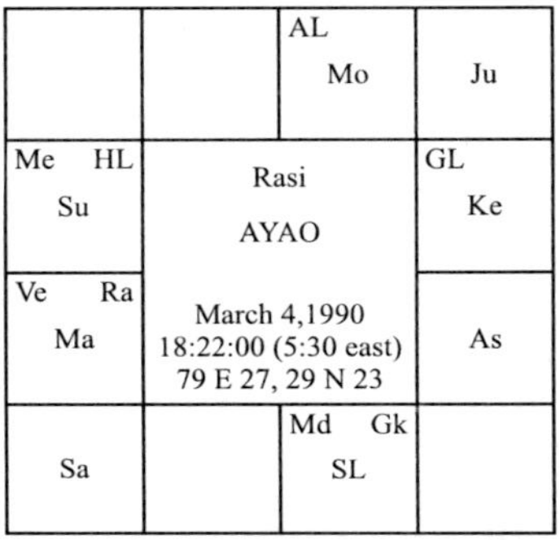

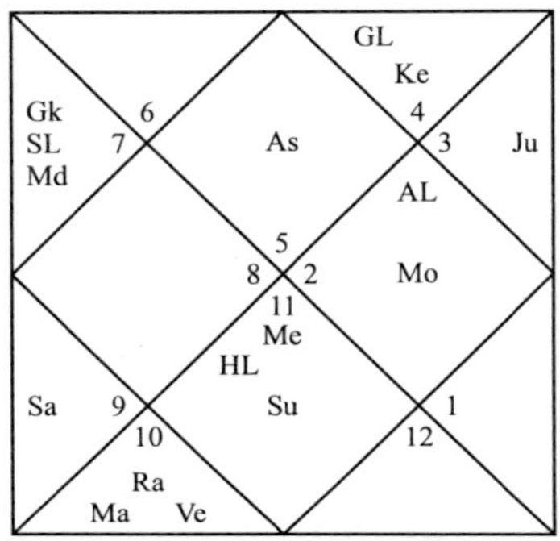

As: 22 Le 42	Su: 19 Aq 58-BK	Mo: 25 Ta 48-AmK	Ma: 1 Cp 01-DK
Me: 7 Aq 41-MK	Ju: 7 Ge 11-PK	Ve: 6 Cp 50-Gk	Sa: 28 Sg 43-AK
Ra: 22 Cp 29-PiK	Ke: 22 Cn 29	HL: 10 Aq 57	GL: 28 Cn 09

Mars is the 4th and 9th lord, with 10th, 3rd lord Venus in 6th, the dispositor of Mars; Saturn is in mutual aspect relationship with 8th and 5th lord Jupiter. Saturn is also related with 11th, 2nd lord Mercury and ascendant lord Sun.

So, the link of mars with 3rd, 5th, 6th, 8th, 10th, 11th is established, a requirement for career in army.

Government job combination is also there the lord od 5th connects to 11th through Saturn, while the 10th Venus is also linked through Saturn the 6th, 7th lord.

POLICE OFFICERS

Example 16: Investigative work requires association of hidden or 3, 6, 8, 12.

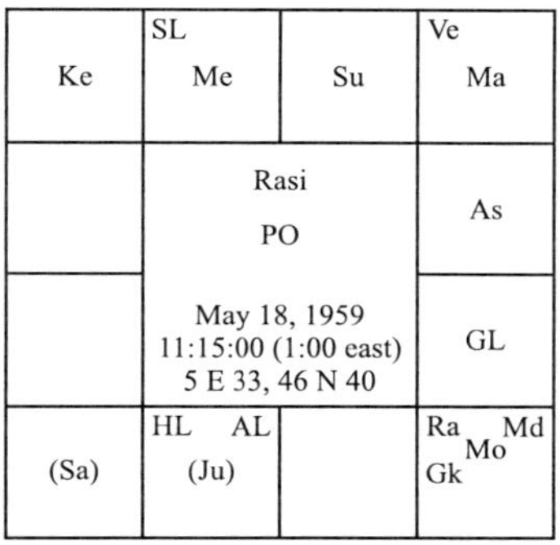

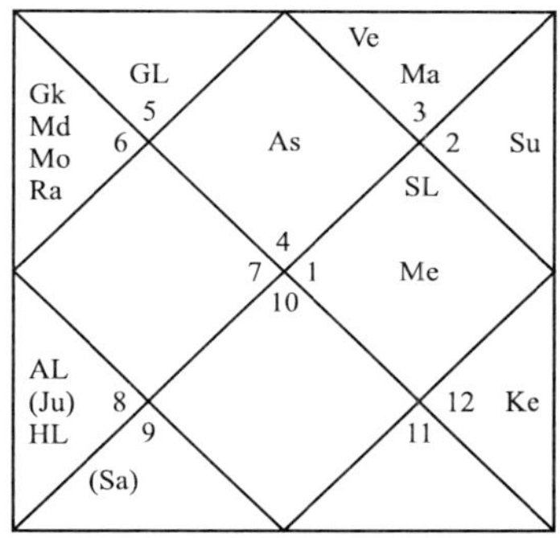

As: 25 Cn 37	Su: 3 Ta 27-DK	Mo: 6 Vi 12-PK	Ma: 28 Ge 37-AK
Me: 16 Ar 20-AmK	Ju (R): 3 Sc 53-GK	Ve: 15 Ge 30-BK	Sa (R): 12 Sg 59-MK
Ra: 18 Vi 57-PiK	Ke: 18 Pi 57	HL: 7 Sc 23	GL: 13 Le 40

Mars is the lord of 5th and 10th, aspects the 3rd and 6th. In exchange relationship with 3rd and 12th Mercury and dispositor to 6th, 9th lord Jupiter. Saturn the lord of 7th, 8th is related to Mars (mutual aspect) while 11th, 4th Venus is in the same sign thus related to Mars.

Mars is linked to 3, 5,6,8,10,11 and 12th house lords.

Investigative work requires association of hidden or 3, 6,8,12.

Government t job – Lord of 5th, 10th and 11th are linked.

Example 17: Ex police officer and Private detective

Mars aspects the 5th lord Sun and 6th, 3rd Mercury, Mars is the lord of ascendant and 8th, so the 5th 8th link with as required for armed forces is present. Mars is placed in sign owned by Jupiter the 9th, 12th lord which is related to 2nd, 7th lord Venus, 10th, 11th lord Saturn, and 4th lord Moon. There is an exchange relationship between Jupiter and Venus. Mars links to planets in the second house and the Venus through Jupiter.

Mars is linked to 3, 5,6,8,10,11 and 12th house lords.

Investigative work requires association of hidden or 3, 6, 8, 12.

Government job – Lord of 5th, 10th and 11th are linked. (through Venus)

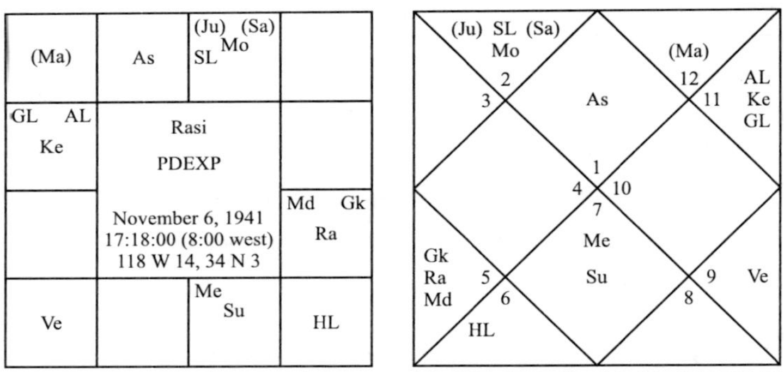

As: 29 Ar 28	Su: 21 Li 12-BK	Mo: 23 Ta 29-AmK	Ma (R): 18 Pi 06-MK
Me: 3 Li 39-PK	Ju (R): 27 Ta 08-AK	Ve: 7 Sg 39-PiK	Sa (R): 2 Ta 53-GK
Ra: 28 Le 13-DK	Ke: 28 Aq 13	HL: 19 Vi 05	GL: 1 Aq 35

Example 18: LAPD (Police officer)

Mars is in relationship with Saturn the 6th, 7th lord, Mars also aspects 10th, 3rd Venus and 11th, 2nd Mercury. Mars is in Kendra relationship with Venus and Mercury. Saturn is Kendra to Jupiter and is its dispositor. Jupiter the 5th, 8th is in Kendra to Mars. Jupiter is also related to Venus and mercury.

Mars is linked to 3rd, 5th, 6th, 8th, 10th, 11th, 12th Moon (through the Venus)

Govt Job- 5th lord Jupiter is linked to 10th and 11th lords Venus and Mercury.

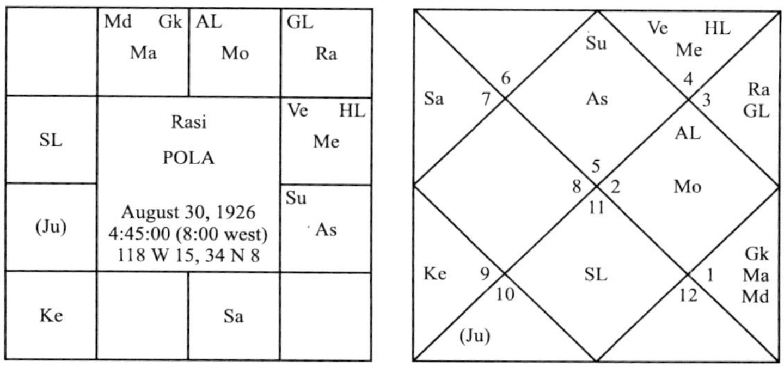

As: 4 Le 29	Su: 13 Le 33-GK	Mo: 17 Ta 36-PK	Ma: 20 Ar 50-PiK
Me: 26 Cn 34-BK	Ju (R): 27 Cp 31-AmK	Ve: 22 Cn 14-MK	Sa: 27 Li 41-AK
Ra: 22 Ge 19-DK	Ke: 22 Sg 19	HL: 21 Cn 08	GL: 18 Ge 55

Example 19: An Ex IPS from India

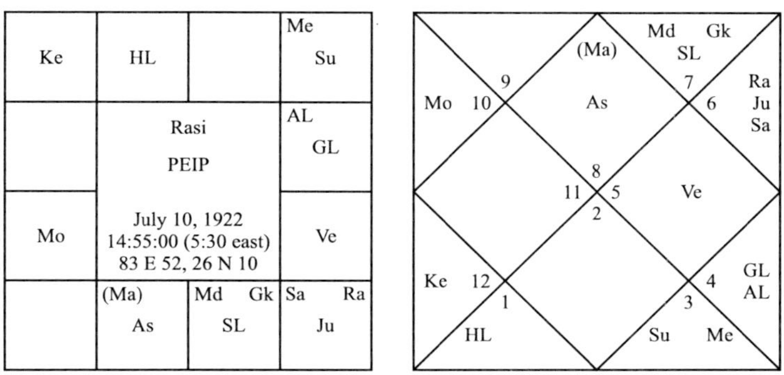

As: 2 Sc 26	Su: 24 Ge 33-AK	Mo: 9 Cp 17-PiK	Ma (R): 18 Sc 38-BK
Me: 3 Ge 49-GK	Ju: 17 Vi 52-MK	Ve: 1 Le 42-DK	Sa: 9 Vi 10-PK
Ra: 9 Vi 57-AmK	Ke: 9 Pi 57	HL: 15 Ar 14	GL: 1 Cn 51

Mars is the ascendant and 6th lord it, aspects the 10th lord Sun and 8th, 11th lord Mercury. Mercury is dispositor for 10th lord Sun, 3rd, 4th lord Saturn and 2nd,

5th lord Jupiter. Saturn the 3rd aspects Mars and carries the influence of related planet Jupiter to Mars. Moon the 12th is in the sign owned by Saturn and is under aspect by Jupiter a planet related to its dispositor Saturn.

Mars is 6th lord, linked to 10th, 11th, 8th, 5th, 3rd and 12th.

Govt Job- 5th lord Jupiter, 10th lord sun and 11th all are linked through the sign placement in mercury signs.

Example 20: An IPS officer

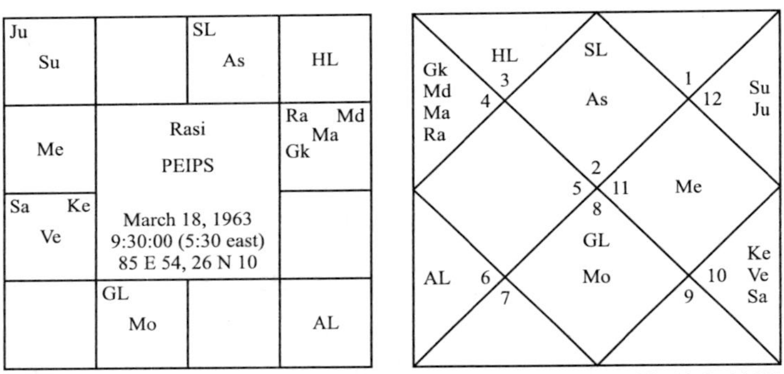

As: 10 Ta 23	Su: 3 Pi 30-GK	Mo: 29 Sc 39-AK	Ma: 12 Cn 01-PK
Me: 21 Aq 47-PiK	Ju: 2 Pi 35-DK	Ve: 22 Cp 38-MK	Sa: 25 Cp 22-BK
Ra: 4 Cn 19-AmK	Ke: 4 Cp 19	HL: 19 Ge 38	GL: 29 Sc 02

Mars is the lord of 12th, 7th, Aspects 6th house, 5th lord Mercury, 6th lord Venus, 10th lord Saturn, while the 8th, 11th lord Jupiter aspects Mars.3rd lord Moon is related to Mars because of a sign exchange. Mars is linked to 3rd, 5th, 6th, 8th, 10th, 11th, and 12th.

Govt job- Mars is related to 10th lord Saturn, (Mutual aspect) and Aspects 5th lord Mercury as related planet of 10th Saturn, While 11th aspects Mars. Saturn aspects the 11th Jupiter.